Questions of Cinema

Stephen Heath

MACMILLAN

First published 1981
Reprinted 1985

Published by
Higher and Further Education Division
MACMILLAN PUBLISHERS LTD
Houndmills, Basingstoke, Hampshire RG21 2XS
and London
Companies and representatives
throughout the world

Printed in Hong Kong

ISBN 0-333-26122-4 (hardcover)
ISBN 0-333-26123-2 (papercover)

Contents

Preface

In 1973 I began an association with the journal *Screen* which led, amongst other things, to my participating in its work by writing a number of essays towards the development of a critical and theoretical account of cinema and film able to engage cultural and political issues. This book is a result of that writing, a selection from those essays and from others written with the same purpose and over the same period of the last six or seven years for other magazines or occasions.

Selection means omissions, some of which — early pieces on the semiology elaborated by Christian Metz, discussions of Brecht and cinema, a long analysis of Orson Welles's *Touch of Evil* — are to be retrieved elsewhere. In fact, the present volume comprises only two essays originally published in *Screen*, the majority coming from those other magazines or appearing here for the first time (details of publication are given at the head of the 'Notes' section for each essay). Apart from minor stylistic changes or small corrections of detail and unless otherwise specified, the previously published pieces are printed in their original form. Repetitions have generally been allowed to stand: from one piece to the next, an idea or theme is taken up and set out in a new context, a different discussion, in a way that will perhaps, hopefully, have something of a cumulative explanatory effect. Each essay exists as a separate entity but joins with the others in what is, the intended unity of the book, a series of questions of cinema. Some of those questions are raised from the consideration of particular films, some from the consideration of particular issues or of particular theoretical concepts that have been important in film theory; all of them spill out of

any narrowly defined field of cinema and its study, involve —
in differing ways and in respect of the development of the
critical and theoretical account mentioned above — Marxism,
psychoanalysis, semiology. Leaving aside the desire to choose
from and bring together some of the more scattered pieces,
the selection was made too, finally, in the interests of
providing a perspective on that development: the questions
of cinema and a little history of the terms of their debate.

There are many people I should acknowledge and thank
for help of every kind in connection with the writing of these
essays; too many for a list not to be an inadequate means of
acknowledging and thanking any one of them. Thus I should
simply like this book, for those people, they who knew and
who miss him, to be in memory of Martin Walsh.

January 1980   STEPHEN HEATH

NOTE

Details of references are given in full in the 'Notes' section at
the end of each essay. In the case of references to works in
languages other than English, details are also given of translations when these exist, are known to me and are readily
available. The translation of any quotation here, however,
will often be my own or a modified version of the available
published translation and will thus not necessarily correspond
to the latter.

Chapter 1

On Screen, in Frame: Film and Ideology

Something changes between 22 March and 28 December 1895. Between the scientific and industrial presentation (the first Lumière demonstration of the cinématographe for the Société d'encouragement à l'industrie nationale) and the start of commercial exploitation (the first public performance in the Grand Café), the screen is fixed in what will come to be its definitive place. The spectators are no longer set on either side of a translucent screen but have been assigned their position in front of the image which unrolls before them — *cinema* begins.

There are any number of anecdotal items which might have their significance in this context — the Japanese audiences to whom it used to be necessary to explain the facts of projection prior to the showing of a film, the organization of shadow theatre in certain cultures where the screen divides the audience into two with only the men allowed to move freely from one side to the other, to go behind the screen (much of the significance of these items is in their non-Western reference) — but more immediately important here are the images of screen and position in Marx and Freud and what they have to suggest for a consideration of film and ideology.

In Marx, of course, it is precisely the description of ideology which, in a well-known passage of *The German Ideology*, runs into such terms: 'Consciousness can never be anything else than conscious existence, and the existence of men is

their actual life-process. If in all ideology men and their circumstances appear upside down as in a camera obscura, this
phenomenon arises from their historical life-processes just as
the inversion of the retina does from their physical life-process.
... We begin with real, active men, and from their real
life-process show the ideological reflexes and echoes of this
life-process. The phantoms of the human brain also are
necessary sublimates of men's material life-process, which can
be empirically established and which is bound to material
preconditions. Morality, religion, metaphysics and other
ideologies no longer retain therefore their appearance of
autonomous existence. They have no history, no development.
... '[1] Men and their circumstances appear upside down as in
a camera obscura — everything is projected in the darkened
room but inverted. The conception is clear yet difficult in
the comparison with the camera obscura: the match between
idea and model, as it were, makes the problem, shows the
work to be done. As the individual faces the screen of ideology
— the wall, the side of the machine onto which the image is
projected — he or she sees a real image, in true, aligned, and
him/herself in position with it, screened too, presented and
represented. There is no turning round (or back) to reality as
to a direct source of light, no putting the eye to a hole in
another wall so as to see the world outside. Ideology arises
from the historical life-processes taken up in it, the struggle
is in reality which includes ideology as a real component of
its presence, historical, social and subjective. The model of
the camera obscura stops on the screen, hypostasizes subject
and reality in the simple figure of inversion at the very
moment that it seeks to stress the relations of their production,
a process that crosses subject and reality in ideology.

It is the process of the subject, its construction, that
occupies Freud in the elaboration of psychoanalysis and it is
the displacement of the subject from a simple coherence of
consciousness which leads to the introduction of terms of
screen and position. Mental processes exist to begin with in
an unconscious phase, only from which do they pass over
into the conscious phase, 'just as a photographic picture
begins as a negative and only becomes a picture after being
turned into a positive'. Once this photographic comparison

has been made in the *Introductory Lectures on Psycho-Analysis*, Freud faces the problem of the selection of the conscious 'images' with a spatial picture, another image: 'The impulses in the entrance hall of the unconscious are out of sight of the conscious, which is in the other room; to begin with they must remain unconscious. If they have already pushed their way forward to the threshold and have been turned back by the watchman, then they are inadmissible to consciousness; we speak of them as *repressed*. But even the impulses which the watchman has allowed to cross the threshold are not on that account necessarily conscious as well; they can only become so if they succeed in catching the eye of consciousness. We are therefore justified in calling this second room the system of the *preconscious*.'[2] The subject is no longer given in front of the screen of ideology but divided in the very process of its construction for that confrontation. The camera obscura becomes a series of chambers with negatives and positives, movements and repressions, screenings for and from the eye of consciousness. The irony is that it is just this kind of image - there is a similar one a few years earlier in the *Five Lectures on Psycho-Analysis*,[3] again a more popularizing exposition — that is filmable in Freud, that attracted the attention of directors and producers from Goldwyn to Pabst. There is something absolutely right and wrong in Goldwyn's approach to Freud (something of the enormity of Laemmle greeting Eisenstein by asking whether Trotsky could manage to knock up a script for him, but more so): film and psychoanalysis join and disjoin on the image, the subject, the reality of their positions.

Thus, already, we have a certain power of cinema: just after Marx, just before Freud (or contemporaneously with him), it furnishes another image, *the* image ('the discovery of the universal language!', cries one spectator to his neighbour in the Grand Café), in movement and set firm on the screen. The images of Marx and Freud — camera obscura, photographic printing, the dark chambers which filter material to catch the eye of consciousness — bear exactly on the image, bear against the phantoms or the phantom of consciousness. Hence these — their own — images are at once necessary and dangerous (witness Freud's reaction of refusal to the filming of the

metaphors he proposes), explicit and complicit. It is this encounter of images, this crisis of complicity, that can guide us.
Cinema brings historical materialism and psychoanalysis
together in such a way that the consideration of film and
ideology begins from and constantly returns us to their conjuncture, in such a way that from the analysis of cinema, of
film, we may be able to engage with theoretical issues of a
more general scope, issues crucial for a materialist analysis of
ideological institutions and practices.

Let us start with the classic — 'naïve' — thesis (often adopted
as a version of 'content analysis' by those who none the less
refuse it). Film, a film, is precisely an image, the image of an
image (of reality), the reproduction of existing representations:
in short, a reflection. Since we have been occupied with
beginnings, it may as well be said that this conception is that
of Louis Lumière but taken one notch down. Instead of
holding to a reproduction of life (Lumière was adamant in
later years: 'the film subjects I chose are the proof that I only
wished to reproduce life'[4]), it holds to a reproduction of the
image of life. Of Lumière one has the right to demand to
know where this 'life' comes from — and the answer is certainly not from itself, for life is composed on the screen of
representations of work, family and leisure, *La Sortie des
usines*, *Le Repas de bébé* and *L'Arroseur arrosé*, chosen subjects indeed. Of the reproduction thesis one has the right to
demand to know where the image comes from and what it is
doing in the film.

This last question is important, and first and foremost in
that it prevents us from stopping at the image, at the idea of
the image, obliges us to specify the *work* of ideology in the
film, of the film in ideology, its production and productions,
its multiple determinations (by what it is determined and
what it determines). There is a Biograph film listed for 1902
(it may recall a scene in Godard's *Les Carabiniers*) entitled
Uncle Josh at the Moving Picture Show: a 'country bumpkin
who becomes so overwhelmed by watching his first motion
picture from a stage box that he tears down the screen in his

enthusiasm to help the heroine of one of the films'. Uncle Josh can see well enough that it is the screen that is at stake, but then he only sees its images (which he loves) and so misses it completely, passes through it. The image goes on, *continues* (doubtless the self-confirming force of the demonstration, the reason why it figures in the film, in this film and in others) — and at the very moment that Uncle Josh pulls away the screen or that the ideologist notes the illusion to lift it off as unreal. Uncle Josh should have turned, as we must turn, in the other direction: the need is to work out the screen, hollow in the image, examine the relations — the real relations —it sustains (produced and producing), what it sets up, the complex of representations, positions and movements, the machinery of cinema (and of film as cinema). The initial question is not 'where is reality?' but 'how does this function?', 'where is the reality *in that*?'.

A second thesis here requires attention. In ideology, it is said, is represented the imaginary relation of individuals to the real relations under which they live. It has also to be stressed, however, that this imaginary relation in ideology is itself real, which means not simply that the individuals live it as such (the mode of illusion, the inverted image) but that it is effectively, practically, the reality of their concrete existence, the term of their subject positions, the basis of their activity, in a given social order. The imaginary is not just in ideology (it is in relations) and ideology is not just reducible to the imaginary (it is that real instance in which the imaginary is realized). What is held in ideology, what it forms, is the *unity* of the real relations and the imaginary relations between men and women and the real conditions of their existence. All of which is not to forget the economic instance nor to ideologize reality into the status of an impossible myth; rather, it is to bring out ideology in its reality and to indicate that reality — as against ideology, as its truth — is posed only in process in the specific contradictions of a particular socio-historical moment.

Thus ideology is to be seen as itself productive within a mode of production, taking the latter — Marx's *Produktionsweise* — to refer precisely in historical materialism to the articulation of the economic, political and ideological instances;

the ideological instance determines the definition, the reproduction, of individuals as agents/subjects for the mode of
production, in the positions it assigns them. To acknowledge
this is to recognize the materiality of ideology and to grasp
analysis accordingly: ideology is not a kind of cloud of ideas
hanging over the economic base and which analysis can 'dispel'
to reveal the coherent image of a simple truth but a specific
social reality given in a specific set of institutions (or 'ideological state apparatuses'); to analyze an ideology involves its
analysis in this existence within the dynamic of a mode of
production. When Marx comments that ideologies 'have no
history', he means that their history is to be understood
exactly in the analysis of the dynamic (the task of historical
materialism) and not in some pure autonomy. At the same
time, however, the recognition of the material existence and
function of ideology demands — and this will be important
for thinking about film — the understanding also of a certain
historicity of ideological formations and mechanisms in
relation to the processes of the production of subject-meanings
(meanings for a subject included as the place of their intention),
demands, in other words, the understanding of the *symbolic*
as an order that is intersected by but is not merely reducible
to the ideological (ideology works *over* the symbolic *on* the
subject *for* the imaginary). A history of cinema could be
envisaged in this perspective which would be not that of the
straight reflection of ideological representations, nor that of
the simple autonomy of an ideality of forms, but, as it were,
the history of the productions of meaning assumed and
established by cinema in specific relations of the individual to
subjectivity.

There are one or two remarks which follow immediately
from these initial emphases. Firstly, it must be seen that the
notion of determination which has proved — or been made to
prove — such a stumbling block for ideological analysis cannot be conceived of as a problem in cause-and-effect with its
answer an explanation from an absolute point of origin (as
though historical materialism were to be, in Engels's words,
'easier than the solution of a simple equation of the first
degree'[5]). Analysis will be concerned not with determinations
in this mechanistic sense but with contradictions, it being in

the movement of these contradictions that can be grasped the *set* of determinations – the 'structural causality' – focused by a particular social fact, institution or work. Secondly, inevitably, a broad conception is emerging of what might be the *critical* role of art, of a practice of cinema, and in terms precisely of a production of contradictions against the fictions of stasis which contain and mask structuring work, in terms of a fracturing of the vision of representation so as to show, as Brecht puts it, that 'in things, people, processes, there is something that makes them what they are and at the same time something that makes them other'.[6] This last remark which engages the very *edge* of the present paper, its constant horizon, leads moreover from the more general discussion of ideology to the necessity to consider the vision of cinema, the nature and the area of its intervention. What is the role of cinema in capitalist society as a point of investment and a form of representation and meaning production? What does it sell on? At what levels – how – does analysis need to operate?

The distinction can be made between industry, machine and text. *Industry* refers to the direct economic system of cinema, the organization of the structure of production, distribution and consumption. Studies have shown that such organization has, at least in Britain and America, by and large conformed to typical patterns of capitalist activity. The *text*, the film, is a particular product of that industry. Currency is occasionally given to the idea that the film industry is one of 'prototypes' ('every film a new film'), but it is clear that the optimal exploitation of the production apparatus, which ties up considerable amounts of capital, requires the containment of creative work within established frameworks and that genres, film kinds, even so-called 'studio styles', are crucial factors here. As for the *machine*, this is cinema itself seized exactly between industry and product as the stock of constraints and definitions from which film can be distinguished as *specific signifying practice*. That formulation in turn needs to be opened out a little. *Signifying* indicates the recognition of film as system or series of systems of meaning, film as articulation. *Practice* stresses the process of this articulation, which it thus refuses to hold under the assumption of notions such as 'representation' and 'expression'; it takes film as a work of production of meanings and in so doing brings into the analysis the question of the positionings of the subject within that work. *Specific* is the necessity for the analysis to understand film in the particularity of the work it engages, the difference of its conjuncture with other signifying practices. This last does not entail pulling film as specific signifying practice towards some aesthetic idea of a pure cinematicity (on a line with the idea of 'literarity' derived in literary criticism from Russian Formalism and often become a way of avoiding issues of ideology in its appeal to a technicist 'structuralist poetics'); specificity here is semiotic, and a semiotic analysis of film — of film as signifying practice — is the analysis of a heterogeneity, the range of codes and systems at work in the film-text; specificity, that is, is at once those codes particular to cinema (codes of articulation of sound and image, codes of scale of shot, certain codes of narrative arrangement, etc.) *and* the heterogeneity in its particular effects, its particular inscriptions of subject and ideology, of the subject in ideology.

These effects of inscription are fundamental, the area of the intersection of film in ideology by industry and machine as institution of the subject, as institution of image and position and their shifting regulation *on* the figure of the subject. The hypothesis, in short, is that an important — determining — part of ideological systems in a capitalist mode of production is the achievement of a number of machines (institutions) which move, which *movie*, the individual as subject — shifting and placing desire, the energy of contradiction — in a perpetual retotalization of the imaginary. The individual is always a subject of ideology but is always more than simply the figure of that representation (just as the social cannot be reduced to the ideological which is nevertheless the very form of its representation as society): what the machine involves is the realignment of such excess — desire, contradiction, negativity. As far as analysis is concerned, the hypothesis tends to suggest a kind of returning movement whereby the industry is to be grasped (in terms of 'film and ideology') from the point of the ideological determination of the institution-machine and the latter from the point of its textual effects. In fact, of course, this complexity, this *complex*, may be broken by analysis into its own levels of contradiction: each film is specific in the ideological operation of its text *and* in its operation of the ideological specificity of film. The aim now must be to sketch something of these limits as the necessary focus for critical — creative — resistance.

To focus limits, in other words, is not to declare cinema by nature reactionary but to attempt to exploit understanding dialectically in the interests of a demonstration-transformation of the cinematic institution in its ideological effects. Yet the difficulties should be remembered and they can be seen by considering for a moment the example of Brecht. It is the question of limits that occupies Brecht in his thinking on cinema: the terms of his assessment alter, but in Hollywood he comes to regard cinema as inevitably regressive (identificational) in so far as it cuts off the spectator from production, from performance: 'the public no longer has any opportunity to modify the actor's performance it is confronted not with a production but with the result of a production, produced in its absence'.[7] This 'fundamental reproach' gains in intensity in the light of the fundamental importance attached by Brecht in his theatrical practice to the *Lehrstück* — and not finally to the epic theatre play — as 'model for the theatre of the future': the purpose of the *Lehrstück*, the 'learning-play' (Brecht's own preferred translation), is 'to show a politically wrong mode of behaviour and hence to teach a correct mode of behaviour', the realization of such a purpose lying 'in the fact that it is acted, not in the fact that it is seen'; 'it completely transforms the role of acting; it suppresses the system actor/spectator, knows only actors who are at the same time apprentices';[8] as model for the future, the *Lehrstück* is thus, in fact, a kind of school of dialectics. Nothing of the sort in film: cinema as art of the product, the public screened from production, fixed in the image. Brecht poses the problem, the difficulties, precisely with regard to subject-position and the implication of cinema in a founding ideology of vision as

knowledge, the specularization of reality for the coherence of
a subject outside contradiction; the assessment, the reproach,
follows from that relation.

What are the terms of this relation of vision? Those of a
memory, the constant movement of a retention of the individual as subject, framed and narrated.

The screen is the projection of the film frame which it
holds and grounds (hence the urgency of the need to fix the
position, to forbid the other side). It is not by chance that
the word 'frame' — which etymologically means 'to advance',
'to further', 'to gain ground' — should emerge from painting
to describe the material unit of the film ('the single transparent
photograph in a series of such photographs printed on a
length of cinematographic film', 'twenty-four frames a second')
and that it should then be used to talk about the image in its
setting, the delimitation of the image on screen (for an Arnheim, for instance, 'frame' and 'delimitation' are synonymous),
as well as to provide an expression for the passage of the film
in the projector relative to the aperture, 'in frame', and for
the camera viewpoint, 'framing' and 'reframing'. In an Eisenstein, moreover, there is a veritable aesthetics of the staging
of the frame, of *mise en cadre* ('Just as *mise en scène* will be
taken to mean the placing of elements, temporally and
spatially, on the theatre stage, so we will call *mise en cadre*
the placing of these elements in the shot'[9]).

It is the differences in frame between film and painting that
are generally emphasized: film is limited to a standard screen
ratio (the three to four horizontal rectangle) or, as now, to a
number of such ratios (Eisenstein in Hollywood proposes a
square screen — the 'dynamic square' — which would permit
the creation of rectangles of any proportion by the use of
masks); film destroys the ordinary laws of pictorial composition because of its moving human figures which capture
attention against all else. In his essay on 'The Work of Art in
the Age of Mechanical Reproduction', Walter Benjamin has
a comparison of film and painting which develops their
incompatibility in this way from the position of the specta-

tor: 'The painting invites the spectator to contemplation; before it the spectator can abandon himself to his associations. Before the movie frame he cannot do so. No sooner has his eye grasped a scene than it is already changed. It cannot be arrested. . . . The spectator's process of association in view of these images is indeed interrupted by their constant sudden change.'[10] There is much there that would call for comment (the comparison stems from the initial valuation of cinema by Brecht and Benjamin as a new mode of organizing and defining artistic production and, in fact, as a potentially epic mode — a conception that the *Threepenny Opera* lawsuit had begun to call into question even before Benjamin's essay was written); what needs to be stressed here, however, is the insistence of the frame which stays in view throughout the comparison, in place, the constant screen. The same constancy (or consistency) carries over the other classic comparison, that of film and theatre. Where the stage has 'wings', fixed limits, the screen in this comparison is said to be lacking in any frame, to know only the implied continuation of the reality of the image. Thus Bazin will write: 'The screen is not a frame like that of a picture, but a mask which allows us to see a part of the event only. When a person leaves the field of the camera, we recognize that he or she is out of the field of vision, though continuing to exist identically in another part of the scene which is hidden from us. The screen has no wings. . . . '[11] Once again, however, the frame simply stays put, transposed as the field of vision of the camera, and there is no necessity to emphasize the importance of what Vertov calls 'theatrical cinema' (not least in Bazin with his consecration of the deep focus scene in the films of a Welles or a Wyler). Moreover, the illimitation which the theatre comparison seeks to stress is exactly the confirmation of the force of the frame, its definition as a 'view' that has ceaselessly to counter absence by the assertion of the coherence of its presence, its 'being-in-frame'.

In frame: the place of image and subject, view (in early French catalogues a film is called a *vue*) and viewer; frame, framing, is the very basis of disposition — German *Einstellung*: adjustment, centring, framing, moral attitude, the correct position. Nijny reports a remark of Eisenstein's to the effect that metaphor is often the key to solutions of problems in *mise en cadre*; what can be added is that the frame itself is the constant metaphor, the transfer — the *metaphora* — of centre and eye (the early circular masks, shaped mattes, etc., are so many signs of this veritable drama of the centred eye — a film like *Grandma's Reading Glass* still has its lessons, its resonances).

The stake of the frame is clear (it is this that is finally crucial in Marx's camera obscura, not the inversion): the frame is the reconstitution of the scene of the signifier, of the symbolic, into that of the signified, the passage through the image from other scene to seen; it ensures distance as correct position, the summit of the eye, *representation*; it redresses (here, paradoxically, is the inversion) reality and meaning, is the point of their match. Analysis must then begin (and much has been done in this field) to examine the history, the techniques, the movements, of the alignment of cinema-eye and human-eye and subject-eye (where Vertov wished to give the disalignment, the difference of the first two in order to displace the subject-eye of the individual into an operative — transforming — relation to reality), must trace the windowing identity of subject and camera, the setting of the gaze to accompany the play of 'point of view' between characters in the diegetic space of the film (always the drama of the eye) which organizes the images in the coherence of the fiction.

The fiction, the view, of the characters — the human figures who enter film from the very first, as though of right, spilling out of the train at La Ciotat, leaving the Lyons factory or the photographic congress (is the fascination with people 'arriving' in film simply coincidental?) and who can only be evacuated with great difficulty, in certain modern, 'experimental' films — encloses the film as narrative, establishes that diegetic space. Specifying cinema the machine as mode of communication at the start of *Langage et cinéma*, Metz comments that it has 'no particular sector of meaning (no portion of the matter of content in Hjelmslevian terms)'.[12] Yet narrative is there immediately in film, in cinema, to lay out the images, to support the frame against its excess, to suggest laws to hold the movement, to ensure continuity, to *be* 'cinematic form' (thus for Lawson, 'The total rejection of a story, and the accompanying denial of syntax or arrangement, can only lead to the breakdown of cinematic form.'[13]). In the inter- mittence of its images (Benjamin's 'constant sudden change'), film is a perpetual metonymy over which narrative lays as a model of closure, a kind of conversion of desire (metonymy is the figure of desire in psychoanalytic theory) into the *direc- tion* of the subject through the image-flow (representation, the positioning of the subject, is as much a fact of the organi- zation of the images as of the fact of the image itself).

Narrative, that is, may be seen as a decisive instance of framing in film (the determining links between narrative con- straint and conventions of framing have often been stressed); its economy — a relation of transformation between two homogeneities ('beginning' and 'end') in which the second is the replacement of the first, a reinvestment of its elements — *checks* the images, centring and containing, prescribing a reading as correlation of actions and inscribing a subject as, and for, the coherence of that operation, carried through against possible dispersion, the multiple intensities of the text of the film. Frame, narrative placing, subject inscrip- tion cut short the interminable movement of the signifier, impose — subject-in-position, on screen, in frame — precisely the continuousness of representation.

The narrative elision of the image-flow, the screening of point of view as the ground of the image, the totalizing of image and space in the frame of field/reverse field — these are some of the procedures that have been described in terms of *suture*, a stitching or tying as in the surgical joining of the lips of a wound. In its process, its framings, its cuts, its intermittences, the film ceaselessly poses an absence, a lack, which is cease- lessly bound up in and into the relation of the subject, is, as it were, ceaselessly recaptured *for* the film. Formulated thus, the description is both important — since it can bring us round again to the articulation of film and ideology on the figure of the subject — and inadequate — since it misses, or masks, a functioning which may perhaps have implications for thinking that articulation.

In psychoanalysis, 'suture' names the relation of the individual as subject to the chain of its discourse where it figures missing in the guise of a stand-in (its place is taken and it takes that place); the subject is an effect of the signifier in which it is represented, stood in for. Ideological representation depends on — supports itself from — this 'initial' production of the subject in the symbolic (hence the crucial role of psychoanalysis, as potential science of the construction of the subject, within historical materialism), directs it as a set of images or inversions, of *fixed* positions, metonymy stopped in coherence. What must be emphasized, however, is that the stopping — the functioning of the suture in imaginary, frame, narrative, etc. — is exactly a *process*: it counters a productivity, an excess, that it states and restates in the very moment of rejection in the interests of coherence — thus the film frame, for example, mined from within by the outside it delimits and poses and has ceaselessly to recontain. The process never ends, the construction-reconstruction has always to be restarted: the machines, cinema included, are there for that. Ideology is *in* the suture.

Coming back to cinema, moreover, it can be seen that in a sense the cinematographic apparatus itself is nothing but an operation of suture. To cross the coherence of a patient's discourse in the analytic situation at the point of its process of suture (the point of construction and hence of exposure, of weakest resistance) is to grasp 'the structure of the subject articulated as a "flickering in eclipses"', like the movement that opens and closes number, delivering the lack in the form of the 1 to abolish it in its successor'.[14] The description has all the echoes of Bouly's patent of 1892 with its *'mouvement saccadé'*: 'The movement of the strip in the apparatus is jerky; that is to say, it is immobile for the time sufficient to register the image and mobile while the shutter closes the access of light.'[15] The images registered in their continuity as differences are then placed in another apparatus for reproduction in that continuity by a similar mechanism on the basis of these very differences. All in all, from machine to film with its own tie procedures, cinema develops as the apparatus of a formidable memory, the tracing of a subject defined, to quote the psychoanalytic account of suture once again, 'by attributes

whose other side is political, disposing as of powers of a faculty
of memory necessary to close the set without the loss of any
of the interchangeable elements'.[16] Or, as Godard once put
it, more succinctly, 'je pense, donc le cinéma existe'.

It is here that the hypothesis of machines for the shifting
regulation of the individual as subject can be specified. The
imaginary — the stand-in, the sutured coherence, the fiction
of anticipated totality — functions over and against the symbolic, the order of language, the production of meanings,
within which the subject is set as the place of an endless movement (identify as a function of repeated difference) and
from which, precisely, there is image and desire and suture.
The subject thus placed supports and is supported by ideological formations as the prospect — the perspective — of
desire, its images. The 'attributes' of construction described
by psychoanalysis are at once formal and 'political' (ideological) — 'the other side', like the recto and verso of a piece
of paper. The individual as subject is simultaneously a subject-
support, and the images of the one are the terms of the other's
representation. Cinema, with its screen, its frames, its binding
memory, is perhaps *the* image machine; not because it is the
'good object' (conditioned by the desire exposed in the symbolic, the energy of division, the imaginary is not to be
equated with the 'good object' in a straight Kleinian sense),
but because it holds the subject — on screen, in frame — in
the exact turning of symbolic and suture, negativity and coherence, flow and image (the 'screen' as it figures in various
Lacanian diagrams has a similar kind of ambivalence: locus of
a potentially ludic relation between the subject and its
imaginary captation, and the sign of the barrier — the slide —
across the subject and object of desire).

Which is why care is needed with such received ideas as
that of a simple commitment in the mainstream development
of cinema to the effacement of the marks of cinematic practice
in favour of a transparent presentation of 'reality' (cinema —
'the art of the real'). Continuity, invisible editing, matches,
and so on are important (indeed, they have here been stressed)
but there is a sense in which the point of cinema was always
this very process itself. D. W. Griffith will furnish an emblem-
atic example. We know that, along with others of his time,

he was apparently opposed to pans on the grounds that they showed up the mechanics of film (there are films where pans have been truncated in the editing as soon as they begin); we also know that in 1913 Griffith took a full page in the *New York Dramatic Mirror* to announce the break with Biograph, ostentatiously listing his claimed inventions — 'the large or close-up figures, distant views as represented first in *Ramona*, the "switch-back", sustained suspense, the "fade-out" and restraint in expression' (*Biograph Bulletin* entries often drew attention to striking innovations or filmic achievements). The conjuncture of the two facts gives something of the feel: the displayed jubilation in the 'modern techniques of the art' and the limits of that display, and then the realization anyway of those techniques (as in the Griffith list) as procedures of suture. The display differs, the balance varies (from the outset almost the problem is the variation of the limits); genres are instances of equilibrium, characteristic relatings — specific relations — of subject and machine in film as particular closures of desire, forms of pleasure (the other factor in a double determination, conjoining with the need for industrial optimalization mentioned earlier); what is constant is film as narration of subject and desire.

Constant narration, different narratives: each text has its particular operation, its particular ideological intersections, its constancies and differences, its terms and their reworking of limits. The analysis in the text of film and system is always imperative, the premise of any consideration of film, of a film, in its specific signifying practice.

The limits sketched out here have done no more than to envisage the ideological place of cinema as an aid to such a consideration and as a response to a Brechtian principle: 'For as long as one does not criticize the social function of cinema, all film criticism is only a criticism of symptoms and has itself a merely symptomatic character.'[17] Is this to come back finally to the 'fundamental reproach'? Yes, perhaps, but displaced a little in its working out, the beginnings of an understanding to be exploited. The problem, the political

problem, for film in its intervention can be given as the transformation of the relations of subjectivity and ideology.
Question of limits: open within the limits — film as theoretical
fiction, sociological experiment, learning play, history lesson
— the other scene, another memory, a new subject, in process,
transforming. Once again, Brecht has outlined the term and
the task:

> All the productivity of men is not contained in the actual
> production, which is always limited. Those elements that
> are not entirely absorbed into it, however, do not simply
> fall outside, they contradict; they are not simply lacking in
> meaning, they disturb. Thus only a very attentive scheme
> will be able to grasp their activity, and you need an ear
> which is extremely sensitive to what is productive. It is a
> real achievement to keep these elements from destruction,
> that is, from destroying *and* being destroyed.[18]

Notes

Opening address at the 'International Symposium on Film Theory and
Criticism', Center for Twentieth Century Studies, University of
Wisconsin—Milwaukee, November 1975; published in *Quarterly Review
of Film Studies* vol. 1 no. 3 (August 1976) pp. 251—65. The reference
to Brecht can be followed through in 'Lessons from Brecht', *Screen* vol.
15 no. 2 (Summer 1974) pp. 103—28; and 'From Brecht to Film',
Screen vol. 16 no. 4 (Winter 1975/6) pp. 34—44.

1. Karl Marx and Frederick Engels, *The German Ideology* (London:
Lawrence & Wishart, 1965) pp. 37—8.
2. S. Freud, *Introductory Lectures on Psycho-Analysis* (1916—17),
The Standard Edition of the Complete Psychological Works vol. XVI
(London: Hogarth Press, 1963) pp. 295—6. Freud is apparently em-
barrassed by this comparison even as he conveniently allows it: 'The
crudest idea of these systems is the most convenient for us — a spatial
one. . . . I know that [these ideas] are crude: and, more than that, I
know that they are incorrect. . . . '
3. S. Freud, *Five Lectures on Psycho-Analysis* (1910), *Standard
Edition* vol. XI (London: Hogarth Press, 1957) pp. 25—7. This image
lacked the reference to negative—positive developing and was more
visibly dramatic (the struggle to remove an 'interrupter', the posting of

guardians — 'three or four strong men' — at the door). For Freud's brushes with cinema mentioned here below, see Ernest Jones, *Sigmund Freud: Life and Work* vol. 3 (London: Hogarth Press, 1957) pp. 121–2. Goldwyn approached Freud in 1925 with an offer of $100,000 for co-operation in a film that would depict scenes from famous love stories, beginning with Antony and Cleopatra; Freud declined to see Goldwyn and telegrammed a famous refusal. Freud was more ambiguous with what was to be Pabst's *Geheimnisse einer Seele* (*Secrets of a Soul*), completed in 1926, but remained unwilling to give any authorization. Jones notes that 'his main objection was his disbelief in the possibility of his abstract theories being presented in the plastic manner of a film' (p. 121).

4. Cit. Georges Sadoul, *Histoire générale du cinéma* vol. I (Paris: Denoël, 1963) p. 288.

5. F. Engels, Letter to J. Bloch (September 1890), *K. Marx – F. Engels Selected Works* (London: Lawrence & Wishart, 1968) p. 692.

6. Bertolt Brecht, *Gesammelte Werke* (Frankfurt am Main: Suhrkamp, 1967(vol. XVI, pp. 925–6).

7. B. Brecht, *Arbeitsjournal* vol. I (Frankfurt am Main: Suhrkamp, 1973) p. 400.

8. Brecht, *Gesammelte Werke* vol. XVII, pp. 1022–34.

9. S. M. Eisenstein and V. Nijny, *Mettre en scène* (Paris: Union Générale d'Editions, 1973) p. 254. The reference to metaphor as solution quoted later is from p. 198.

10. Walter Benjamin, 'Das Kunstwerk im Zeitalter seiner technischen Reproduzierbarkeit', *Gesammelte Schriften* vol. 1.2 (Frankfurt am Main: Suhrkamp, 1974) p. 502; translation, 'The Work of Art in the Age of Mechanical Reproduction', *Illuminations* (London: Fontana, 1973) p. 240.

11. André Bazin, 'Théâtre et cinéma', *Qu'est-ce que le cinéma?* vol. II (Paris: Cerf, 1959) p. 100.

12. Christian Metz, *Langage et cinéma* (Paris: Larousse, 1971) p. 27; translation, *Language and Cinema* (The Hague and Paris: Mouton, 1974) p. 38.

13. J. H. Lawson, *Film: The Creative Process* (New York: Hill & Wang, 1964) p. 289.

14. Jacques-Alain Miller, 'La suture', *Cahiers pour l'analyse* no. 1 (1966) p. 49 translation, 'Suture', *Screen* vol. 18, no. 4 (Winter 1977/8) p. 34.

15. Brevet 219350, *Bulletin officiel de la propriété industrielle et commerciale* (1892) p. 34.

16. Miller, op. cit. p. 41; translation, p. 27.

17. Brecht, *Gesammelte Werke* vol. XVIII p. 168.

18. Ibid. vol. XIX p. 408.

Chapter 2

Narrative Space

'It is precise that "events *take place*" ' Michael Snow

At a climactic point in Hitchcock's *Suspicion*, Lina (Joan Fontaine) receives a visit from two police inspectors come to inform her of the death of a friend in circumstances which cannot but increase her fears concerning the probity – the rectitude – of her husband Johnnie (Cary Grant). The scene finds its centre in a painting: the massive portrait of Lina's father which bears with all its Œdipal weight on the whole action of the film – this woman held under the eye of the father (the name as crushing as the image: General *MacLaidlaw*), sexuality in place as transgression ('Lina will never marry, she's not the marrying sort . . . Lina has intellect and a fine solid character', declares the General early on in the film), as radically 'impossible' (leaving her father for Johnnie, Lina is henceforth racked by doubt, a suspicion that is irresolvable, for her and the film) – and before which she now positions herself to read the newspaper report of the friend's death and to gather strength enough to face the scrutiny of the law, the look relayed from portrait to police and to portrait again (Stills 1, 2, 3, 4). Thus centred, the scene is set out according to that unity so characteristic of classical cinema in its narrative spectacle: the new arrives – the visit, the death, the doubt augmented – and the action is continued, pushed forward, but within a movement of rhyme and balance, of

1

2

3

4

sustained coherence: on either side of what Lina is here given to see (the insert 'Stop Press' report for which she puts on her glasses, catching up one of the basic figures of the film, and which we share from her reading, as previously we share the photo of Johnnie in the society magazine or his telegram on the eve of the Hunt Ball), from the entry of the two inspectors back to their departure at the end of the scene, a perfectly symmetrical patterning builds up and pieces together the space in which the action can take place, the space which is itself part of that action in its economy, its intelligibility, its own legality.

Consider simply in this respect, across the scene, the shots at the start and close of the visit (Still 5, 6). The coherence is clear – the end comes round to the beginning, one shot echoing the other in the resolution of rhyme – at the same time that the distance travelled forward in the scene is registered, space redefined in the light of the dramatization effected – alone, diminished by the high angle, Lina is helplessly entangled in the network of shadows, enmeshed in 'the spider's web' of her doubt (the image is common in critical

5   6

discussions of the film). Moreover, the first shot itself is
immediately and dramatically exhaustible in its situation in
the film: the maid, Ethel, announces the visitors and functions globally as a comic turn — 'Oh! Mr Aysgarth! What will
my young man think!' — in what is, after all, a Hollywood
version of England in the 1930s; the dog, another turn, is an
impetuous present from Johnnie to Lina; the house is an
example of Johnnie's profuse irresponsibility ('Johnnie,
you're a baby', comments Lina, dumbfounded, when he
shows her the house after the honeymoon). Everything is
placed, there is nothing out of line. And yet, something does
jar, already, in this first shot. The composition is faultless,
the framing describes the theatricality of the inspectors'
entry (the ring at the door, the interruption, the unknown),
with the columns, steps and walls providing a stage effect, the
characters are centred, perspective is sharp: the image is in
every sense clearly directed. But not quite. Out of the action,
breaking the clarity of direction, obstinately turned away,
one of the inspectors is pulling to the left, gazing abruptly at
something hidden from us, without reason in this scene.

If a painting stands straight at the centre of the scene, the
look that holds Lina's reception of the news, that organizes
the scene itself, it goes askew at the edges of the beginning
and end, instants indeed of another painting. What occupies
Benson, the gazing inspector, lost in a kind of fascinated
panic, is precisely this other painting, hung on the side wall
behind the column by the front door and with a little —
repeated — scene of its own within the larger scene in which
it is somehow included (Stills 7, 8, 9, 10 and 11, 12, 13). At
the beginning, just after Lina asks the maid to show the

7

8

9

10

11

12

13

inspectors in, there is a shot of the latter still waiting by the front door but from an angle that now reveals the post-cubist, Picasso-like painting[1] that is the object of Benson's gaze (Still 7); the next shot cuts in closer to give the painting in detail while Benson cranes forward to see it (Still 8), a brief piano phrase totally different to the expressive orchestrations elsewhere dominant emerging on the sound track; cut back to the angle and distance of the previous shot as the maid comes to take the inspectors in to her mistress, Benson turning round with a look of shock on his face (Still 9) and then back to the painting again before following the maid and his colleague, continuing nevertheless to throw backward glances at the painting (Still 10). Similarly at the end of the scene: Lina accompanies the inspectors to the door and, while she and the other inspector, Hodgson, are exchanging a few words, Benson once more pulls to the very edge of the frame, towards the disconcerting painting (Still 11); cut to a shot of him craning, with the brief piano phrase, exactly parallel to the one at the beginning (Still 12, cf. Still 8); cut back to the medium three-shot, Benson totally disframed, Hodgson having literally to order him back into the scene, into the action (Still 13).

The play here is complex: this other painting has no reason, is 'useless' (isolated, without resonance over the film, marked off by the piano phrase and by the fact of its link with Benson who remains more or less apart in the main substance of the scene, out of frame and with only one line of any significance), beyond the limits of the film; and yet it arrives in the film, set into the rhyming balance of the scene, serving to demonstrate the rectitude of the portrait, the true painting at the centre of the scene, utterly in frame in the film's action. A 'Hitchcock joke'? Perhaps. But a joke that *tells* in a film that hesitates so finely in its enclosure of space, the terms of its points of view. Organized from Lina's point of view (in so far as we have the scenes that she has with respect to her husband, never seeing him separately in a way that might decide the sense of his actions, break the doubt) but under the inspection of an eye (the portrait its mirror) that gives the theatre of the suspicion, the setting of Lina's career, the film as story is easy in its ambiguity: no matter if Johnnie is crooked or not, the picture — from portrait to film — is straight, receivable, readable, psychologically and dramatically; Lina's character, her doubt, our experience of that are in place and it is this place that is important, that is the *film's* reason. Hence, however, a problem of *ending* (it is contingently interesting in this connection that Hitchcock had an alternative ending, that an attempt was made by cutting to produce a version that would eliminate any equivocation as to Cary Grant-as-Johnnie's honesty, that there were difficulties). Lina and Johnnie struggle in the car, Johnnie explains, Lina's doubt is resolved, the car U-turns to take them back together. The unity of the place — containing transgression and sexuality and doubt and guilt, the whole family romance — splits, the perspective now lost, the picture of ambiguity broken in the absolute-since-here-arbitrary 'banality' of the enforced happy ending (the constraint of 'Cary Grant') which brings back, as its contradiction, the memory of the 'original' struggle outside the church when, in an abrupt moment of violence, Lina is suddenly somewhere else, fighting off Johnnie in the distance of a shot and a space (a windswept empty wasteland in the middle of an English village hitherto and thereafter presented with all the cosy sporting bucolicness one might expect) that is never finally recaptured in — *for* — the film, remains left over within it, a kind of missing spectacle. Benson's painting too — 'his' in so far as it catches him out in his gaze — has its effect as missing spectacle: problem of point of view, different framing, disturbance of the law and its inspectoring eye, interruption of the homogeneity of the narrative economy, it is somewhere else again, another scene, another story, another space.

Snow's stress: events take place. What, then, is this 'taking place' in film? *Suspicion* suggests such a question, its action so tightly dependent on the construction and holding of place, its references to painting in the course of that construction and holding, its points of joke or difficulty, excess or otherness. A question that is today posed with insistence, practically and critically, in film-making and film theory. Annette

Michelson, for instance, describing the achievement of the work of Snow himself, writes that he 'has redefined filmic space as that of action', has refound 'the tension of narrative' in 'the tracing of spatio-temporal *données*'.[2] Snow's example, which is indeed crucial in this respect, can serve here as a simple reminder of the importance of a whole number of differing explorations in independent cinema of space and time, narrative and place. Equally, attention has been directed in film theory to 'spatial and temporal articulations', to 'kinds of space' and their narrative determinations or disruptions. The basic text of such an attention is Noël Burch's *Theory of Film Practice*[3] and something of its implications — its positions — can be seen in the work on Ozu Yasujiro by Edward Branigan, David Bordwell and Kristin Thompson; work which hinges on the demonstration of a certain 'foregrounding' of space in Ozu's films and on the argument that this foregrounding confirms Ozu as a 'modernist' film-maker: 'the modernity of Ozu's work involves the úse of specific spatial devices which challenge the supremacy of narrative causality'; 'space, constructed alongside and sometimes against the cause/effect sequence, becomes "foregrounded" to a degree that renders it at times the primary structural level of the film'; 'it is this foregrounding of the spatial code in Ozu's films that justifies us in classifying Ozu as a "modernist" film-maker',[4] work which in its example in the field of theory again underlines the insistent actuality of the question of space in film and the 'taking place' of events.

If that same question were posed to the start of cinema's history, the answer would come easily enough, without problem: the space of film is the space of reality, film's ambition and triumph is 'to reproduce life' (Louis Lumière); 'nature caught in the act', as a spectator put it after one of the first Cinématographe showings in the Grand Café, while another extolled the finding at last of the 'universal language', 'la langue universelle est trouvée!'.[5] As its source and authority (its very 'author'), the universal language has no less than the universe itself, the world embraced by the eye of the camera and delivered over on screen, the world in views (films are listed as *vues* in early French catalogues). The long shot is there in classical narrative cinema as it subsequently develops as the constant figure of this embracing and authoritative vision, providing the conventional close to a film, the final word of its reality.

That reality, the match of film and world, is a matter of representation, and representation is in turn a matter of discourse, of the organization of the images, the definition of the 'views', their construction. It is the discursive operations that decide the work of a film and ultimately determine the scope of the analogical incidence of the images; in this sense at least, film is a series of languages, a history of codes. The universalist temptation, of course, is exactly the grounding in analogy: film works with photographs and, in the technological, economic and ideological conjuncture of the birth and exploitation of cinema, the photograph is given as the very standard of the reproduction of the real ('photographic realism'). Scientifically, the addition of movement to the photograph to give a picture of life as we see it in the hustle and bustle of the arrival of the train at La Ciotat could be regarded as without interest; illusion is not analysis: Marey, the chronophotographer, has no time for the cinema in the development of which he nevertheless plays a part. Ideologically, the addition of movement (as later the addition of sound to the moving picture) is the possibility of the investment of the photograph as currency of the real in systems of representation that can engage that reality and the guarantee of its vision in a constant — industrial — production of meanings and entertainment within the terms of those meanings.

Meaning, entertainment, vision: film produced as the realization of a coherent and positioned space, and as that realization *in movement*, positioning, cohering, binding in. The passage from views to the process of vision is essentially that of the coding of relations of mobility and continuity. Early film space tends simply to the tableauesque, the set of fixed-camera frontal scenes linked as a story ('The Original Comedy Chase/The Most Familiar and Laughable Incident in the Whole List of Childhood Tales/Shown in Eight Snappy Scenes'[6]). Evidently, the tableau has its structure of representation but that structure misses the subject in the very moment of the movement it now offers: the spectator is placed in respect of the scene but the movement is potentially and perpetually excessive. To link scenes as story is not yet to contain that excess in the achievement of a homogeneously continuous space, the spectator cut in as subject precisely to a process of vision, a positioning and positioned movement. It is here that we touch on the history of cinema in its development of codes and systems: beneath that, on the fact of cinema as order of space and time: 'film is not a sum of images but a temporal form'; 'movement is not just perceived in itself but localized in space ... the spectator is not just responsive to what is moving but also to what stays in place and the perception of movement supposes fixed frames'.[7] Such phenomenological descriptions insist on the interlocking spatio-temporality of film and suggest in their turn something of the general area of the problems of film in this connection, those problems that are currently and rightly important. Bearing in mind the particular points of the emergence of that current importance, the aim in what follows will be to provide a descriptive and theoretical context for understanding the debate and to indicate, in so doing, certain critical conclusions with regard to film as 'narrative space'.

Photography and cinema share the camera. Photography is a mode of projecting and fixing solids on a plane surface, of producing images; cinema uses the images produced by photography to reproduce movement, the motion *of* the flow of the images playing on various optical phenomena (φ-effect, retinal persistence) to create the illusion of a single movement *in* the images, an image of movement. Phenomenologically, the result is characterized as 'neither absolutely two-dimensional nor absolutely three-dimensional, but something between'.[8] The 'something between' is the habitual response to the famous 'impression of reality' in cinema and it is this impression, this reality that are of concern here in their implications for a consideration of space in film.

Stress has been laid in recent work on the situation of cinema in terms of a development of codes of figuration inherited from the Quattrocento, notably codes of perspective.

The focus of attention thus defined is, exactly, the camera: 'a camera productive of a perspective code directly constructed on the model of the scientific perspective of the Quattrocento' (Marcelin Pleynet);[9] the stress, in other words, is on the camera as machine for the reproduction of objects (of solids) in the form of images realized according to the laws of the rectilinear propagation of light rays, which laws constitute the perspective effect. In this connection, there are already a number of remarks and clarifications to be made, remarks that will bear on Quattrocento perspective, the photograph and cinema, and in that order.

The perspective system introduced in the early years of the fifteenth century in Italy (developing above all from Florence) is that of *central projection*: 'It is the art of depicting three-dimensional objects upon a plane surface in such a manner that the picture *may* affect the eye of an observer in the same way as the natural objects themselves. . . . A perfectly deceptive illusion can be obtained only on *two conditions*: (a) the spectator shall use only one eye, (b) this eye has to be placed in the central point of perspective (or, at least, quite near to this point)'.[10] The component elements of that account should be noted: the possible exact match for the eye of picture and object, the deceptive illusion; the centre of the illusion, the eye in place. What is fundamental is the idea of the spectator at a window, an *'aperta finestra'* that gives a view on the world – framed, centred, harmonious (the *'istoria'*). Alberti, in his treatise *Della Pittura* written circa 1435, talks of the picture plane as of a pane of glass on which the world in view can be traced: 'Painters should only seek to present the form of things seen on this plane as if it were of transparent glass. Thus the visual pyramid could pass through it, placed at a definite distance with definite lights and a definite position of centre in space and a definite place in respect to the observer.'[11] The cost of such fixed centrality is the marginal distortion which ensues when the observer's eye is not correctly in position in the centre of the perspective projection but pulls to the edge (like Benson's gaze in *Suspicion*, which then receives the shock of another – confusing – painting). Anamorphosis is the recognition and exploitation of the possibilities of this distortion; playing between 'ap-

pearance' and 'reality', it situates the centre of the projection
of the painting (or of a single element, as in Holbein's 'The
Ambassadors' in the National Gallery) obliquely to the side,
the sense of the painting — its representation — only falling
into place (exactly) once the position has been found. Galileo
abhorred these perversions of the 'normal' view into a turmoil
of lines and colours ('una confusa e inordinata mescolanza di
linee e di colori'[12]) but, developed in the course of the six-
teenth century and particularly appreciated in the following
two centuries, they can be seen as a constant triumph of
central perspective, a kind of playful liberation from its constraints that remains nevertheless entirely dependent on its
system, a ceaseless confirmation of the importance of centre
and position. What must be more crucially emphasized is that
the ideal of a steady position, of a unique embracing centre,
to which Galileo refers and to which anamorphosis pays its
peculiar homage, is precisely that: a powerful *ideal*. To say
this is not simply to acknowledge that the practice of painting
from the Quattrocento on is far from a strict adherence to
the perspective system but demonstrates a whole variety of
'accommodations' (in certain paintings, for example, buildings
will be drawn with one centre according to central perspective
while a separate centre will then be chosen for each set of
human figures); it is also to suggest that there is a real utopianism at work, the construction of a code — in every sense a
vision — projected onto a reality to be gained in all its hoped-
for clarity much more than onto some naturally given reality;
a suggestion that merely repeats the conclusions of Francastel
in his study of the birth of Quattrocento space: 'It was a
question for a society in process of total transformation of a
space in accordance with its actions and its dreams. . . . It is
men who create the space in which they move and express
themselves. Spaces are born and die like societies; they live,
they have a history. In the fifteenth century, the human
societies of Western Europe organized, in the material and
intellectual senses of the term, a space completely different
from that of the preceding generations; with their technical
superiority, they progressively imposed that space over the
planet.'[13] For five centuries men and women exist at ease in
that space; the Quattrocento system provides a practical

representation of the world which in time appears so natural as to offer its real representation, the immediate translation of reality in itself.

The conception of the Quattrocento system is that of a scenographic space, space set out as spectacle for the eye of a spectator. Eye and knowledge come together; subject, object and the distance of the steady observation that allows the one to master the other; the scene with its strength of geometry and optics. Of that projected utopia, the camera is the culminating realization (the camera obscura, described by Giambattista della Porta in 1589 in a treatise on optics, commands attention in the wake of the spread of the Quattrocento system); the images it furnishes become, precisely, the currency of that vision, that space: 'Strong as the mathematical convention of perspective had become in picture making before the pervasion of photography, that event definitely clamped it on our vision and our beliefs about "real" shapes, etc. The public has come to believe that geometrical perspective, so long as it does not involve unfamiliar points of view, is "true", just as a long time ago it believed that the old geometry of Euclid was "the truth" '; 'Every day we see photographs which are central perspective images. If another system were applied to the art of painting one could believe that one was living in a bilingual country.'[14] In so far as it is grounded in the photograph, cinema will contribute to the circulation of this currency, will bring with it monocular perspective, the positioning of the spectator-subject in an identification with the camera as the point of a sure and centrally embracing view (Metz draws further conclusions from this identification in his essay 'The Imaginary Signifier').[15]

'Our field of vision is full of solid objects but our eye (like the camera) sees this field from only one station point at a given moment. . . . '[16] The comparison of eye and camera in the interests of showing their similarity has come to seem irresistible: our eye like the camera, with its stationary point, its lens, its surface on which the image is captured, and so on. In fact, of course, any modern scientific description of the eye will go on to indicate the limits of the comparison. Our eye is never seized by some static spectacle, is never some motionless recorder; not only is our vision anyway binocular,

but one eye alone sees in time: constant scanning movements
to bring the different parts of whatever is observed to the
fovea, movements necessary in order that the receptive cells
produce fresh neuro-electric impulses, immediate activity of
memory inasmuch as there is no brute vision to be isolated
from the visual experience of the individual inevitably engaged in a specific socio-historical situation. In a real sense,
the ideological force of the photograph has been to 'ignore'
this in its presentation as a coherent image of vision, an image
that then carries over into a suggestion of the world as a kind
of sum total of possible photographs, a spectacle to be
recorded in its essence in an instantaneous objectification for
the eye (it would be worth considering the ideological determinations and resonances of the development and commercialization of polaroid photography); a world, that is, conceived outside of process and practice, empirical scene of the
confirmed and central master-spectator, serenely 'present' in
tranquil rectilinearity (a curvilinear perspective, for which
arguments of 'optical realism' can be adduced if need be,
comfortably rejected as out of true, as 'wrong').

Cinema is involved with photograph and camera, its principal matter of expression that of moving photographic images
('principal' as we know it in its history), its prime achievement
that of the creation of the 'impression of reality' — 'neither
absolutely two-dimensional nor absolutely three-dimensional,
but something between'. The latter description reads in many
ways like an account of the effect of depth of field which
gives very much the possibility of a cued construction of
space in accordance with the Quattrocento system. Yet
cinema can also use in one and the same film quite other
projections (lenses with long focal length, for example), projections which approximate more or less, but differently,
to the perspective model; simply, angles and distances change,
the centre shifts its points. It may well be that classically
cinema acquires 'the mobility of the eye' while preserving the
contained and delimited visual field on which 'correct' perspectives depend, but the mobility is nevertheless difficult:
movement of figures 'in' film, camera movement, movement
from shot to shot; the first gives at once a means of creating
perspective (the movements of the figures in a shot can 'bring

out' the space, show relative positions, suggest depth) and a problem of 'composition' (film is said to destroy the 'ordinary laws' of pictorial organization because of its moving figures which capture attention against all else); the second equally produces problems of composition and, though often motivated in the manuals by some extension of the eye-camera comparison (the camera executes the same movements as the head; horizontal panning is turning the head, etc.), is strictly regulated in the interests of the maintenance of scenographic space (the version of space, indeed, which determines the justifying comparison); the third, again apt to receive the comparative motivation ('In so far as the film is photographic and reproduces movement, it can give us a lifelike semblance of what we see, in so far as it employs editing, it can exactly reproduce the *manner* in which we normally see it'[17]), effectively indicates the filmic nature of film space, film as constantly the construction of a space (thus Branigan will conclude that 'that space exists only at twenty-four frames per second'[18]). The ideal of space remains that of photographic vision which brings with it the concern to sustain the camera as eye; in the sense of the detached, untroubled eye discussed earlier, an eye free from the body, outside process, purely looking (no matter, finally, if the falsity of the eye-camera comparison be admitted since it can be retrieved with a confirming twist: the eye in cinema is the *perfect* eye, the steady and ubiquitous control of the scene passed from director to spectator by virtue of the cinematic apparatus: 'The director's aim is to give an *ideal* picture of the scene, in each case placing his camera in such a position that it records most effectively the particular piece of action or detail which is dramatically significant. He becomes, as it were, a ubiquitous observer, giving the audience at each moment of the action the best possible viewpoint.'[19] The ideal, however, is a construction, the mobility acquired is still not easy, the shifting centre needs to be settled along the film in its making scenes, its taking place; space will be difficult.

To put it another way: mobility is exactly what is *possible* in film, complicit — the possibility of holding film within a certain vision, thereby 'perfected' — and radical — the possibility of film disturbing that vision, with which none the less it is immediately involved, historically, industrially, ideologically. Cinema is not simply and specifically ideological 'in itself'; but it is developed in the context of concrete and specific ideological determinations which inform as well the 'technical' as the 'commercial' or 'artistic' sides of that development. For Marey, cinema did nothing 'to rid the eye of any of its illusions' since set up precisely to play on the illusions of a conventional vision, to 'reproduce life' as Lumière put it; for Vertov, cinema could be made to challenge that vision by constructions of dissociations in time and space that would produce the contradictions of the alignment of camera-eye and human-eye in order to displace the subject-eye of the social-historical individual into an operative — transforming — relation to reality. Film is dominantly articulated in the interests of the 'theatrical cinema' Vertov sought to shatter, the world of the scene and the stasis of its relations of vision, but Brecht, and Benjamin with him, will see in the very fact of the succession of film images a certain contradiction to be exploited against that theatre, for a different vision. a different space. In its developments and possibilities, its constraints and disruptions, it is the whole question of space in film that must now be examined further.

The examination of space in film may be divided for the moment into two: the examination of space 'in frame', of the space determined by the frame, held within its limits; the examination of space 'out of frame', the space beyond the limits of the frame, there in its absence and given back, as it were, in the editing of shot with shot or in camera movement with its reframings. The division can be maintained long enough to allow an order for the remarks that follow, remarks which will finally suggest more clearly its inadequacy.

Screen, frame: Notions of screen and frame are fundamental in the elaboration of the perspective system. Leonardo da Vinci writes: 'Perspective is nothing else than seeing a place (or objects) behind a pane of glass, quite transparent, on the surface of which the objects behind that glass are drawn.

These can be traced in pyramids to the point in the eye, and
these pyramids are intersected on the glass pane.'[20] The pane
is at once a frame, the frame of a window, and a screen, the

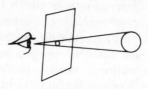

area of projection on which what is seen can be traced and
fixed; from the Quattrocento on, the 'pane' delimits and holds
a view, the painter's canvas as a screen situated between eye
and object, point of interception of the light rays (see figure).
It is worth noting, indeed, in Renaissance (and post-Renais-
sance) painting the powerful attraction of the window as
theme, the fascination with the rectangle of tamed light, the
luminously defined space of vision. In Ghirlandaio's 'Vecchio
e bambino' (Louvre, Paris), Titian's 'Isabel di Portogallo'
(Prado, Madrid) or Dürer's 'Selbstbildnis' (Prado), for
example, a window opens to the right, behind the figure por-
trayed, on to the perspective of a distant horizon; the figure
placed almost as by a cinema screen, the sudden illumination
of another view, a frame of light to which we are invited to
attend. More important, however, is to grasp the very idea of
the frame as fully historical in the developments it is given.
Before the fifteenth century, frames hardly exist, other than
as the specific architectural setting that is to be decorated
(wall, altarpiece, or whatever); it is during that century that
frames begin to have an independent reality, this concomitant
with the growth of the notion itself of 'a painting' (the first
instance of the use of the word 'frame' in an artistic sense
recorded by the *Oxford English Dictionary* is *c*. 1600). The
new frame is symmetrical (the centred rectangle, clearly
'composable') and inevitable (the Quattrocento system cannot be realized without it, it becomes a reflex of 'natural'
composition). Significantly, it brings with it the easel (first
recorded instance *c*. 1634 – 'a frame or easel called by
artists'), 'significantly' because the easel is precisely dependent
on the idea of 'a painting' as single, central view. The painter
stands as spectator in front of his easel (in this history it is

men who are the professionals of painting, the authoritative
gaze), capturing on the canvas screen the scene behind onto
which it gives and which it sets as such; no longer englobed in
the area of the painting (dome or arch or ceiling), the painter
is definitely upright, an eye on the world, an eye that stations
itself, with the easel carried from place to place, much like a
tripod. Easel painting, that is, established along with perspective system and camera obscura (the latter itself rapidly becomes a portable apparatus for the mobile painter), is a step
in the direction of the camera, a camera that will provide
screen and frame and the image reflected, fixed, painted with
light: a camera that will culminate this whole vision.

'Frame' describes the material unit of film ('the single
transparent photograph in a series of such photographs printed
on a length of cinematographic film', 'twenty-four frames a
second') and, equally, the film image in its setting, the delimitation of the image on screen (in Arnheim's *Film as Art*,
for example, 'frame' and 'delimitation' are assumed as synonymous). Framing, determining and laying out the frame, is
quickly seen as a fundamental cinematic act, the moment of
the very 'rightness' of the image: 'framing, that is to say,
bringing the image to the place it must occupy', a definition
taken from a manual for teachers written in the 1920s.[21]
Quickly too, and in consequence, it becomes the object of an
aesthetic attention concerned to pose decisively the problems
of the composition of the frame, of what Eisenstein calls
'mise en cadre'.

'There it is, our 1.33 to 1 rectangle, it will tolerate precious
little tampering with at all' (Hollis Frampton).[22] The compositional rectangle is there, carried through into cinema;
space is structured within its frame, areas are assigned position in relation to its edges. In a sense, moreover, the constraint of the rectangle is even greater in cinema than in
painting: in the latter, its proportions are relatively free; in
the former, they are limited to a standard aspect ratio
(Frampton's 1.33 to 1 rectangle, the aptly named 'academy
frame') or, as now, to a very small number of ratios,[23] with
techniques such as masking the sides of the frame to change
the size of the rectangle in general disfavour. Hence the rectangle must be mastered – 'Maîtriser le rectangle', the title

of one of the key sections in a modern manual for young
people. Hence the rules for mastery, rules which come straight
from the Quattrocento system, its balanced vision and the
composition of the clarity thus decided; so, from the same
modern manual: 'To consider the rectangle as a surface
crossed by lines of force . . . and with strong points (the
points of intersection of those lines) is to guarantee it a solid
base structure and to refuse the notion of it as a sort of visual
hold-all'; 'If, therefore, we have to place an actor in this rectangle, one of the best places will be that which follows one
of the lines of force in question. And the face, "strong point"
of the human person, will be placed at one of the strong
points of the rectangle'; 'A second character will naturally be
placed at one of the strong points . . . '; 'Let us quickly note
when we come to "landscapes" how inharmonious is a division
of the surface which does not correspond to the famous
"third" and how placing the horizon midway in the frame is
only apparently logical.'[24] In cinema, however, these rules
also have their 'excess', there is always a further court of
appeal – life itself, the very aim of cinema: 'But cinema is
life, is movement. The cinéaste must not fall into the traps of
a plastic aesthetic. Failure to remember the rules of framing
will often bring agreeable surprises, for it is not without truth
that the world is already, in itself, harmonious.'[25]

If life enters cinema as movement, that movement brings
with it nevertheless its problems of composition in frame, as
was mentioned earlier in the discussion of perspective. In fact,
composition will organize the frame in function of the human
figures in their actions; what enters cinema is a logic of movement and it is this logic that centres the frame. Frame space,
in other words, is constructed as narrative space. It is narrative
significance that at any moment sets the space of the frame to
be followed and 'read', and that determines the development of
the filmic cues in their contributions to the definition of space
in frame (focus pull, for example, or back-lighting). Narrative
contains the mobility that could threaten the clarity of vision
in a constant renewal of perspective; space becomes place –
narrative as the taking place of film – in a movement which is
no more than the fulfilment of the Renaissance impetus, an
impetus that a De Kooning can describe as follows: 'It was up

to the artist to measure out the exact space for a person to die in or to be dead already. The exactness of the space was determined or, rather inspired by whatever reason the person was dying or being killed for. The space thus measured out on the original plane of the canvas surface became a "place" somewhere on the floor.'[26] What is crucial is the conversion of seen into scene, the holding of signifier on signified: the frame, composed, centred, narrated, is the point of that conversion.

Cinema as 'life in its truth as scene', the frame as the instance of such a vision. Metz talks here of the regime 'of the primal scene and the keyhole': 'the rectangular screen permits every type of fetishism, all the effects of "just-before", since it places at exactly the height it wants the sharp vibrant bar which stops the seen. . . . '[27] The fascination of the scene is there, and from the beginnings of cinema with its tableaux, its dramatic masks (including the keyhole-shaped matte; as in *A Search for Evidence*, AM & B 1903), its occasional thematic directnesses (in *Gay Shoe Clerk*, Edison Co. 1903, which involves a flirtatious shoe clerk, an attractive young lady and her chaperone armed with an umbrella, a cut-in close-up shows the young lady's ankle with the clerk's hand gripping her foot into the shoe[28]); the fetishism is there, with the edge, the limit, the setting, the careful place, and from Alberti on — witness that whole series of machines and devices for the production of a certain distance of image, a sure illusion of scrutiny. Simply, the 'just-before' in film is spatially moving, the itinerary of a fixity perpetually gained, and the frame stands — acts — in relation to that.

As for the screen, it receives and gives the frame, its flatness halts the image and lays the base of that triangle for which the spectator's eye provides the apex. Doubtless there is a sheer pleasure for the position of the eye in the very fact of the projection of the frames onto and from the screen, in their 'hitting the screen';[29] a space is established with no 'behind' (it is important that the Lumière brothers should set the screen as they do in the Grand Café and not with the audience on either side of a translucent screen, that cinema architecture should take its forms in consequence, that there should be no feeling of machinery to the side of or beyond the screen, that the screen should be one of the most stable elements in cinema's history), a pure expanse that can be invested with depth. The screen, that is, is at once ground, the surface that supports the projected images, and background, its surface caught up in the cone of light to give the frame of the image. Ground and background are one in the alignment of frame and screen, the 'on screen in frame' that is the basis of the spatial articulations a film will make, the start of its composition.[30]

Psychoanalysis, it may be briefly added, has come to stress the dream as itself projected on a screen: the *dream screen*, blank surface present in dreams though mostly 'unseen', covered over by the manifest content of the projected dream; a screen that represents the breast (infinitely extensive centre of the baby's visual space) and then also sleep (the desire for sleep) as an original ground of pleasure 'before' difference, 'before' identity, 'before' symbolization.[31] In cinema, the images pass (twenty-four per second), the screen remains; covered but there, specified — the images of this or that film — but the same — the satisfying projection of a basic oneness. The force of this relation, however, must be understood: it is the passing of the images that produces the constancy of the screen; without those images the screen is 'empty', with them it is an impression, a surface-ground that the film and the spectator find as the frames hit the screen, that they find intact, safely *in* the background (revealing and disturbing moment when a character in a film throws something, as is said, 'at the screen').[32]

Movement, transitions: From the very first, as though of right, human figures enter film, spilling out of the train, leaving the factory or the photographic congress, *moving* — this is the movies, these are moving pictures. The figures move in the frame, they come and go, and there is then need to change the frame, reframing with a camera movement or moving to another shot. The transitions thus effected pose acutely the problem of the filmic construction of space, of achieving a coherence of place and positioning the spectator as the unified and unifying subject of its vision. It is this process of construction, indeed, which is often regarded as the power of cinema and as defining the overall reality of film as that of a kind of generalized 'trick effect': 'if several successive images represent a space under different angles, the spectator, victim of the "trick effect", spontaneously perceives the space as unitary. . . .'[33]

Early films are typically organized as a series of fixed scenes, with a strict unity of time and place. The example was cited above of *Tom, Tom, The Piper's Son* which tells the well-known story in 'eight snappy scenes', simply joined the one after the other as so many *tableaux*. The actions of the characters in frame, as though on a stage, make out the sense of the image, centre the eye in paths of reading, but within the limits of the distance of the fixed frontal view which creates difficulties of effectively maintaining such a centred perception given the continual wealth of movements and details potentially offered by the photographic image (Ken Jacobs in his film of the same title minutely explores the surface of *Tom, Tom, The Piper's Son*, refilming from the screen and finding in so doing not just 'other' actions but also 'central' actions not easily grasped or possibly even missed in the original – as, for instance, the handkerchief stealing in the opening shot). Those difficulties, in the context of its commercial exploitation, are fundamental for cinema's development. The centre is the movement, not movements but the logic of a consequent and temporally coherent action. The vision of the image is its narrative clarity and that clarity hangs on the negation of space for place, the constant realization of centre in function of narrative purpose, narrative movement: 'Negatively, the space is presented so as not to distract attention from the dominant actions: positively, the space is "used up" by the presentation of narratively important settings, character traits ("psychology"), or other causal agents.'[34] Specific spatial cues – importantly, amongst others, those depending on camera movement and editing – will be established and used accordingly, centring the flow of the images, taking place.

Which is to say, of course, that the *tableau* space of the early films is intolerable in its particular fixity, must be broken up in the interests of the unity of action and place and subject view as that unity is conceived from the narrative models of

the novelistic that cinema is dominantly exploited to relay
and extend. Burch puts it well: 'It was necessary to be able to
film objects or people close up — to isolate a face, a hand, an
accessory (as the discourse of the novel does) — but avoiding
any disorientation of the spectator in respect of his or her
own "reasoned" analysis of the spatial continuum. . . .'[35]
The need is to cut up and then join together in a kind of
spatial *Aufhebung* that decides a superior unity, the binding
of the spectator in the space of the film, the space it realizes.
In the late 1930s and early 1940s, the average shot length of
a full-length Hollywood film has been estimated at about
9—10 seconds,[36] but that fragmentation is the condition of a
fundamental continuity.

    'There are no jerks in time or space in real life. Time and
space are continuous. Not so in film. The period of time that
is being photographed may be interrupted at any point. One
scene may be immediately followed by another that takes
place at a totally different time. And the continuity of space
may be broken in the same manner.'[37] Why is it, Arnheim
goes on to ask, that the 'juggling with space' possible in film
(and including the breaking of a single 'real life' space into
'several successive images . . . under different angles') does
not cause discomfort? The answer refers back to the 'some-
thing-between' status of film previously mentioned: 'Film
gives simultaneously the effect of an actual happening and of
a picture. A result of the "pictureness" of film is, then, that a
sequence of scenes that are diverse in time and space is not
felt as arbitrary. . . . If film photographs gave a very strong
spatial impression, montage probably would be impossible. It
is the partial unreality of the film picture that makes it possible.'[38] The emphasis on the 'pictureness' of the image is
crucial here (there would be problems of cutting for spatial
unity with holography): the space constructed in film is
exactly *a filmic construction*. Thus Mitry, for example, will
write that shots are like 'cells', 'distinct spaces the succession
of which, however, reconstitutes a homogeneous space,
but a space *unlike* that from which these elements were
subtracted'.[39]

    The conception at work in such descriptions can be seen
(even if in this or that writer that conception may be inflected

'aesthetically', turned in the direction of film as 'art'). The filmic construction of space is recognized in its difference but that difference is the term of an ultimate similarity (indeed, a final 'illusion'); the space is 'unlike' but at the same time 'reconstitutes', using elements lifted from real space. In fact, we are back in the realm of 'composition', where composition is now the laying out of a succession of images in order to give the picture, to produce the implication of a coherent ('real') space; in short, to create continuity.

The compositional rules for spatial clarity and continuity are sufficiently well known not to need extended discussion at this stage; it will be enough merely to stress one or two of their determinations. Firstly, the establishment of fixed patterns of clarity for the variation of scale of shot in a scene: there are 'normal ways' of organizing dialogue scenes, action scenes, and so on;[40] these systems allowing for a certain free play — 'exceptions' — within their overall structure in the interests of 'dramatic effect' ('In the normal way, it is almost certainly better to cut the scenes as we have indicated, but ... there may be exceptions when the rules need to be modified to convey certain dramatic effects.').[41] What may be remembered above all in this context is the extreme importance attached to providing an overall view, literally the 'master-shot' that will allow the scene to be dominated in the course of its reconstitution narratively as dramatic unity ('Even where a sequence starts on a detail, it is important that the whole setting should be shown at some stage'[42]). Take the beginning of *Jaws*: a beach party with the camera tracking slowly right along the line of the faces of the participants until it stops on a young man looking off; eyeline cut to a young woman who is thus revealed as the object of his gaze; cut to a high-angle shot onto the party that shows its general space, its situation, before the start of the action with the run down to the ocean and the first shark attack — the shot serves, that is, as a kind of master fold in the sequence, setting it correctly in place. Secondly, the establishment of the 180-degree and 30-degree rules. The former matches screen space and narrative space (the space represented in the articulation of the images), ground and background; with its help, 'one will always find the same characters in the same parts

of the screen'.[43] The 180-degree line that the camera is forbidden
to cross answers exactly to the 180-degree line of the screen
behind which the spectator cannot and must not go, in front
of which he or she is placed within the triangle of representation, the space of the image projected, that is repeated in the
very terms of the fiction of the imaged space. As for the latter,
a 'quick, simple rule that issues directly from the necessities
of cinematic fragmentation' and that avoids the 'disagreeable
sensation' of a 'jump in space',[44] it is finally nothing other
than a specific perspective rule for a smooth line of direction
in film, for the achievement of a smooth line in from shot to
shot. Thirdly and lastly, following on from those more particular remarks, the establishment generally as a powerful
evidence, as a natural basis, of the idea of continuity as
smoothness in transitions: the rules of the filmic construction
of space on screen (master-shot, 180-degree and 30-degree
rules, matching on action, eyeline matching, field/reverse field,
etc.) background the image flow into a unified subject-space,
immediately and fully continuous, reconstitutive: 'Making a
smooth cut means joining two shots in such a way that the
transition does not create a noticeable jerk and the spectator's
illusion of seeing a continuous piece of action is not interrupted.'[45]

Continuity in these terms is also decisive with regard to
transitions and changes of frame effected by camera movement. 'Imperceptible' reframing movements, more definite
pans and tracking shots are developed in the interests of the
narrative composition of space in relation to the actions of
the characters;[46] here, too, rules are elaborated accordingly,
the camera having, for instance, to impregnate space with the
anticipation of action: 'if the actor is accompanied by a
movement of the camera, more "room" must be left in front
of him or her than behind, so as to figure sensorially the
space to be crossed'.[47] In this respect, it is worth bearing in
mind the extent to which the sequence-shot-with-deep-focus
long take valued by Bazin in his account of 'the evolution of
cinematic language' can stay within such a conception of
space. The narrative of a Welles or a Wyler in Bazin's account
is carried through in a manner that retains the particular effects
to be derived from 'the unity of the image in time and space',

a manner that refinds and draws out the essential 'realism' of cinema; a realism in which space is all important: 'the cinematographic image can be emptied of all reality save one — the reality of space'.[48] The space of *Citizen Kane* or *The Best Years of Our Lives* is still entirely dramatic, however; heightened indeed in its drama: as was suggested earlier, deep focus allows composition for a high degree of perspective ('depth of field' exactly), and this can be increased over the long take with its potential definition of a complex action in a single shot, its filling out of movements and positions in a temporally visible demonstration of space as narrative place.[49] It should anyway be noted that the average shot length overall of *Citizen Kane* is 12 seconds, 'about average for its period',[50] and it remains true that classically continuity is built on fragmentation rather than the long take — on a segmentation for recomposition that can bind the spectator in the strong articulations of the unity it seeks to create. Elsewhere, Bazin was to refer to the version of the spatial realism he ontologically cherished provided by Italian Neo-Realism; a version that might show the possibilities of the long take away from an absorbed dramatic space; and so, by contrast, the force of the classical continuity in that dependence on segmentation-articulation and its effective inclusion of the longer take within its terms of spatial construction.

Those terms, as they have been described here, are the terms of a constant welding together: screen and frame, ground and background, surface and depth, the whole setting of movements and transitions, the implication of space and spectator in the taking place of film as narrative. The classical *economy* of film is its organization thus as organic unity and the *form* of that economy is narrative, the *narrativization* of film. Narrative, as it were, determines the film which is contained in its process in that determination, this 'bind' being itself a process — precisely the narrativization. The narration is to be held on the narrated, the enunciation on the enounced; filmic procedures are to be held as narrative instances (very much as 'cues'), exhaustively, without gap or contradiction.

What is sometimes vaguely referred to as 'transparency' has its meaning in this narrativization: the proposal of a discourse that disavows its operations and positions in the name of a signified that it proposes as its pre-existent justification. 'Transparency', moreover, is entirely misleading in so far as it implies that narrativization has necessarily to do with some simple 'invisibility' (anyway impossible — no one has yet seen a signified without a signifier). The narration may well be given as visible in its filmic procedures; what is crucial is that it be given as visible *for the narrated* and that the spectator be caught up in the play of *that* process, that the *address* of the film be clear (does anyone who has watched, say, *The Big Sleep* seriously believe that a central part of Hollywood films, differently defined from genre to genre, was not the address of a process with a movement of play and that that was not a central part of their pleasure?).

Within this narrativization of film, the role of the character-look has been fundamental for the welding of a spatial unity of narrative implication. In so many senses, every film is a veritable drama of vision and this drama has thematically and symptomatically 'returned' in film since the very beginning: from the fascination of the magnifying glass in *Grandma's Reading Glass* to Lina's short-sightedness in *Suspicion* to the windscreen and rear-view mirror of *Taxi Driver*, from the keyhole of *A Search for Evidence* to the images that flicker reflected over Brody's glasses in *Jaws* as he turns the pages of the book on sharks, finding the images of the film to come and which he will close as he closes the book; not to mention the extended dramatizations such as *Rear Window* or *Peeping Tom*. How to make sense in film if not through vision, film with its founding ideology of vision as truth? The drama of vision in the film returns the drama of vision of the film: the spectator will be bound to the film as spectacle as the world of the film is itself revealed as spectacle on the basis of a narrative organization of look and point of view that moves space into place through the image-flow; the character, figure of the look, is a kind of perspective within the perspective system, regulating the world, orientating space, providing directions — and for the spectator.

Film works at a loss, the loss of the divisions, the discontinuities, the absences that structure it — as, for example, the 'outside' of the frame, off-screen space, the *hors-champ*. Such absence is the final tragedy of a Bazin, who wants to believe in cinema as a global consciousness of reality, an illimitation of picture frame and theatre scene — 'The screen is not a frame like that of a picture, but a mask which allows us to see a part of the event only. When a person leaves the field of the camera, we recognize that he or she is out of the field of vision, though continuing to exist identically in another part of the scene which is hidden from us. The screen has no wings . . . '[51] — but who can only inspect the damage of 'camera angles or prejudices',[52] acknowledge none the less the frame, the scene, the mask, the hidden, the absent. The sequence-shot-with-deep-focus long take functions as a utopia in this context — the ideal of a kind of 'full angle', without prejudices, but hence too without cinema; the ideal recognized in *Bicycle Thieves*, 'plus de cinéma'.[53]

Burch writes that 'off-screen space has only an intermittent or, rather, *fluctuating* existence during any film, and structuring this fluctuation can become a powerful tool in a film-maker's hands'.[54] The term 'fluctuation' is excellent, yet it must be seen that the work of classical continuity is not to hide or ignore off-screen space but, on the contrary, to contain it, to regularize its fluctuation in a constant movement of reappropriation. It is this movement that defines the rules of continuity and the fiction of space they serve to construct, the whole functioning according to a kind of metonymic lock in which off-screen space becomes on-screen space and is replaced in turn by the space it holds off, each joining over the next. The join is conventional and ruthlessly selective (it generally leaves out of account, for example, the space that might be supposed to be masked at the top and bottom of the frame, concentrating much more on the space at the sides of the frame or on that 'in front', 'behind the camera', as in variations of field/reverse field), and demands that the off-screen space recaptured must be 'called for', must be 'logically consequential', must arrive as 'answer', 'fulfilment of promise' or whatever (and not as difference or contradiction) — must be narrativized. Classical continuity, in other words, is an order of the pregnancy of space in frame; one of the narrative

acts of a film is the creation of space[55] but what gives the
moving space its coherence in time, decides the metonymy as
a 'taking place', is here 'the narrative itself', and above all as
it crystallizes round character as look and point of view. The
fundamental role of these is exactly their pivotal use as a
mode of organization and organicization, the joining of a
film's constructions, the stitching together of the overlaying
metonymies.

'If in the left of the frame an actor in close-up is looking
off right, he has an empty space in front of him; if the following shot shows an empty space to the left and an object
situated to the right, then the actor's look appears to cross an
orientated, rectilinear, thus logical space: it seems to bear
with precision on the object. One has an eye-line match.'[56]
The look, that is, joins form of expression — the composition
of the images and their disposition in relation to one another
— and form of content — the definition of the action of the
film in the movement of looks, exchanges, objects seen, and
so on. Point of view develops on the basis of this joining
operation of the look, the camera taking the position of a
character in order to show the spectator what he or she sees.[57]
Playing on the assumption of point of view, a film has an evident means of placing its space, of giving it immediate and
holding significance; Burch talks of the establishment of an
organization founded on the 'traditional dichotomy between
the "subjective camera" (which "places the spectator in the
position of a character") and the "objective camera" (which
makes the spectator the ideal, immaterial "voyeur" of a profilmic pseudo-reality).'[58]

This account, however, requires clarification. The point-of-
view shot is 'subjective' in that it assumes the position of a
subject-character but to refer to that assumption in terms of
'subjective camera' or 'subjective image' can lead to misunder-
standing with regard to the functioning of point of view.
Subjective images can be many things; Mitry, for example,
classifies them into five major categories: 'the purely mental
image (more or less impracticable in the cinema); the truly
subjective or analytical image (i.e. what is looked at without
the person looking), which is practicable in small doses; the
semi-subjective or associated image (i.e. the person looking +

what is looked at, which is in fact looked at from the view-point of the person looking), the most generalizable formula; the complete sequence given over to the imaginary, which does not raise special problems; and finally the memory image, which is in principle simply a variety of the mental image but, when presented in the form of a flash-back with commentary, allows for a specific filmic treatment which is far more success-ful than in the case of other mental images.'[59] The point-of-view shot includes 'the semi-subjective or associated image' (its general mode) and 'the truly subjective or analytical image' (its pure mode, as it were) in that classification but not necessarily any of the other categories (a memory sequence, for instance, need not contain any point-of-view shots); what is 'subjective' in the point-of-view shot is its spatial positioning (its place), not the image or the camera.

To stress this is to stress a crucial factor in the exploitation of the film image and its relation to point-of-view organization. Within the terms of that organization, a true subjective image would effectively need to mark its subjectivity *in the image itself*. Examples are common: the blurred image of Gutman in *The Maltese Falcon* is the subjective image of the drugged Spade; the blurring of focus marks the subjectivity of the image, exclusively Spade's, and the spectator is set not simply *with* Spade but *as* Spade. They are also limited, since they depend exactly on some recognizable — marking — distortion of the 'normal' image, a narratively motivated aberration of vision of some kind or another (the character is drugged, intoxicated, short-sighted, terrified . . . down to he or she running, with hand-held effects of the image 'jogging', or even walking, with regular speed of camera movement for-ward matched on a shot that effectively establishes the character as in the process of walking; the latter represents the lowest limit on the scale since the camera movement is there a weak subjective marking of the image which itself remains more or less 'normal' — except, of course, and hence this limit position of the banal action of walking, that the normal image is precisely static, that movement in a central perspective system can quickly become a problem of vision). The implication of this, of course, is then the strength of the unmarked image as a constant third person — the vision of

picture and scene, the Quattrocento view, Burch's 'voyeur'
position — *which is generally continued within point-of-view
shots themselves*; the point-of-view shot is marked as subjective
in its emplacement but the resulting image is still finally (or
rather firstly) objective, the objective sight of what is seen
from the subject position assumed. Indicatively enough, the
general mode of the point-of-view shot is the shot which
shows both what is looked at and the person looking. Instances
of the pure shot, showing what is looked at without the person looking, however, are equally conclusive. Take the shot
in *Suspicion* of the telegram that Lina receives from Johnnie
to tell her of his intention to attend the Hunt Ball: the telegram is clearly shown from Lina's reading position and the
end of the shot — the end of the reading — is marked by her
putting down her glasses onto the telegram lying on a table,
the glasses thus coming down into frame; the position of the
shot is marked as subjective with Lina but the image nevertheless continues to be objective, 'the real case' for the narrative.[60]

Point of view, that is, depends on an overlaying of first and
third person modes. There is no radical dichotomy between
subjective point-of-view shots and objective non-point-of-view
shots; the latter mode is the continual basis over which the
former can run in its particular organization of space, its disposition of the images. The structure of the photographic
image — with its vision, its scene, its distance, its normality —
is to the film somewhat as language is to the novel: the
grounds of its representations, which representations can
include the creation of an acknowledged movement of point
of view. This is the sense of the spectator identification with
the camera that is so often remarked upon (Benjamin: 'the
audience's identification with the actor is really an identification with the camera'; Metz: 'the spectator can do no other
than identify with the camera').[61] The spectator must *see*
and this structuring vision is the condition of the possibility
of the disposition of the images via the relay of character look
and viewpoint which pulls together vision and narrative.
Emphasis was laid earlier on the structures of the structuring
vision that founds cinema; what is emphasized now is the
dependence of our very notion of point of view on those

structures; dependence at once in so far as the whole Quattrocento system is built on the establishment of point of view,
the central position of the eye, and in so far as the mode of
representation thus defined brings with it fixity and movement in a systematic complicity of interaction — brings
with it, that is, the 'objective' and the 'subjective', the 'third
person' and the 'first person', the view and its partial points,
and finds this drama of vision as the resolving action of its
narratives.

Identification with the camera, seeing, the 'ideal picture'
of the scene: 'the usual scene in a classical film is narrated as
if from the point of view of an observer capable of moving
about the room'.[62] Such movement may be given in editing
or by camera movement within a shot, and the importance
accruing to some master view that will define the space of the
mobility has been noted. Movement, in fact, will be treated
as a supplement to produce precisely the 'ideal *picture*'
(going to the movies is going to the pictures): on the basis of
the vision of the photographic image, that is, it will provide
the 'total' point of view of an observer capable of moving
about the room without changing anything of the terms of
that vision, the scene laid out for the central observer (and
spectator); every shot or reframing adds a difference, but that
difference is always the same image, with the organization —
the continuity, the rules, the matches, the pyramid structures
— constantly doing the sum of the *scene*.

That said, it remains no less true, as has again been noted
and as will become important later on, that movement represents a potentially radical disturbance of the smooth stability
of the scenographic vision (hence the need for a systematic
organization to contain it). Such a disturbance, however, is
not as simple as is sometimes suggested and it is necessary
briefly to consider at this stage two instances of disturbance
as they are conventionally described; both bear on the mobility of the camera.

The first is that of what Branigan characterizes as the impossible place: 'To the extent that the camera is located in an
"impossible" place, the narration questions its own origin,
that is, suggests a shift in narration'.[63] 'Impossible', of course,
is here decided in respect of the 'possible' positions of the

observer moving about, the disturbance involved seen as a disjunction of the unity of narration and narrated, enunciation
and enounced. Thus defined, impossible places are certainly
utilized in classical narrative cinema, with examples ranging
from the relatively weak to the relatively strong. At one end
of the range, the weak examples would be any high or low
angles that are not motivated as the point of view of a character; or, indeed, any high or low angles that, while so motivated,
are nevertheless sufficiently divergent from the assumed normal upright observing position as to be experienced as in
some sense 'impossible' in their peculiarity (the most cele-
brated — and complex — example is the dead-man-in-the-
coffin point of view in *Vampyr*).[64] At the other end, the
strong examples — those intended by Branigan — can be illus-
trated by a description of two shots from *Killer's Kiss*: (1) as
Davey, the boxer-hero, is seen stooping to feed his goldfish,
there is a cut to a shot through the bowl, from the other side,
of his face peering in as the feed drops down; since the bowl
is on a table against a wall, the place taken by the camera is
not possible; (2) Rappello, the dance-hall owner, furious at
being left by the heroine, is drinking in a back-room, its walls
covered with posters and prints; a close-up of a print showing
two men leering from a window is followed by a shot of Rappello who throws his drink at the camera ('at the screen'!); a
crack appears as the drink runs down a plate of glass; impossibly, the shot was from 'in' the print. The second — and
related — instance of disturbance is that of the development
of camera movement as a kind of autonomous figure; what
Burch calls 'the camera designated as an "omnipotent and
omniscient" (i.e. manipulative and pre-cognitive) presence'.[65]
This presence too is utilized in classical narrative cinema and
weak and strong examples can once more be indicated. In
Taxi Driver, Travis Bickle is seen phoning Betsy after the
porno-film fiasco; as he stands talking into the pay-phone,
fixed on a wall inside a building, the camera tracks right and
stops to frame a long empty corridor leading out to the street;
when Travis finishes his call, he walks into frame and exits via
the corridor. The tracking movement designates the camera
with a certain autonomy — there is an effect of a casual deci-
sion to go somewhere else, off to the side of the narrative —

but the example is ultimately weak: the corridor is eventually brought into the action with Travis's exit and, more importantly, it has its rhyming and thematic resonances — the corridors in the rooming-house used by Iris, the marked existential atmosphere of isolation, nothingness, etc. Stronger examples are provided in the work of an Ophuls or a Welles — the spectacular tracking shot at the start of *Touch of Evil* or the intense mobility in many of the shots at the end of that same film.

These two instances of disturbance have been characterized here in their existence in established cinema simply to make one or two points directly in the context of the present account. Thus, the examples given of autonomy of camera movement are all clearly operating in terms of 'style' (Welles, Ophuls, the tics of a new American commercial cinema that has learnt a consciousness of style). The crucial factor is not the valuation of camera movement, be it autonomous, but the point at which a certain work on the camera in movement produces the normality of the third person objective basis as itself a construction, gives it as role or fiction and breaks the balance of the point-of-view system. Similarly, the examples of the impossible place from *Killer's Kiss*, which also have their reality as stylistic marking in the film, are without critically disruptive extension in themselves, are simply tricks (in the sense of spatial prestidigitations): the impossible place is entirely possible if held within a system that defines it *as such*, that it confirms in its signified exceptionality. The felt element of trick, moreover, raises the general point of the realization of film as process. It is too readily assumed that the operation — the determination, the effect, the pleasure — of classical cinema lies in the attempt at an invisibility of process, the intended transparency of a kind of absolute 'realism' from which all signs of production have been effaced. The actual case is much more complex and subtle, and much more telling. Classical cinema does not efface the signs of production, it contains them, according to the narrativization described above. It is that process that is the action of the film for the spectator — what counts is as much the representation as the represented, is as much the production as the product. Nor is there anything surprising in this: film is not a static and isolated object but a series of relations with the spectator it imagines, plays and sets as subject in its movement. The process of film is then perfectly available to certain terms of excess — those of that movement in its subject openings, its energetic controls. 'Style' is one area of such controlled excess, as again, more powerfully, are genres in their specific version of process. The musical is an obvious and extreme example with its systematic 'freedom' of space — crane choreography — and its shifting balances of narrative and spectacle; but an example that should not be allowed to mask the fundamental importance of the experience of process in other genres and in the basic order of classical cinema on which the various genres are grounded. Which is to say, finally, that radical disturbance is not to be linked to the mere autonomization of a formal element such as camera movement; on the contrary, it can only be effectively grasped as a work that operates at the expense of the classical suppositions of 'form' and 'content' in cinema, posing not autonomies but contradictions in the process of film and its narrative-subject binding.

The construction of space as a term of that binding in classical cinema is its implication for the spectator in the taking place of film as narrative; implication-process of a constant refinding — space regulated, orientated, continued, reconstituted. The use of look and point-of-view structures — exemplarily, the field/reverse field figure (not necessarily dependent, of course, on point-of-view shots)[66] — is fundamental to this process that has been described in terms of *suture*, a stitching or tying as in the surgical joining of the lips of a wound.[67] In its movement, its framings, its cuts, its intermittences, the film ceaselessly poses an absence, a lack, which is ceaselessly recaptured for — one needs to be able to say 'forin' — the film, that process binding the spectator as subject in the realization of the film's space.

In psychoanalysis, 'suture' refers to the relation of the individual as subject to the chain of its discourse where it figures missing in the guise of a stand-in; the subject is an effect of the signifier in which it is represented, stood in for, taken place (the signifier is the narration of the subject).[68]

Ideological representation turns on — supports itself from — this 'initial' production of the subject in the symbolic order (hence the crucial role of psychoanalysis, as potential science of the construction of the subject, with historical material-ism), directs it as a set of images and fixed positions, meto-nymy stopped into fictions of coherence. What must be emphasized, however, is that stopping — the functioning of suture in image, frame, narrative, etc. — is exactly a *process*: it counters a productivity, an excess, that it states and restates in the very moment of containing in the interests of coherence — thus the film frame, for example, exceeded from within by the outside it delimits and poses and has ceaselessly to recap-ture (with post-Quattrocento painting itself, images are multi-plied and the conditions are laid for a certain mechanical reproduction that the photograph will fulfil, the multiplication now massive, with image machines a normal appendage of the subject). The process never ends, is always *going on*; the con-struction-reconstruction has always to be renewed; machines, cinema included, are there for that — and their ideological operation is not only in the images but in the suture.

The film poses an image, not immediate or neutral,[69] but posed, framed and centred. Perspective-system images bind the spectator in place, the suturing central position that is the sense of the image, that sets its scene (in place, the spectator *completes* the image as its subject). Film too, but it also moves in all sort of ways and directions, flows with energies, is potentially a veritable festival of affects. Placed, that move-ment is all the value of film in its development and exploita-tion: reproduction of life and the engagement of the spectator in the process of that reproduction as articulation of co-herence. What moves in film, finally, is the spectator, immobile in front of the screen. Film is the regulation of that movement, the individual as subject held in a shifting and placing of desire, energy, contradiction, in a perpetual retotalization of the imaginary (the set scene of image and subject). This is the investment of film in narrativization; and crucially for a co-herent space, the unity of place for vision.

Once again, however, the investment is in the process. Space comes in place through procedures such as look and point-of-view structures, and the spectator with it as subject

in its realization. A reverse shot folds over the shot it joins
and is joined in turn by the reverse it positions; a shot of a
person looking is succeeded by a shot of the object looked at
which is succeeded in turn by a shot of the person looking to
confirm the object as seen; and so on, in a number of multiple
imbrications. *Fields* are made, *moving* fields, and the process
includes not just the completions but the definitions of
absence for completion. The suturing operation is in the process, the give and take of absence and presence, the play of
negativity and negation, flow and bind. Narrativization, with
its continuity, closes, and is that movement of closure that
shifts the spectator as subject in its terms: the spectator is the
point of the film's spatial relations — the turn, say, of shot to
reverse shot —, their subject-passage (point-of-view organization, moreover, doubles over that passage in its third/first
person layerings). Narrativization is scene and movement,
movement and scene, the reconstruction of the subject in the
pleasure of that balance (with genres as specific instances of
equilibrium) — *for* homogeneity, containment. What is fore-
closed in the process is not its production — often signified as
such, from genre instances down to this or that 'impossible'
shot — but the terms of the unity of that production (narration on narrated, enunciation on enounced), the other scene
of its vision of the subject, the outside — heterogeneity, contradiction, history — of its coherent address.

The role of look and point of view for the holding organization
of space has been heavily stressed; the whole weight of the
remarks made has been on the image and on the laying out of
the images in film. It is important, however, not to overlook
in this context the role played by sound. Hence one or two
indications here concerning sound and film's narrative of
space, indications all the more necessary in that they bear on
the problem of address.

The equivalent of the look in its direction of the image-
track is the voice in its direction of the sound-track. Significantly, there is much less play of process practicable with the
latter in classical cinema than with the former; the sound-track
is hierarchically subservient to the image-track and its pivot is
the voice as the presence of character in frame, a supplement

to the dramatization of space, along with accompanying 'sound effects'. Vertov's loathed 'theatrical cinema' is confirmed in its domination with the arrival of sound and the narrative forms of cinema develop in respect of that theatricality (the truth of the common reference to 'novels dramatized for the screen'). In fact, the regime of sound as voice in the cinema is that of the 'safe place': either in the narrative in its 'scenes', as with the normal fiction film, or in the discourse that accompanies the images to declare their meaning, as with the documentary film which remains marginal in commercial cinema. The safe place is carefully preserved in fiction films. Voice and sound are diegetic (with music following the images as an element of dramatic heightening), generally 'on screen' but equally defined in their contiguity to the field in frame when 'off screen'; voice-over is limited to certain conventional uses (as, for example, the direction of memory sequences, a kind of documentary of the past of a life within the film) which effectively forbid any discrepancy — any different activity — between sound and image tracks (Malick is even reputed to have had trouble in getting Holly's narration in *Badlands* accepted). The stress is everywhere on the unity of sound and image and the voice is the point of that unity: at once subservient to the images and entirely dominant in the dramatic space it opens in them — the film stops when the drama the voices carry in the image ends, when there are no more words, only 'The End'.

In this context, against that unity, it is worth recalling briefly the insistent emphases of Straub—Huillet in their work on the 'directness' of sound: 'Space-off exists. Which is what one discovers when one shoots with sound and what those who shoot without cannot know. And they are wrong to do so, because they go against the essence of cinema. They have the impression that they are only photographing what they have in front of the camera; but that is not true, one also photographs what one has behind and around the frame.'[70] Straub—Huillet disrupt by reference to an extreme of 'truth' (often linked, as here, to a Bazin-like reference to 'the essence of cinema'). Dominant and subservient, the voice drama in the fiction film can be dubbed after the shooting, added on to an image track which, as script, it was anyway controlling (in Italy, where Straub–Huillet work, dubbing is standard practice). Neither dominant nor subservient, sound (which includes a veritable work on the grain of the voice itself, the material rhythms of its existence in language – *Othon*, *History Lessons*, *Moses and Aaron*) in Straub–Huillet *gives space*, not as coherence but as contradiction, heterogeneity, outside (the extreme of 'truth' thus leading away from Bazin): 'Shooting with direct sound, one cannot cheat with space: one must respect it, and, in respecting it, one offers the spectator the possibility of reconstructing it, because a film is made of "extracts" of time and space. One can also not respect the space one films, but one must then offer the spectator the possibility of understanding why one did not respect it. . . . '[71] It is the coherence of the *fiction* that falls: the fiction film disrespects space in order to construct a unity that will bind spectator and film in its fiction; where a Godard breaks space, fragments and sets up oppositions in the interests of analysis ('analysis with image and sound'), Straub–Huillet film a unity, sound and image, in and off, that will never 'make a scene'; in both cases, the address is complex, in process, no longer the single and central vision but a certain freedom of contradictions.[72]

What has been described here is the whole context of the importance of work and reflection on space in film, the whole context of its actuality; Burch, for instance, as film-maker and theorist, can say that 'we are just beginning to realize that the formal organization of shot transitions and "matches" in the strict sense of the word is the essential cinematic task'.[73] What must now be considered are some of the terms in which that actuality has been articulated and, critically, something of the implications of those terms; the examples will be limited, the final argument more general.

It is hardly necessary to underline the extent to which American independent cinema set about destroying the narrative frame in the interests of the action of the film as flow of images (flashes of movement and energy, sheets of rhythmic multiplicity), the perpetual action of an eye for which every object, in Brakhage's words, is 'a new adventure of perception', an eye in panic and fascination (like that of Hitchcock's Benson in front of the troubling picture). There is a sense of re-doing the history of cinema again, from zero; hence, in part and at the same time, the interest accorded to experimental directions indicated and lost in the early moments of that history (including those of 'cubist cinema'; Benson's painting has its specific resonances here and in the radical separation from Quattrocento space that cubism represents[74]) or even to the interrogation of its initial productions (as Jacobs explores and extends *Tom, Tom, The Piper's Son*, finding and creating fresh spaces on screen).

Evidently, the practice of American independent cinema is not to be limited to the simple desire for the capture of the present — the presence — of a phenomenologico-romantic visionary consciousness, what P. Adams Sitney calls 'the cinematic reproduction of the human mind'. At a time when that cinema already has its own history — from *Meshes of the Afternoon* to *Zorns Lemma*, the field covered by Sitney's book[75] —, the very problems of screen and frame, movement and framing, and their narrative-spatial determinations are of increasing concern — and this without being reducible to a category of the 'structural film' type. In Frampton's *Poetic Justice*, nothing but a table with a cup of coffee, a cactus, and in the middle a pile of sheets of paper; silently, the sheets follow one another to the top of the pile and we read — fragments seized at the whim of the succession — the scenario of a film; a rubber glove rests on the last page. In J. J. Murphy's *Print Generation*, a sequence of images is passed through a series of 'generations' until it arrives at a printing close to the 'normal' from which it is run back down to the initial state of luminous abstraction. Two quite different films, but both engaging problems of narrative and frame: in the one, the image is fixed in the frame of a written narrative which makes this film which exceeds it, vacillation of reading the film (where is the point of view to be held?), each viewing varied against the fixity of the image (and not more complete); in the other, the film as the action of a technical process, the image narrated, scales of readings in that action (suspense of the point of recognition of the image), the screen in dots, impressions-pulsations of new spaces.

Those examples were minor, cited as such and a little at random. The films of Michael Snow, on the contrary, are a major example, quite different but again finding their particular force in this connection, with respect to space in film. *Wavelength* gives the economy of the formal explorations of the 'structural film' in a radical work on the problems of the spaces of narrative and the narratives of space. The famous forty-five minute zoom constructs the filmed room (the New York loft) into a *crossing*, a time of continuously jerky spaces – the superimposition of fixed images, the unsteadiness of the regulation of the zoom, the human events that arrive in its path. It is a matter of narrating in the time of the film the space covered, of making that crossing of space – with its frames (the play of the windows onto the street, the photograph picked out on the wall, the events themselves – so many quotations of actions, of commonplaces) and its framings (the changing focal length of the zoom) – the scene of a veritably filmic action, a process without any *single* view. In *La Région centrale*, the programme of 360-degree rotations works at the loss of any perspective frame, as a kind of speed-jubilation of a time of space (landscape as movement, movement as landscape), an impossibly uncentred narrative in which the apparatus (the camera), sole 'character' in the film, serves to disjoin the subject-eye, to open gaps between sight and seen, overturning the technological 'yield' of cinema.

What remains is the difficulty of sound as the address of voice. *Rameau's Nephew by Diderot* (*thanx to Dennis Young*) *by Wilma Schoen* is conceived as a 'real "talking picture" ' (hence the title, Rameau's nephew as the irruption of the body-voice onto the scene of philosophy) and over its twenty-four sections – so many sketches and gags – explores 'image-sound relationships' in the cinema in a way that often connects with the spatial preoccupations to be found in, say, *Wavelength* and *La Région centrale*. The result is something akin to an indefatigably prolonged version of Godard's *Le Gai Savoir*, but lacking the political insistence of any analysis as text; the film talks, jokes, accumulates, overlays, reverses, confuses and tricks as though empty of any reflexive contradiction. Its work, as it were, fails to *carry*, in the sense in which the crucial filmic-narrative concerns of the previous films might have led one to expect, fails to transform — and to transform politically — the cinematic relations of form and content, and the setting of narrative accordingly.

Burch's arguments in *Theory of Film Practice* come together as a central plea — developed via terms such as 'dialectical', 'organic', 'structural', these terms tending to synonymity — for the poetic function of film, 'conflictual organization' as 'unity through diversity': 'Although film remains largely an imperfect means of communication, it is none the less possible to foresee a time when it will become a totally immanent object where semantic function will be intimately joined with its plastic function to create a *poetic function*.'[76] The analysis of spatial tensions and movements is made in this context and *Theory of Film Practice* finally falls within a range of writing on film that would also include, for instance, the work of Arnheim; Burch introduces structural conflict with dialectical relationship, disorientation with dynamic organicism, the ultimate concern always composition, film as *art*. It is easy enough, moreover, to transpose such a concern with its brand of phenomenological formalism, into notions of 'deconstruction' as a formal crisis of codes. Indicating the importance of deconstruction in an interview in 1973 ('I should say right now that this concept of deconstruction is something which is quite important to me'), Burch continues: 'Let's leave the word deconstruction for the moment because it's a more modern word than the actual origin of this concept, which can be traced back to the Prague school and to Jakobson and Mukařovský and work in semiotics which involves the concept that there is an aesthetic message (I'm using the word now in the specifically semiotic sense) if you like, produced through the subversion, through the breaking down of, through creating a crisis in what we call the dominant codes of representation in a given medium. This language can be extended to practically anything.'[77] What is emerging is a potentially critical idea of deconstruction covered by its simple articulation as a poetics, this latter being its history in Burch's work. Thus a description of *Man with a Movie Camera*

as deconstruction film will read exactly as a transposition of
the definition of the poetic function of film the totally immanent object found in *Theory of Film Practice*, with
Jakobson precisely as an underlying presence for both: 'But
it was only with Dziga Vertov's *Man with a Movie Camera*
(1929) that the work of paradigmatic deconstruction of the
illusionist codes gave rise to the constitution of a comprehensive dialetic, informing the totality of the work along the
syntagmatic axis.'[78]

Something of the problems of a formal idea of deconstruction can be seen in the Thompson—Bordwell and Branigan
texts on Ozu. What those texts suggest is a modernity of Ozu's
films based on a foregrounding — here too, it is worth noting
the reference made to concepts derived from literary Formalism — of space that challenges the supremacy of narrative
causality. In fact, there are two components in the argument
developed. The first concerns the demonstration of a certain
autonomy of space: 'Ozu's films include not only the spaces
between points but also spaces *before* and *after* actions occur
there . . . '; 'Ozu's cutaways and transitions usually present
spaces distinct from the characters' personal projects . . . at
the most radical level, in presenting space empty of character
— spaces around characters, locales seen before characters
arrive or after they leave, or even spaces which they never
traverse — Ozu's films displace the illusion of narrative
presence and plenitude.'[79] The second concerns the description of a 360-degree shooting space: 'If Hollywood builds
upon spatial patterns bounded by 180 degrees and 30 degrees,
Ozu's films use limits of 360 degrees and 90 degrees.'[80]

These two components are related in their demonstration
of the importance of space in Ozu but can at the same time
be differentiated a little in a way that will help focus the
problems of that demonstration. Thus, the analysis of the
360-degree shooting space is very much the analysis of a closed
system: 'Ozu's scenic space is systematically built up, modified by subtle repetitions and variations within the limits he
has set for himself.'[81] That system is effectively different
from that of Hollywood (where 360-degree movements are
very conventionally and narratively limited — the slow pan at
the beginning of the drive in *Red River*), which it can serve to

contrast, but the question of its effective functioning, its critical activity, *in the films* is not posed. Indeed, certain formulations imply 360-degree space in Ozu as a formal accompaniment to a content that in itself and in its other devices is very close to Hollywood: 'Once this pattern of circular space is established, Ozu's films use the same devices Hollywood does, but without the axis of action.'[82] The description of the autonomy tends to avoid consideration of its activity outside of formal limits. More radical in a sense is the account of a presence of space based specifically on terms of autonomy, the space that is there, distinct, before and after; this in so far as it suggests an exploration of the tensions between surface and place, screen and frame, economy of the film and economy of narrative. When followed through into the discussion of graphic matches, however, the tensions are once again shown as subdued in a formal independence (near to an art of composition): 'Such graphic play is central to Ozu's modernity because the screen surface itself and the configurations that traverse it are treated as independent of the scenographic space of the narrative.'[83] Spatial nuances are set up as graphic matches in the systematic and repetitious space of the films, but what are the critical tensions of this autonomy in the *action* of the films?

In this respect, the description of the 'most transgressive transition', the baseball-game transition in *An Autumn Afternoon*, is significantly weak: 'Ozu's transition goes first to the place the character is *not*, then to the place where he actually is. This sequence is one of the culminations of Ozu's exercises in moving through spaces between scenes independently of any narrative demands.'[84] Nothing in the description suggests more than an 'exercise'; the transition goes not so much to the place the character is not as to the place *he should have been*, a projected space (Kawai insists that he is going to the game), exactly a simple *place*; certainly there is a play of difficulty in finding the men, but that play — irony and revelation (so Kawai didn't go . . .) — is not transgressive of the terms of the narrative in the terms of the narration it gives. And to pose such a transgressive activity involves an analysis directed not to a unity of dominants and overtones but to the bindings of those terms, to the modes of address of film in its subject-vision relations in narrative space, to the contradictions they contain.

Frames hit the screen in succession, figures pass across screen through the frames, the camera tracks, pans, reframes, shots replace and—according to the rules—continue one another. Film is the production not just of a negation but equally, simultaneously, of a negativity, the excessive foundation of the process itself, of the very movement of the spectator as subject in the film; which movement is stopped in the negation and its centring positions, the constant phasing in of subject vision ('this but not that' as the sense of the image in flow). Such a negativity is the *disphasure* of the subject in process, the fading, the 'flickering of eclipses' or 'time between' that the classical narrative film seeks to contain in *its* process, film aiming thus to *entertain* the subject (etymologically, 'entertainment' is a holding-in and a maintenance — the subject occupied in time). Narrativization is then the term of film's entertaining: process and process contained, subject bound in that process and its directions of meaning. The ideological operation lies in the balance, in the capture and regulation of energy; film circulates — rhythms, spaces, surfaces, moments, multiple intensities of signification — and narrativization entertains the subject — on screen, in frame — in exact turnings of difference and repetition, semiotic and suture, negativity and negation; in short, the spectator is *moved*, and *related* as subject in the process and images of that movement. The spatial organization of film as it has been described here in the overall context of its various articulations is crucial to this moving relation, to the whole address of film: film makes space, takes place as narrative, and the subject too, set — sutured — in the conversion of the one to the other.

In his essay on 'Le cinéma et la nouvelle psychologie', already cited above, Merleau-Ponty writes that 'the aspect of the world would be transformed if we succeeded in seeing as *things* the intervals between things'.[85] The formulation can now be recast: the relations of the subject set by film — its vision, its address — would be radically transformed if the intervals of its production were opened in their negativity, if the fictions of the closure of those intervals were discontinued, found in all the contradictions of their activity. Take the second of the five sections of *Penthesilea* in which Wollen traces a complex itinerary round the sun-and-shadow-strewn house, the camera accompanying, leaving, rejoining him, fixing for itself — in its own time — the memory-cards of the discourse he delivers. A certain influence from films of Snow is clear but difficult: a theoretical narrative of the space of the film — Wollen here 'speaks' his and Mulvey's film — within a constant disframing of the time of that narrative, the shifting choreography of discourse to space in the wake of the camera. The camera has an 'autonomy' — dancing high-angle circles round a table-top, for instance — but that autonomy is given in its history: its history in the sequence, where it slips from classical subordination of movement to character into a rediscovery of the space of the initial sub-ordination through new variations of movement along its path; its history in cinema, Wollen's discourse involving reflection on film space and spaces; its history in this film, which plays systematically across its sections on movement and fixity, scene and space and distance. The autonomy, moreover, is at every moment taken up elsewhere, divided in its articulations within the political action of the film which is itself, exactly, a series of actions, of histories — the women's struggle, Penthesilea, the Amazons, Kleist and psychoanalysis, functions of myth and questions posed to 'feminine' myths, to images and to cinema and to this film with respect to those myths — that includes the action and the history of the camera spacing as a critical term in its reflection — finding the cards, for example, and indicating the problems of voice and image and movement and their material force: what is a film that speaks, speaks politically? how is the point to be arrived at from which such a question can be formulated in film? Hence, indeed, the importance of the final section of *Penthesilea* with its four screens on screen, the film remembered in their separation and relation and working over, the film repeated differently again in this critical inflection of its present struggle: this woman who now faces the camera with the problem of speech, these images, these words and sounds, this film in the intervals of struggle, with the narrative space of the film extended plurally to a movement of spaces and the contradictions of their intersection. *Penthesilea*, finally, marks a recognition, and across the unity of the conventional opposition in film, that to fight for a revolutionary content is also to fight for a revolution of form but that — in a dialectic which defines the work of a specific signifying practice — the content ceaselessly 'goes beyond' (Marx's insistence at the start of *The Eighteenth Brumaire*) and that a *political* struggle is to be carried through in the articulations of 'form' and 'content' at every point of that process.

Which is where it becomes possible to say that the narrative space of film is today not simply a theoretical and practical actuality but is a crucial and political avant-garde problem in a way which offers perspectives on the existing terms of that actuality. Deconstruction is quickly the impasse of formal device, an aesthetics of transgression when the need is an activity of transformation, and a politically consequent materialism in film is not to be expressed as veering contact past internal content in order to proceed with 'film as film'[86] but rather as a work on the constructions and relations of meaning and subject in a specific signifying practice in a given socio-historical situation, a work that is then much less on 'codes' than on the operations of narrativization. At its most effectively critical, moreover, that work may well bear little resemblance to what in the given situation is officially acknowledged and defined as 'avant-garde'; in particular, and in the context of the whole account offered here of film and space, it may well involve an action at the limits of narrative within the narrative film, at the limits of its fictions of unity.

This, to take an example chosen since Japanese films are often used as a contrasting frame of reference in the formal deconstruction arguments, is the radical importance of several of the films of Oshima Nagisa. The *intensity* of Oshima's work lies in a 'going beyond' of content that constantly breaks available articulations of 'form' and 'content' and poses the film in the hollow of those breaks. The films have an immediate presence of narrative articulation but that presence in each case presents the absence of another film the discourse of which, punctuating this film and its space, finds its determinations, its contradictions, its negativity. Split *in* the narrativization, the films are thus out of true with — out of 'the truth' of — any single address: the subject divided in complexes of representation and their contradictory relations.

In *Death by Hanging*, the prisoner refuses to die and the hanging fails: R The Korean (Yun Yun-do), R worker, as the court verdict begins, cannot be hanged again until he is 'conscious', 'himself', fully identical with 'the real R' ('he must realize his guilt is being justly punished'); the officials busy themselves in efforts to restore R, their R, the legal R, and the film builds its immediate narrative round those efforts, organized into sections announced by written titles, stages in the problem of R's identity and identification. At one point, the action leaves the carefully and theatrically structured confines of the execution-chamber and moves outside, still in the interests of the memory of R that must be reawakened in R; the sequence finds shanty town, river bank, station, alley-way, bridge, ice-cream parlour, and school, where the Education Officer (Watanabe Fumio) becomes carried away in his demonstration of the murder of the woman on the roof. One or two remarks must suffice to suggest the difficult space of this sequence.

The first is general: throughout the sequence R is accompanied by a voice, that of the Education Officer who recounts and enacts R's story, where he should be in the space in frame, specifying its place; the Education Officer's voice is literally 'all over the place'—R sits down by the river, the Education Officer joins him to tell what his feelings must have been and must be (since in this acting out R has to be made to coincide exactly with the repeated story); R telephones at the station, the Education Officer, out of frame, calls instructions. Simply, R is never quite there, in the place assigned; the events take place without him and the space-place conversion is troubled in that absence; another film is possible, but only in the hollow of this film, dialectically in its contradiction. R has neither voice nor look: voices are given — that of the Education Officer but also that of the Sister figure (Koyama Akiko) with a direct militant account of R's acts — and R can come to accept (being R for the sake of all Rs, a certain reality in the Sister) and look (into camera, framed in close-up against the Japanese-flag motif at the start of the final — acceptance — section); something remains over, however, something that Oshima's films constantly attempt to articulate as a new content (in Marx's sense of a content that goes beyond) in the exploration of the political relations of the subject and the subjective relations of the political. In that double and simultaneous movement lies a utopianism that is equally constant, the utopianism of another space (remember the utopianism of the perspective system and its centred subject), a radically transformed subjectivity (often formulated by Oshima in terms of the imaginary as in excess of existing definitions of reality and struggle which it sees as both necessary and as alienating in those definitions — the whole play between R and the Sister figure, between the original news story of the Korean, the reactions to the story in contemporary Japan, and Oshima's film). The work of Oshima is political and obliquely political, a return of the one on the other through questions posed to meanings, images, fictions of unity, the questions of subject relations and transformations.

The second remark is particular: a quotation from within the sequence as a kind of coda. R is never quite there, in the place assigned. R is seen coming along the river bank followed by the compact group of uniformed officials, the Education Officer on a bicycle narrating the story, R eventually bringing the group to a halt by sitting down (Stills 14, 15); the Education Officer sits down in his turn by the side of R, the camera having been repositioned to hold the two men in left profile in near shot but still facing in the direction from which the

14   15

group arrived, R turns to look back over his right shoulder
(Still 16); a cat is revealed as the object of R's gaze by a
straightforward transition answering to the orientation of
space established by that gaze in the previous shot (Still 17);
R is now seen from a position behind him and the Education
Officer, R continuing to look back (Still 18); the cat (Still
19); R in close-up seen looking, the camera here positioned
to his right (Still 20); the cat (Still 21); a long shot from
behind the cat which shows the group of officials, the Education Officer's bicycle, R sitting looking and the Education
Officer stretched out beside him in a line across the frame
from left to right, with the bridge beyond in the background

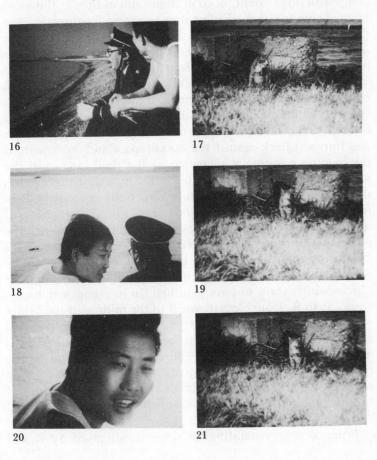

16   17

18   19

20   21

22

and the cat in the centre foreground (Still 22); the shots are
linked by cuts and the camera is fixed in every shot. The
composition is evident, both in frame and in the development
of the shots together, the last shot reversing the direction and
the positions in frame — note the group of officials — of the
first; in three shots, punctuated by the cat shots, the camera
moves a half circle round R, enacting a little narrative on its
own, and of R on his own, taken away from the Education
Officer, more and more distant from the story relayed by his
voice until the separation of the close-up. What then breaks
the R/cat exchange, gives the distancing of R one more turn
and brings it back against the overall space and movement of
this sequence within a sequence, is the final long shot: the
match of look and object is interrupted by a shot that catches
the cat itself as look in another direction; in front of R in
frame, with R and along the line of his look, the cat gazes off
into camera, to something never seen, abruptly absent. The
place of the camera, moreover, is impossible: object of R's
gaze, the cat is seen against a little 'wall' of concrete blocks;
gazing, the cat is seen free in its space, from behind the
blocks which seem to have vanished. In its composed lines —
from cat to R, from bicycle wheel to the middle of the bridge
— the shot offers a perfect perspective, but a perspective that
runs short in the completion it seeks the scene opened out —
intervalled — in its focus of address, a sudden pull to the
relations of space, to the elements therein, to the places they
take, and for whom (as Oshima's voice over at the close of
the film turns its action to the audience — 'and you too, and
you too, and you too . . . ').

From Benson's painting to this cat, glimpsed by R and

pulled out of his gaze, framed elsewhere. Thus pulled, thus framed, the cat says something important that has been the whole insistence here: events take place, a place for some one, and the need is to pose the question of that 'one' and its narrative terms of film space.

Notes

Published in *Screen* vol. 17 no. 3 (Autumn 1976) pp. 68–112. An initial version of the discussion of avant-garde film and *Penthesilea* appeared in French as 'Espaces du récit dans le cinéma indépendent américain', *Art Press* no. 7 (1977) pp. 24–5. Further consideration of *Suspicion* can be found in 'Droit de regard', in Raymond Bellour (ed.), *Le Cinéma américain, analyses de films* vol. 2 (Paris: Flammarion, 1980) and of *Death by Hanging* in 'Anata mo', *Screen* vol. 17 no. 4 (Winter 1976/7) pp. 49–66.

1. Cf. Picasso's 'Nature morte au pichet, bol et fruit' 1931 (Picasso Collection).

2. Annette Michelson, 'Toward Snow', *Artforum* (June 1971) p. 32; reprinted in Peter Gidal (ed.), *Structural Film Anthology* (London: British Film Institute, 1976) p. 41.

3. Noël Burch, *Theory of Film Practice* (London: Secker & Warburg, 1973); first published in French as *Praxis du cinéma* (Paris: Gallimard, 1969).

4. Kristin Thompson and David Bordwell, 'Space and Narrative in the Films of Ozu', *Screen* vol. 17 no. 2 (Summer 1976) pp. 42, 45; Edward Branigan, 'The Space of *Equinox Flower*' ibid. p. 104.

5. Cf. Georges Sadoul, *Histoire générale du cinéma* vol. 1 (Paris: Denoël, 1963) pp. 288, 290.

6. American Mutoscope and Biograph Company *Bulletin* account of *Tom, Tom, The Piper's Son*, made in 1905 cf. Kemp R. Niver, *The First Twenty Years: A Segment of Film History* (Los Angeles and Berkeley: University of California Press, 1968) p. 88.

7. M. Merleau-Ponty, 'Le cinéma et la nouvelle psychologie', in *Sens et non-sens* (Paris: Gallimard, 1948) p. 110; P. Francastel, 'Espace et illusion', *Revue internationale de filmologie* II–5 (1948) p. 66.

8. R. Arnheim, *Film as Art* (London: Faber, 1969) p. 20.

9. Cf. M. Pleynet, interview (with Gérard Leblanc), *Cinéthique* no. 3 (1969).

10. G. Ten Doesschate, *Perspective: Fundamentals, Controversials, History* (Nieuwkoop: B. de Graaf, 1964) pp. 6–7.

11. Leon Battista Alberti, *On Painting* (New Haven and London: Yale U.P., 1966) p. 51.

12. Galileo, *Opere*, ed. A. Favaro, vol. IX (Florence: Edizione nazionale, p. 129. [A recent book by Ernest B. Gilman, *The Curious Perspective: Literary and Pictorial Wit in the Seventeenth Century* (New Haven and London: Yale U.P., 1978), stresses—as in effect does Galileo—a parodic, almost subversive implication of the use of anamorphosis: 'Although the curious perspective system would have been impossible without the achievement of a systematic linear perspective in the earlier Renaissance, its effect was to parody, question, and even undermine the central cognitive assumption behind perspective representation' (p. 233). It remains, however, that the 'wit' of anamorphosis is constantly a reference to a rational and stable system that it assumes in the very moment it parodies or questions and is thus always available as a final image of order; as witness the idea of anamorphosis in a passage from Leibniz on universal harmony quoted by Gilman (p. 97); 'It is as in the inventions of perspective, where certain lovely drawings appear only as confusion, until one finds their true point of view or sees them by means of a certain glass or mirror. . . . Thus the apparent deformities of our little world come together as beauties in the greater world, and there is nothing opposed to the unity of a universally perfect principle.' What is clear and important is that the Renaissance perspective system opens the way to an assurance and a trap for the look, the vision of the subject, to an *illusion* of *reality*, in the play of which two terms a whole problematic of representation is established—a problematic in which cinema is engaged, *moves*.]

13. P. Francastel, *Études de sociologie de l'art* (Paris: Denoël, 1970) pp. 136–7.

14. W. M. Ivins, *Art and Geometry* (New York: Dover, 1964) p. 108; Ten Doesschate, op. cit. p. 157.

15. C. Metz, 'Le signifiant imaginaire', *Communications* no. 23 (1975) pp. 35–7; translation, 'The Imaginary Signifier', *Screen* vol. 16 no. 2 (Summer 1975) pp. 52–4.

16. Arnheim, op. cit., p. 18.

17. E. Lindgren, *The Art of the Film* (London: Allen & Unwin, 1948) p. 54.

18. Branigan, 'The Space of *Equinox Flower*', p. 104.

19. K. Reisz and G. Millar, *The Technique of Film Editing* (New York and London: Hastings House, 1968) p. 215.

20. J. P. Richter (ed.), *The Literary Works of Leonardo da Vinci* vol. 1 (London: Oxford U.P., 1939) p. 150. The figure is Leonardo's own, ibid. [Leonardo was much exercised by difficulties in the match between the Albertian perspective system and visual appearances, exploring elsewhere the possibility of an alternative system based on a spherical optics; cf. J. White, *The Birth and Rebirth of Pictorial Space* (Boston: Boston Book and Art Shop, 1967) pp. 207–15.]

21. E. Reboul, *Le Cinéma scolaire et éducateur* (Paris: Presses Universitaires de France, 1926).

22. Hollis Frampton, interview with Simon Field and Peter Sainsbury, *Afterimage* no. 4 (Autumn 1972) p. 65.

23. Frampton writes elsewhere: 'The film frame is a rectangle, rather anonymous in its proportions, that has been fiddled with recently in the interests of publicising, so far as I can see, nothing much more interesting than the notions of an unbroken and boundless horizon. The wide screen glorifies, it would seem, frontiers long gone: the landscapes of the American corn-flats and the Soviet steppes; it is accommodating to the human body only when that body is lying in state. Eisenstein once proposed that the frame be condensed into a "dynamic" square, which is as close to a circle as a rectangle can get, but his arguments failed to prosper.' 'The Withering Away of the State of Art', *Artforum* (December 1974) p. 53.

24. *Apprendre le cinéma*, special issue of *Image et son*, no. 194 bis (May 1966) pp. 119, 121.

25. Ibid. p. 123.

26. Quoted by Rosalind Krauss in 'A View of Modernism', *Artforum* (September 1972) p. 50. Krauss comments: 'Perspective is the visual correlate of causality that one thing follows the next in space according to rule . . . perspective space carried with it the meaning of narrative: a succession of events leading up to and away from this moment; and within that temporal succession—given as a spatial analogue—was secreted the "meaning" of both that space and those events.'

27. C. Metz, 'Histoire/discours', in J. Kristeva, J.-C. Milner and N. Ruwet (eds), *Langue, discours, société* (Paris: Seuil, 1975) p. 304; translation, 'History/Discourse', *Edinburgh '76 Magazine* (1976) p. 23.

28. A still from the shot can be found in Niver, op. cit. p. 36.

29. 'There must be a lot of essential pleasure just in the films when they hit the screen—I heard this expression yesterday, "to hit the screen", that's fantastic in English. Hit the screen—this is really what the frames do. The projected frames hit the screen.' Peter Kubelka, interview with Jonas Mekas, *Structural Film Anthology* p. 102.

30. It can be noted that much independent film work has been concerned to experience dislocations of screen and frame; Sharits, for example, writes: 'When a film "loses its loop" it allows us to see a blurred strip of jerking frames; this is quite natural and quite compelling subject material. When this non-framed condition is intentionally induced, a procedure I am currently exploring, it could be thought of as "anti-framing".' Paul Sharits, 'Words per page', *Afterimage* no. 4 (Autumn 1972) p. 40. For an attempt by a film-maker to provide a theoretical formulation of such dislocation using the notion of a 'second screen' (in fact, the frame on screen in a narrative coherence of ground/background) that independent cinema will destroy ('in independent cinema, there is no second screen'), see Claudine Eizykman, *La jouissance-cinéma* (Paris: Bourgois, 1976) esp. pp. 147—51.

31. B. D. Lewin, 'Sleep, the Mouth, and the Dream Screen', *Psychoanalytic Quarterly* vol. XV (1946) pp. 419—34.

32. Discussion of screen and dream screen is suggested at the close of

a recent article by Guy Rosolato, 'Souvenir-écran', *Communications* no. 23 (1975) pp. 86—7. See also my 'Screen Images, Film Memory', *Edinburgh '76 Magazine* (1976) pp. 33—42.

33. C. Metz, *Essais sur la signification au cinéma* vol. II (Paris: Klinck-sieck, 1972) p. 189.

34. Thompson and Bordwell, 'Space and Narrative in the Films of Ozu', p. 42. For an initial discussion of procedures of image centring ('specification procedures'), see my 'Film and System: Terms of Analysis' part II, *Screen* vol. 16 no. 2 (Summer 1975) pp. 99—100.

35. Noël Burch, 'De *Mabuse* à *M*: le travail de Fritz Lang', in *Cinéma Théorie Lectures*, special issue of the *Revue d'Esthétique* (Paris: Klinck-sieck, 1973) p. 229.

36. See Barry Salt, 'Statistical Style Analysis of Motion Pictures', *Film Quarterly* (Fall 1974) pp. 13—22.

37. Arnheim, op. cit. p. 27.

38. Ibid. p. 32.

39. J. Mitry, *Esthétique et psychologie du cinéma* vol. II (Paris: Editions Universitaires, 1965) p. 10.

40. Branigan gives the schema of the inverted pyramid structure characteristic of classical Hollywood film, art. cit. p. 75. ('1. Establishing Shot (a major variant: we see a detail of the scene, then pull back or cut to the establishing shot) 2. Long Shot (master shot) 3. Medium Two-Shot 4. Reverse Angles (over-the-shoulder shots) 5. alternating Medium Close-ups 6. Cut-away (or Insert) 7. alternating Medium Close-ups 8. Re-establishing Shot (usually a reverse angle or two-shot).')

41. Reisz and Millar, op. cit. pp. 224—5.

42. Ibid. pp. 225—6.

43. *Apprendre le cinéma*, p. 142.

44. Ibid. p. 151.

45. Reisz and Millar, op. cit. p. 216. To emphasize the reality of this smoothness as construction rather than 'reflection', it can be noted that the Navajo Indians studied by Worth and Adair, though capable of producing the 'correct' continuity (for example, by matching on action), were very far from the 'rules' in their films, articulating another system of space as an area of action (in which 'jumps' from the standpoint of the vision of the rules became essential continuities); cf. Sol Worth and John Adair, *Through Navajo Eyes* (Bloomington: Indiana U.P., 1972) p. 174 and stills 22—35, 35—40.

46. Barry Salt has pointed to the importance of the outdoor-action subject film (notably the Western) historically in this development; 'The Early Development of Film Form', *Film Form* no. 1 (Spring 1976) pp. 97—8.

47. *Apprendre le cinéma*, p. 125 ('an orientated empty space is a promise').

48. André Bazin, *What is Cinema?* vol. I (Los Angeles and Berkeley: University of California Press, 1967) p. 108.

49. Which is not, of course, to say that deep focus must necessarily be used in this way; for analysis of 'a refusal of perspective within

depth of field', see Cl. Bailblé, M. Marie and M.-C. Ropars, *Muriel*
(Paris: Galilée, 1974) pp. 128—36.

50. Salt, 'Statistical Style Analysis', p. 20.

51. André Bazin, *Qu'est-ce que le cinéma?* vol. II (Paris: Cerf, 1959)
p. 100.

52. Bazin, *Qu'est-ce que le cinéma?* vol. IV (Paris: Cerf, 1962) p. 57.

53. Ibid. p. 59. For discussion of Bazin on Neo-Realism, see Chrisopher
Williams's article of that title in *Screen* vol. 14 no. 4 (Winter 1973/4)
pp. 61—8.

54. Burch, *Theory of Film Practice*, p. 21.

55. Branigan, art. cit. p. 103.

56. *Apprendre le cinéma*, p. 148.

57. For a detailed analysis of the point-of-view shot, see Edward
Branigan, 'Formal Permutations of the Point-of-View Shot', *Screen*
vol. 16 no. 3 (Autumn 1975) pp. 54—64.

58. Noël Burch and Jorge Dana, 'Propositions', *Afterimage* no. 5
(Spring 1974) p. 45.

59. As summarized by Metz in his 'Current Problems in Film Theory',
Screen vol. 14 no. 1/2 (Spring/Summer 1973) p. 49.

60. In fact, and not surprisingly, the less narratively 'metonymical'
and the more 'metaphorical' is what is looked at in the pure point-of-
view shot (without the marking of image distortion), the nearer such a
shot will come to subjectivizing the image. Released from prison at the
beginning of *High Sierra*, Roy Earle is shown walking through a park,
breathing the air of freedom; shots of him looking up are followed by
shots of tree tops against the sky, with a certain effect of subjectivization
in so far as the tree tops against the sky are outside the immediate
scope of the movement of the narrative and, objectively useless (unlike
Lina's telegram in *Suspicion*), belong only for Roy's character (he was
born of a modest farming family and is not the hardened criminal his
reputation would have him be).

61. Walter Benjamin, *Illuminations* (London: Fontana, 1970) p. 230;
C. Metz, 'Le signifiant imaginaire', p. 35; translation, p. 52.

62. Edward Branigan, 'Narration and Subjectivity in Cinema', mimeo-
graphed (University of Wisconsin—Madison, 1975) p. 24.

63. Ibid.

64. Discussed by R. Barthes, 'Diderot, Brecht, Eisenstein', *Screen* vol.
15 no. 2 (Summer 1974) p. 38; Branigan, 'Formal Permutations', p. 57;
and M. Nash, '*Vampyr* and the Fantastic', *Screen* vol. 17 no. 3 (Autumn
1976) pp. 32—3, 54—60.

65. Burch and Dana, art. cit. p. 45.

66. Salt distinguishes three varieties of field/reverse field and assigns
an order and approximate dates for their respective appearances: 'It is
necessary to distinguish between different varieties of angle — reverse-
angle cuts; the cut from a watcher to his point of view was the first to
appear; the cut from one long shot of a scene to another more or less
oppositely angled long shot, which must have happened somewhat later
— the first example that can be quoted is in *Røverens Brud* (Viggo

Larsen, 1907); and the cut between just-off-the-eye-line angle — reverse-angle shots of two people interacting — the earliest example that can be quoted occurs in *The Loafer* (Essanay, 1911).' 'The Early Development of Film Form', p. 98.

67. For details of the introduction and various accounts of suture, see 'On suture', present volume pp. 86—101.

68. Cf. J.-A. Miller, 'La suture', *Cahiers pour l'analyse* no. 1 (1966) pp. 37—49; translation, 'Suture', *Screen* vol. 18 no. 4 (Winter 1977/8) pp. 24—34.

69. 'Another characteristic of the film image is its neutrality.' *Encyclopaedia Britannica* (Macropaedia) vol. 12 (Chicago, etc., 1974) p. 498.

70. 'Entretien avec Jean-Marie Straub et Danièle Huillet)', *Cahiers du cinéma* no. 223 (August—September 1970) p. 54.

71. 'Sur le son (entretien avec Jean-Marie Straub et Danièle Huillet)', *Cahiers du cinéma* no. 260—1 (October—November 1975) p. 49.

72. No mention has been made in this section of the difficult problem of the verbal organization of the image according to 'inner speech'; see Paul Willemen, 'Reflections on Eikhenbaum's Concept of Internal Speech', *Screen* vol. 15 no. 4 (Winter 1974/5) pp. 59—70; and 'Language, Sight and Sound', present volume, pp. 204—17. Worth and Adair note examples of Navajo Indians who judged certain *silent* films incomprehensible because 'in English', op. cit. p. 130.

73. Burch, *Theory of Film Practice*, p. 11.

74. Cubism as 'construction of deformable and varied worlds, subject to non-Euclidian but extremely topological notions of proximity and separation, succession and surrounding, envelopment and continuity, independently of any fixed schema and of any metrical scale of measurement', Francastel, op. cit, p. 142; cf., in the same volume, the chapter entitled 'Destruction d'un espace plastique', pp. 191—252.

75. P. Adams Sitney, *Visionary Film* (New York and London: Oxford U.P., 1974).

76. Burch, *Theory of Film Practice*, p. 12; in her 'Introduction', Annette Michelson writes: 'his voice puts forth a claim for total structural rigor and authenticity . . . ', p. xv. It should be noted: firstly, that the remarks made here consider only the implications of Burch's arguments and do not touch on the value of his working out of those arguments; secondly that Burch himself, in the 'Preface' to this English version of his initial French publication (pp. xvi—xx), is retrospectively critical of the book, though within limits which actually close the distance from it he now asserts and bring the intended criticism very near to the formulations of the original.

77. 'Beyond *Theory of Film Practice*: an interview with Noël Burch', *Women and Film* no. 5—6 p. 22.

78. Burch and Dana, art. cit. p. 44 (Jakobson: 'The poetic function projects the principle of equivalence from the axis of selection into the axis of combination.' 'Linguistics and Poetics', in T. A. Sebeok (ed.), *Style in Language* (Cambridge, Mass.: M.I.T. Press, 1960) p. 358).

79. Thompson and Bordwell, art. cit. pp. 52, 54.

80. Ibid. p. 58.

81. Ibid.

82. Ibid. p. 60.

83. Ibid. p. 70.

84. Ibid. p. 51; full details of the transition discussed here can be found on this same page. [Thompson and Bordwell have since returned to the terms of their account of Ozu's 'modernism', taking up points made here; see Kristin Thompson, 'Notes on the Spatial System of Ozu's Early Films', *Wide Angle* vol. 1 no. 4 (1977) pp. 8–17 (especially pp. 8–9); David Bordwell, 'Our Dream Cinema: Western Historiography and the Japanese Film', *Film Reader* no. 4 (1979) pp. 45–62 (especially p. 54).]

85. Merleau-Ponty, op. cit. p. 98.

86. 'The structural/materialist film must minimise the content in its over-powering, imagistically seductive sense, in an attempt to get through this miasmic area of "experience" and proceed with film as film. Devices such as loops or seeming loops, as well as a whole series of technical possibilities, can, carefully constructed to operate in the correct manner, serve to veer the point of contact with the film past internal content. The content thus serves as a function upon which, time and time again, a film-maker works to bring forth the filmic event.' Peter Gidal, 'Theory and Definition of Structural/Materialist Film', *Studio International* (November–December 1975) p. 189; reprinted in *Structural Film Anthology*, p. 2.

Chapter 3
On Suture

Use has been made in preceding pages of the idea of a suturing activity involved in the relations a film sustains and is constructed to sustain with its spectator. Suture was initially introduced as a concept within the field of psychoanalysis in an article by Jacques-Alain Miller, the subsequent editor of Lacan's seminar, and then translated into film theory by the *Cahiers du cinéma* critic Jean-Pierre Oudart. The currency that has now been achieved for suture as a concept in film theory, in both French and Anglo-American writing, has not gone without ambiguities and misunderstandings. The following notes try to provide a context for understanding suture, to indicate something of the terms of its original psycho-analytic elaboration and of its subsequent utilization to specify the functioning of cinematic discourse. The first section, which deals with the former, is thus a somewhat 'technical' exposition of certain aspects of Lacanian theory and difficult in this; those aspects are important, however, for grasping where suture comes from into thinking about cinema and the problems it can raise.

I

Miller's article 'La suture' was published in the first issue of *Cahiers pour l'analyse* in 1966 and is based on a paper delivered the previous year to Lacan's seminar at the École Normale Supérieure.[1] Its concern is to propose suture as a necessary concept in the development of 'a logic of the signifier', a concept that Miller sees as being at every moment present in Lacan's work though never there named as such (a point to be qualified below). The article should thus be read as a contribution to Lacanian theory and is, in fact, a commentary on the account of the causation of the subject offered by Lacan in his seminar in 1964 (to which Miller makes direct reference throughout the final section on the relation of subject and signifier), generally available today in two versions: the transcript of the seminar itself and the paper 'Position de l'inconscient' written up in the same year (*SXI*, 185–208/203–29; *É*, 829–50).[2] To understand Miller's introduction of suture, therefore, is inevitably to turn back to the psychoanalytic theory of the subject as set out by Lacan.

The impetus of that theory is, of course, the experience of the unconscious. How then does psychoanalysis conceive of the position of the unconscious (to adopt the title of the paper by Lacan just mentioned)? 'The unconcious *is* a concept forged on the trace of what operates to constitute the subject; the unconscious *is not* a case defining in psychical reality the circle of that which does not possess the attribute (or the virtue) of consciousness' (*É*, 830). The unconscious is in no way 'first', 'in the beginning', or whatever; *it* does not constitute the subject, is not a simple divison from consciousness; on the contrary, it is a concept *forged on the trace of what operates to constitute the subject*. The operation here is that of the order of the symbolic, language as 'cause of the subject' (*E*, 830), and the place of the symbolic, the locus of its operation, is the place of the Other. Hence there are two 'domains': the subject and the Other, with the unconscious 'between them their active break' (*É*, 839). Rather than a topic (leading so often in Freud to difficulties of fixed spatialization, of rigid spatial imagery; as, for instance, the visualization of the unconscious as a dark chamber before the room of the preconscious beyond which lies conscious awareness), description of the psychical apparatus demands, exactly, a logic, a logic of the signifier capable of following out the endless movement of the constitution of the subject, or, as later developed by Lacan, a topology, able to hold to the mobile surface of the subject's articulation.

As active break, the unconscious is finally not so much a position as an *edge*, the junction of division between subject and Other, a process interminably closing. In this connection, Lacan has a passage which, while pointing explicitly to a topology, nevertheless involves stresses and terms that are important for Miller: 'The place in question [the place from which it — *ça, Es* — speaks] is the entrance to the cave in regard to which Plato, as we know, guides us towards the exit, while one imagines seeing the psychoanalyst enter there. But things are less easy, because it is an entrance at which one only ever arrives at closing time (so this place will never be much good for tourists) and because the sole way to have it open a little is to call from within. All of which is not insoluble, if the 'open, sesame!' of the unconscious is its having effect of speech, its being structure of language, but demands of the analyst that he or she come back on the mode of its closure. Gaping, flickering, an alternating suction . . . that is what we have to give account of, which is what we have undertaken by founding it in a topology. The structure of that which closes is inscribed in a geometry wherein space is reduced to a combining: strictly, it is what is called an *edge*' (*É*, 838).

The 'open, sesame!' of the unconscious is its being structure of language, effect of speech or discourse. From this recognition emerge the two repeated emphases in Lacan's elaboration of the idea of the unconscious as a concept forged on the trace of what operates to constitute the subject: the unconscious is the discourse of the Other; the unconscious is structured as a language. The Other is the domain of the symbolic as 'locus of the signifying cause of the subject' (*É*, 841), distribution-circulation of signifiers within which the subject is produced — 'the locus from which the question of its existence may be posed it' (*É*, 549/194). Thus, crucially, the Other in Lacan is the radical thesis with respect to language of the 'primacy' and 'materiality' of the signifier: 'language imposes being' (*SXX*, 44). Far from the necessity that being be for me to speak of it, I must first of all speak for the problem of being to arise, the problem, for instance, of whether or not anything exists which corresponds to or satisfies what I am saying (hence Miller will consider truth as supported from the relations of subject and signifying chain). I must first of all speak, and first of all be spoken, be *bespoken*: produced from and for the Other, the order of discourse that I maintain (*I* as the very index of suture). Outside and given in the symbolic, turning point, the subject is a category of division, of lack (the lack in being that is the subject's place and experience in language – 'the drama of the subject in language is the experience of this *manque-à-être*' *É*, 655 – and the structure of its desire, its want – 'the desire of man is the desire of the Other' *É*, 268): between subject and Other, the unconscious is the breaking edge, a constant flickering of the subject, *flickering in eclipses* (to take up a term from Miller). The unconscious is nowhere present, is only in the relations of the symbolic and the individual effected as subject in those relations, their structuring of desire – the unconscious exactly as discourse of the Other.

The subject is thus nothing other than that which 'slides in a chain of signifiers' (*SXX*, 48), its cause is the effect of language: 'by this effect, it is not cause of itself, carries in it the worm of the cause of its splitting' (*É*, 835). The unconscious is the fact of the constitution-division of the subject in language; an emphasis which can even lead Lacan to propose replacing the notion of the unconscious with that of the subject in language: 'it is a vicious circle to say that we are speaking beings; we are "speakings", a word that can be advantageously substituted for the unconscious'.[3] Veritable treasure of signifiers, the unconscious is structured as a language; psychoanalysis, the 'talking-cure', developing precisely as an acute attention to the movement of the subject in the signifying chain.

It can be objected here that the idea of psychoanalysis as talking-cure in no way implies a 'linguistic version' of the unconscious and that Lacan is far from the substance of Freud's own account in this respect, Freud insisting, for example, that the unconscious knows only 'thing-presentations' not 'word-presentations' which are the province of the preconscious-conscious.[4] Such an objection, however, is raised from a fixed and secondary conception of language (the conception of linguistics itself). To say that the unconscious is structured as a language is not, for Lacan, to say that it is simply 'linguistic': the rhetoric of unconscious operations, the primary processes and their effects of meaning, requires an idea of linguistic activity vastly more complex and extensive than that involved in the language-object-of-study defined by linguistics (where is the linguistics that deals with the question of the construction of the subject?).[5] Radically in excess of the linguistic thinking of its time, Freud's work is nevertheless bound by the terms of that thinking and thus often issues in formulations which repeat a limited objectification of language. Lacan's own emphasis, moreover, is still today given as a displacement of linguistics: Saussure and Jakobson are used, are important, but shifted critically, recast by the psychoanalytic insertion of that question of the subject. Most recently, indeed, Lacan has employed the term *lalangue* specifically to indicate shift and recasting, over and against the distinction *langue/parole* (and its variants) with which linguistics works at the expense of an understanding of the subject in language. Where *langue* is a formal system to be described and *parole* its use by communicating agents, *lalangue* is an 'inconsistent multiplicity', neither system nor use but production, area of the problematic of subject and truth opened by psychoanalysis: 'The unconscious is a knowledge, a know-how with *lalangue*. And what is known-how-to-do with *lalangue* far exceeds what can be accounted for under the heading of language. *Lalangue* affects us first by everything it contains as effects that are affects. If we can say that the unconscious is structured as a language, it is in that the effects of *lalangue*, already there as knowledge, go well beyond everything the being who speaks is capable of stating.' (*SXX*, 127.)

'Everything arises from the structure of the signifier' (*SXI*, 188/206). Given the preceding remarks, let us now come to the actual terms of Lacan's account of the causation of the subject in two fundamental operations which stand in a circular though not reciprocal relation (to quote Miller quoting Lacan; cf. *SXI*, 188/207 and *É*, 840).

The first of these operations is referred to by Lacan as

alienation: the originating division of the subject with itself by virtue of its appearance in the play of signifiers. 'The signifier occurring in the place of the Other not yet grasped has the subject emerge there from the being as yet without speech, but at the price of fixing it. What *there was* there ready to speak — in the two senses the French imperfect gives to *il y avait*: putting it in the moment before (it was there and is there no longer) but also in the moment after (a little more and it was there from having been able to be there) — what *there was* there disappears from being now only a signifier.' (*É*, 840–1.) This alienation is not the fact of the Other (there is no notion of 'enmity', 'inauthenticity', or whatever) but the fact of the subject. Effect, the subject is subject by division, division in the symbolic, is *cut out* by the signifier, represented and excluded, becoming some *one* by its constitution as *less-than-one* — 'the subject is first constituted as minus one'.[6] Since the system of signifiers is by definition complete, the subject can only be entered there as this structure of lack-in-being: 'a trait which is traced from its circle without being able to be counted there; symbolizable by the inherency of a (-1) in the set of signifiers' (*É*, 819/316). What makes the symbolic force of castration is then, as it were, its revelation of lack, its summary metaphor of the division of the subject: 'the phallus functions as signifier of the lack in being that its relation to the signifier determines in the subject' (*É*, 710); 'the phallus . . . is the signifier of the very loss that the subject suffers from the fragmentation of the signifier' (*É*, 715).

Lacan provides this definition of the alienation of the subject with little illustrations-cum-demonstrations. Consider, for instance, the conjunction 'or'. It is possible to distinguish an exclusive 'or' (I'll go to Glasgow or Edinburgh': the choice is absolute, to go to the one is to not go to the other), an equivalent 'or' ('I'll do it one way or another': which way is unimportant, all ways are as equal in the interests of doing it 'somehow') and, less commonly perceived, an 'or' which Lacan likens to the Latin *vel*: 'Your money or your life!' — choose money and you lose life and money; choose life and you lose the money, your life is reduced thereby, and anyway death will still be your lot. Lacan characterizes this as the

'alienating vel' and moves it across into his account of the
operation of the subject in language: 'the *vel* which con-
demns the subject to appear only in this division — if on one
side the subject appears as meaning, produced by the signifier,
on the other it appears as *aphanisis*' (*SXI*, 191/210; aphanisis
is a word borrowed from Ernest Jones to refer to the constant
eclipsing, the *fading* of the subject). At which point, set
theory is called upon to add further clarification, Lacan giving
a Venn diagram for the union and intersection of classes:

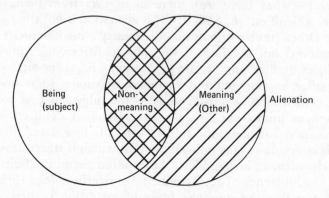

'Let us illustrate the *vel* by what concerns us: the being of
the subject, the subject which is there under meaning. If we
choose the being, the subject disappears, escapes us, falls into
non-meaning; if we choose the meaning, then meaning is only
left curtailed of the part of non-meaning which is, strictly
speaking, what constitutes, in the realization of the subject,
the unconscious. In other words, it is in the nature of this
meaning such as it emerges in the field of the Other to be in
a large part of its field eclipsed by the disappearance of being
induced by the very function of the signifier.' (*SXI*, 192/211.)
In other words again, forged on the trace of what operates to
constitute the subject, the unconscious between subject and
Other is the *action* of division: 'so if I talk of the unconscious
as of that which opens and closes, this is because its essence is
to mark that time by which, born with the signifier, the subject is born divided; the subject is that occurrence which just
before, as subject, was nothing, but which, scarcely has it
appeared, sets as signifier' (*SXI*, 181/199).

The second fundamental operation in the causation of the subject is described as that of *separation*, a term stretched on the racks of equivocation and etymology to mean not simply 'separation' but also 'to put on', 'to parry', and 'to engender' — how does the subject *procure itself* in the signifier? Separation is the moment of the shift in what Miller will call 'the time of the engendering'.

Effect of the signifier under which it slides, the subject comes back on — 'attacks' — the intervals of the signifying chain, takes up the desire of the Other: *what does it want in what it says*? 'It is in the interval between the signifiers of its alienating articulation that lies the desire offered for the subject to grasp in the experience of the discourse of the Other, of the first Other with which it has to deal, let us say, for illustration, here the mother. It is in so far as its desire goes beyond or stays this side of what she says, what she intimates, what she brings out as meaning, in so far as her desire is unknown, in this lack or want, that is constituted the subject's desire. The subject — by a process not without its trickery, not without presenting that basic torsion thanks to which what the subject finds is not what inspired its movement of finding — thus returns to the starting-point, which is that of its lack as such, the lack of its *aphanisis*.' (*SXI*, 199/218–19.) The separation of the subject is thus its passage in this metonymy of desire, its self-procuration from and for the Other in a kind of interminable rerun of the signifiers in which it is originally divided and to which it is thereby subordinated for a second time; the subject now taking place in relation to the Other, to what it finds wanting in the discourse of the Other, separating, responding, parrying, putting on images, caught in a specific problematic of representation ('a signifier represents a subject for another signifier' (*É*, 840)) and fantasy (the postponement of the truth of division, of *aphanisis*): 'this second subordination does not simply loop round to complete the effect of the first by projecting the topology of the subject in the instant of fantasy; it seals it, refusing to the subject of desire that it know itself effect of speech, what it is to be nothing other than the desire of the Other' (*É*, 835–6). In the separation of the subject, its passage, is given the *encroachment* of the unconscious, the permanent action of the edge: one lack covers another (the originating division of the subject in the signifier run over by the division — the gaps, the desire — to which the subject replies in the signifier), which indeed is the whole expense of the subject, thenceforth held in the ceaselessly displacing join of symbolic and imaginary, the very *drama*: 'The drama of the subject in language is the experience of its lack-in-being. . . . It is because it parries this moment of lack that an image comes to the position of bearing all the cost of desire: projection, function of the imaginary. As against which, there is an index at the core of being, designating its breach: introjection, relation to the symbolic.' (*É*, 655.)

It is to this account of the causation of the subject that Miller's introduction of the concept of suture is proposed as a contribution. Via reference to Frege and number theory (indications for which reference are to be found in Lacan; see, for example, *SXI*, 205/226), to the double movement of the zero lack and the zero number, Miller's purpose is precisely to describe the relation of subject and signifier, the metaphor/metonymy of the subject in the signifying chain: 'If the series of numbers, metonymy of the zero, begins with its metaphor, if the 0 member of the series as number is only the standing-in-place suturing the absence (of the absolute zero) which is carried on under the chain according to the alternating movement of a representation and an exclusion, then what is there to stop us from seeing in the restored relation of the zero to the succession of numbers the most elementary articulation of the subject's relation to the signifying chain?'

The specific concern of the article is thus the symbolic and its operation; hence, indicatively, the recourse to mathematical logic and the insistence on the general extension of the suturing function: 'Suture names the relation of the subject to the chain of its discourse: we shall see that it figures there as the element which is lacking, in the form of a stand-in. For, while there lacking, it is not purely and simply absent. Suture by extension, the relation in general of the lack to the structure of which it is an element, inasmuch as it implies position of a taking-the-place-of.' The logic of the signifier within which suture is to exist as a concept is a 'general logic', the formal disposition of all fields of knowledge. To instance suture, Miller points at once, as though to its immediate index, to the 'I' of an utterance: the utterance states a place of the subject at the same moment that it splits from that place by the very fact of the place of the utterance itself, the place from which the statement is made; the subject of the enounced and the subject of the enunciation never fully come together, are always in the *distances* of the symbolic, the subject not one in its representation in language. In the light of which instance, however, it can be seen that the appeal to logic, to the idea of a logic, is simultaneously the emergence of a question that disrupts any notion of a closed formal system (so that extension and generality are them- selves the terms of the insertion of that question into all fields); much in the way Lacan himself, in a rarely mentioned essay on 'Le temps logique' (*É*, 197–213), opens up in logic the time of the enunciation, inserts a reflection on the 'I'. The dimension of truth to which Miller adapts the concept of suture in this dimension not of logic in its classic accounts but, exactly, of the *logic of the signifier*, that is, of psycho- analysis. When Lacan talks of 'the division of the subject between truth and knowledge' (*É*, 864), the truth is that of psychoanalysis as attention to the drama of the subject, is that of the knowledge made possible by such an attention, radically other to the knowledge of the subject's self-possession as 'I' ('we cannot ask it of the subject as I' (*É*, 819/317)). Thus it is not surprising that in reaction to Miller's paper, the psychoanalyst Leclaire should be found eager to insist that the analyst be recognized as, by definition, the person who *'does not suture'*.[7]

Not surprising because the concept of suture, specifying the relation of the subject to the chain of its discourse, can- not be a concept merely for the symbolic (is not a concept of logic). Suture names not just a structure of lack but also an availability of the subject, a certain closure, much as the turn of the second fundamental operation in Lacan procures the subject: the 'I' indicates lack and availability well enough. It is not surprising again, therefore, that Lacan's own use of the term 'suture' (prior to Miller's paper and in the course of a discussion in which Miller participates) gives it the sense of

a 'pseudo-identification', defines it as 'junction of the
imaginary and the symbolic' (*SXI*, 107/117), nor that subsequent examples of its use by Lacanian theorists should be
with this same stress. Jean-Claude Milner, for example,
writing of the objectification of language by linguistics, the
limit of its knowledge of language as that of the 'speaking
subject', comments: 'the speaking subject, point without
dimension, desire or unconscious, is strictly tailored to the
measure of the subject of the enunciation and is made to
mask it, or more exactly to suture it'.[8] The stake is clear:
the 'I' is a division but joins all the same, the stand-in is the
lack in the structure but nevertheless, simultaneously, the
possibility of a coherence, of the *filling in*. At the end of the
suturing function is the ego, the *me*: 'it's me!', the little
linguistic scenario of the ego — that *I* am the only one who
can say, can say in so far as I am *one*. The ego is not to be
confused with the subject: it is the fixed point of imaginary
projection and identification, where the subject as such is
always on the side of the symbolic, the latter the order of its
very constitution; but then, precisely, there is no ego without
a subject, terrain of its necessity and its hold: function of the
symbolic, suture is towards the imaginary, the moment of
junction — standing in, a taking place, a something, a *some
one there*.

II

It is from this psychoanalytic context that Oudart lifts the
concept of suture into the field of film theory in the 1969
Cahiers du cinéma article mentioned above.[9] As a result of
that article (and of a number of subsequent pieces by Oudart
developing his initial formulations[10]), the concept has at-
tained the currency referred to at the beginning of these
notes; currency in France, particularly, of course, amongst
writers involved with or close to *Cahiers du cinéma*,[11] and,
following an influential exposition in English of Oudart's
work by Daniel Dayan in 1974, in theoretical writing in
Britain and North America. The notes that follow in no way
attempt to repeat Oudart or to set out all the detail of the

various subsequent positions (Dayan's exposition, important
arguments against Oudart and Dayan made by William Rothman, and so on); simply, they try to demonstrate something
of what is at stake in the concept of suture in relation to film,
hoping to add clarifications here and there, raising one or two
questions, perhaps advancing a little.[12]

In his article, Oudart offers a description of the movement of
the constitution of the cinematic and its subject in the process
of reading a film. Suture now specifies the logic of the signifier in cinema ('the logic of the cinematic'): 'suture represents
the closure of the cinematic enounced in conformity with the
relationship sustained with it by its subject (the filmic subject
or rather the cinematic subject), recognized and set in its
place, the spectator'.

   As described by Oudart, the process of reading a film goes
in stages, the first of which is a moment of sheer jubilation *in*
the image (the spectator 'fluid, elastic, expanding' — see his
account of the experience of a shot from *The General*); a
moment, as it were, untroubled by screen and frame, prior to
the articulation of cinema. Awareness of the frame then
breaks this initial relation, the image now seen in its limits;
the space which, just before, was the pure extent of the spectator's pleasure becomes a problem of representation, of being-
there-*for* — there for an absent field, outside of the image
('the fourth wall'), for the phantom character that the spectator's imagination poses in response to the problem: 'the
Absent One'. Crucially, what this realization of absence from
the image at once achieves is the definition of the image as
discontinuous, its production *as signifier*: the move from
cinema to cinematic, cinema as discourse: 'The revelation of
this absence is the key-moment in the fate of the image, since
it introduces the image into the order of the signifier and
cinema into the order of discourse.' What then operates,
classically, is the effacement (or filling in) of the absence, the
suturing of the discourse — its movement as in a continuity
of articulation — by the reappropriation of the absence within
the film, a character in the film coming to take the place of
the Absent One posed by the spectator; suture as 'the abolition of the Absent One and its resurrection in some one': 'the

pure field of absence becomes the imaginary field of the film and the field of its imaginary'.

The major emphasis in all this is that the articulation of the signifying chain of images, of the chain of images as signifying, works not from image to image but from image to image through the absence that the subject constitutes. Cinema as discourse is the production of a subject and the subject is the point of that production, constantly missing in and moving along the flow of images, the very assurance of the flow, with suture, as it were, the culmination of that assurance: '[*The Trial of Joan of Arc*] reveals by and for whom the operation of suture works: the filmic subject, the spectator, and from a place which, although remaining empty when he-she goes to vanish into the filmic field, must nevertheless be reserved for him-her throughout the film if he-she is not to refrain from fulfilling his-her role of imaginary subject of the cinematic discourse'. The awareness of absence breaks the immediate delight in the image; that absence is posed by the spectator as an absence of, the absent field of an Absent One; that absent field is reappropriated into the film, the place of the Absent One is filled by a character in the film; thus the pure field of absence becomes the imaginary field of the film, given as absent *from* the film, and the field of its imaginary, given in terms of the film's fiction; thus the break in the initial relation with the image is sutured, sutured across the spectator constituted as cinematic or filmic subject,[13] essential to the realization of image as signifier and to the articulation of shots together. Which is Oudart's reference to Miller: the subject is a moving function of the signifying chain (where a signifier represents a subject for another signifier), its structure a 'flickering in eclipses' (an expression cited and used by Oudart); here, the subject is ceaselessly in and out of the film, the ceaseless position of *exchange*: 'that "exchange" of which Bresson talks, thanks to which the *signified* truly appears'. The subject makes the meanings the film makes for it, is the *turn* of the film as discourse: 'the key to the process of any cinematic reading is provided by the subject, itself not knowing, while carrying it out, that it is its function which is operating and which is there represented'. This position of exchange, this turn, moreover, is the determination of the *obliquity* stressed by Oudart: the spectator is neither character nor Absent One: 'the spectator does not identify with the character located in the invisible field of the film, occupies a position out of place with it, staggered from that of the Absent One who is only imaginarily there when the character is not there and whose place this latter takes'. The imaginary of the spectator and the imaginary of the film move apart together: the spectator poses the Absent One for the movement of the fiction of the film which filling in its place — the suture as character for Absent One, from the imaginary field of the film to the field of its imaginary — frees the spectator's imaginary once again for the renewal of the movement.

It can thus be noted that suture for Oudart is very much a concept relating to the junction of the symbolic and the imaginary, with the emphasis in fact falling on its support of the imaginary. Suture closes cinematic discourse (the articulation of cinema as discourse), closes the spectator-subject in that process, ceaselessly, throughout the time of the film which then sets out a constant repetition of the subject as difference and a constant reappropriation of that difference in the passage across the spectator from Absent One to some one. What is quite difficult immediately in Oudart's account, however, is the status given to the concept — a difficulty which can be demonstrated by considering how Bresson is used in the article.

In Miller the concept of suture is not evaluative but descriptive, introduced to specify the logic of the signifier, the relation of the subject in the signifying chain; in Oudart, tracing the logic of the cinematic, it becomes at once involved with 'the tragic and vacillating nature of the image', with 'the specifically tragic nature of cinematic language'. Cinema as discourse, that is, is seen as implicated in loss, the loss of the totality of the image, the loss of the extreme pleasure of absorption in the image as the spectator is set as the subject of the film: 'the cinema is characterized by an antinomy of reading and pleasure'. If this is the case, however, it is then necessary to develop an effective theory of the different instances of pleasure in the cinema, to offer an adequate account, for example, of the field of the imaginary of a film. Despite scattered indications and a final note pointing to something of the problem, Oudart does not do this, a failure which is symptomatic of a certain slide in the terms of the article. Thus, when Oudart describes the spectator's initial possession of the image (the spectator totally possessed by the image), the terms he uses are those of the child's experience in the mirror-phase: dual — dyadic — relation, jubilation, totality, a kind of extensiveness of pleasure, imaginary. At the same time, indicatively, the moment of possession in these terms is qualified as 'purely mythical'; 'indicatively', because the symbolic cannot be made to follow the imaginary in cinema in this way: cinema is not the mirror-phase, which any spectator-subject of a film has already accomplished (as against the little infant who can come to the film but not come as its spectator), being always already in reading. In this sense, the moment of the image Oudart stresses is not 'before' but 'after' the symbolic, is much more the dispersion of the subject-ego than the anticipation of its mastery (look again at the passage devoted to *The General*). Or rather, since the point is not to shift to a simply contrary position, what is in question is a complex and multiple play of symbolic and imaginary, the production of the spectator as subject in the film in that play: it is not the spectator's imaginary, as Oudart at times appears to state, which sutures the discourse; rather, the suturing function includes the spectator as part of an imaginary production.

In this respect, then, the reference continually made to Bresson's work becomes somewhat problematic. Bresson is presented as the discoverer of suture, the cineaste who realizes the existence and operation of the cinematic subject, the passage across the spectator (hence the displacement of simple notions of 'subjective cinema'). *The Trial of Joan of Arc* is important as 'the first film to submit its syntax to the cinema's necessary representation of the subject's relation to its discourse'. Leaving aside the usual doubts as to the idea of 'the first film', it could be accepted with Oudart that Bresson's film does provide an effectively visible demonstration of the process of the articulation of cinema as discourse and its suture. What is less easy is to understand why, in contrast,

Au hasard, Balthazar should be criticized as a film which, 'purely linear' but also 'a decomposition of syntagms', does not suture, does not fill in its absences, 'a representation which cannot be resolved because suture is impossible, because the imaginary field is always that of an absence': 'the camera movements in *Balthazar* are precisely, by the absence they create at every moment and which is only filled in in rare scenes recalling *The Trial of Joan of Arc* (the meeting between Gérard and Marie), what prevent the spectator's imaginary from working and suturing the discourse'. The problem is the evaluation, with behind that the status accorded suture in the description given. *The Trial of Joan of Arc* is praised because, within the system of the suture, it assumes the specifically tragic nature of cinematic language; *Au hasard, Balthazar* is condemned because it does not, because it fails fully to realize the properties of that language, 'its discourse endlessly signifies itself, dead letter, and its syntax emerges at every instant as the only signified of the film'. The system of the suture seems in this context to be something of an essence of cinema, its veritable 'passion' (note here the manner in which the presence or absence of a feature like depth of field can provide Oudart with an immediate criterion for judgement: the use of images without depth in modern cinema hides the fundamental movement of cinema; *Balthazar* is characterized by an irritating abandon of all depth of field; and so on). Part of the praise for *The Trial of Joan of Arc*, however, is in so far as it demonstrates the system, exposes it, laying out the process of reading a film and thereby offering a certain experience of the symbolic: 'far removed from the complacencies of a cinema such as that of Flaherty, who claimed to recreate the very event of communication, Bresson allows himself only to show us its signs; but he does so within a cinematic field which, because it makes no attempt to give the illusion of its immediacy, restores to it a symbolic dimension revealed in the actual process of its reading'. The wavering mesh of formulations seems finally to depend on a kind of estimation of a potentiality of cinema, almost a poetics of film (not without echoes of the 'poetic function' perspective of Noël Burch's contemporary *Praxis du cinéma*): 'Now that all its properties are recognized, we look to that speech to recreate not an object but a site, a cinematic field which will no longer be the privileged means of realizing a fiction but that for cinema's speech to unfold itself according to its properties, since it is through space that the cinema is born into the order of discourse, from the place whose absence it evokes that it is designated as speech and that its imaginary is deployed.'

Elsewhere, Oudart is perfectly clear that the system of the suture is a particular cinematic writing (even if that writing be largely dominant) and it is this emphasis that is developed by Dayan in his indicatively entitled piece 'The Tutor-Code of Classical Cinema'. The references to tragedy and Bresson are dropped, the term 'ideology' taken up: the system of the suture is grasped as the ideological operation of the process of cinematic discourse; the operation, in fact, of a constant unity of the subject, a certain bind of coherence that Oudart describes as 'theological' (hence, probably, the capital letters accorded to 'absence' and 'the absent one' in the original article): 'An essentially theological cinema, intended for a profoundly religious spectator, in the Lacanian sense of someone who leaves to the Other (God, the Artist, the Absent One) the burden of the cause, demanding of that Other the guarantee of a meaning supposed not to be produced by any scriptural work, supposed to proceed directly from a vision, from *a look which gives meaning to things*. A theological cinema again in that its writing comes down to proving the visible by the invisible and vice versa: cinema of revelation, incarnation and grace. Writing which has had as its function to transform a fantasy into fiction and a fiction into vision, the Absent One into someone, the spectator into a double of him-herself and the doubling of the filmed object. . . . '[14]
    The question as to the status of suture must be considered further in this context. Characterized as 'the tutor-code of classical cinema', the system of suture is defined as a historical articulation of cinema as discourse, as a writing in the sense in which Barthes uses the term in *Writing Degree Zero*;[15] one can thus talk of 'the cinema of suture' and stress, for example, shot/reverse shot as its exemplary figure. Dayan, however, hesitates: on the one hand, there are other cinematic systems besides that of the suture;[16] on the other, the system of the

suture is to classical cinema as verbal language is to literature.[17]
The latter notion is important in its confusion. Verbal language
is the matter of expression of literature, its ground and horizon, the system or code of any discursive realization (literature being a whole set of discursive realizations). While the
problem of the relations of linguistic system and social-
ideological formation is a difficult and fully contemporary
one, the terms of that problem are not such as simply to
equate language and ideology. If the system of the suture is a
particular ideological system (a 'writing'), it cannot be compared with verbal language. That Dayan does so compare it is
symptomatic of the muddled status of the concept: in Miller
and some Oudart, suture is descriptive of the production of
the very possibility of significaton; in some Oudart and most
Dayan, suture is an ideological operation, which the 'privileged example'[18] of shot/reverse shot demonstrates and
resumes (so much so that Rothman is later able to take
'system of the suture' as synonymous with 'point-of-view
cutting[19]).

What is at stake here, the real problem, is exactly the
understanding of cinema as discourse, of *enunciation and
subject of enunciation* in cinema. In an early essay, Metz
insisted on a correspondence between the filmic image
and the sentence in natural language; the image is always
actualized: 'A close-up of a revolver does not mean "revolver"
(a purely virtual lexical unit) but at the very least, and
without speaking of the connotations, it signifies "Here is a
revolver!" '[20] Both Dayan and Rothman are in agreement
that this must be regarded as mistaken: the single shot is
grammatically incomplete; it is the sequence of shots which is
a 'statement' (Dayan) or a 'sentence' (Rothman).[21] The
terminology is confused and confusing: a sentence is a
methodological abstraction of linguistics; outside of that abstraction, there is no sentence which is not an utterance, the
term of an act of enunciation. What Metz points to is the fact
of a shot as utterance, its being-there-for, its address; every
image is the force of an event, not some simple presence of a
word. That force, however, comes with a certain 'innocence'
(the ideological potential of the photographic and filmic
image), the marks of enunciation are relatively unspecified in

the image (there are no equivalents, for instance, to the pro-
nouns in language); we know how to contradict a linguistic
utterance, we are much less sure with a single image (hence
the common tendency to see the image as corresponding to a
word, hence notions of cinema as 'a system of signs where
the object is the sign of the object itself'[22]), are confronted
with its apparent completeness *as image* (hence the problem
for a Godard of 'sounds which are already right on images
which are still false': the image will always be false inasmuch
as it brings with it an effacement of the act of its proposition;
truth is to be grasped not simply in the enounced but equally
in the enunciation, in the distances, gaps, contradictions of the
two). Which completeness, coming back once more on the
image as utterance, is, precisely, only apparent: the image is
never complete in itself (if it were, there would be no place
for a viewer, hence, finally, no place for any image) and its
limit is its address (the limit where it enters the chain, completes with the subject it thus entertains). To understand
cinema as discourse, the general aim of the Oudart article, is
to understand the relation of that address in the movement
of the image, in the movement of and between shots.

The realization of cinema as discourse is the production at
every moment through the film of a subject address, the specification of the play of incompleteness-completion. What
suture can serve to name is this specification, variously articulated but always a function of representation (the play for a
subject, its taking place). The difficulty in the Oudart lies in
the collapse of the process of specification into the single
figure of the absent one, a figure to which Miller's account of
suture as necessary concept for a logic of the signifier makes no
appeal, referring solely to the Other as site of the distribution-
circulation of signifiers. Oudart, beginning effectively from
the demonstration of a particular film (*The Trial of Joan of
Arc*) and the perspective offered by that demonstration on
the historical development of cinema as discourse, describes a
specific regime of the junction of symbolic and imaginary, a
specific return on the subject (heavily dependent on the
exploitation of point-of-view cutting), and in so doing,
given the terms of this — dominant — specification, asserts
the absent one (or the Absent One) for the Other, the latter

then disappearing from the argument. The system Oudart considers is one in which difference is taken up within a structure of absence and the making up of absence in the interests of guaranteeing the constancy — the *consistency* (the definition of the imaginary is that it consists, that it hangs together) — of the returned subject; the absent one is an element in that structure of guarantee, covers the symbolic: the spectator is to be implicated, as subject of the film, and by the investing of the very movement which is cinema's supplement to the photograph, the motion of the picture, the succession of shots, *in* a narrative action and *as* the true vision of that action, the dual representation — *of* and *to* the subject — to which Oudart's description responds with its stress on inclusion and obliquity.

Two kinds of problem can thus be distinguished: those concerning the description of the particular discursive specification of cinema; those concerning characterization of a general logic of cinematic discourse. Attention must now be given to one or two points relating to the former, points indeed that also bear on the latter, to which they will eventually lead.

Consider the 'privileged example' of shot/reverse shot to which reference has already been made. For Oudart, that figure stands in some sort as the very fact of the suturing operation he describes, its ideal: 'the ideal chain of a sutured discourse, articulated in figures which it is no longer appropriate to call shot/reverse shot but which mark the need, so that the chain can function, for an articulation of space such that the same portion of space be represented at least twice, in the filmic field and in the imaginary field (with all the variations of angle that the obliqueness with regard to the place of the subject allows) . . . ' It is the obliqueness that renders the term 'shot/reverse shot' inappropriate: leaving aside the scattered examples of the *Kriemhild's Revenge* variety ('aberrations', 'the aberrant series in *Kriemhild's Revenge*, where the protagonists seem unreal because of Lang's categorical refusal to allow the camera to move from the position of their viewpoint'), the position of the camera is always more or less different from that of the character's look, and it is with this difference that the system of suture is described as working; as Dayan puts it: 'The absent-one's glance is that of a nobody which becomes (with the reverse shot) the glance of a somebody (a character present on the screen). Being on screen he can no longer compete with the spectator for the screen's possession. The spectator can resume his previous relationship with the film. The reverse shot has "sutured" the hole opened in the spectator's imaginary relationship with the filmic field by his perception of the absent-one.'[23]

There are two highly critical assessments of this discussion of suture and shot/reverse-shot which need to be considered here, one by Rothman in the article already cited, the other by Barry Salt in a paper on 'Film Style and Technology in the Forties'.[24] Salt has carefully studied the development of 'angle-reverse less angle cutting' ('taken to include all cuts which change the camera angle from a direction which is within 45 degrees of the eyeline of a person appearing in a shot through a sufficient angle to fall within 45 degrees from the eyeline of the other direction . . . the general category of "angle-reverse angle" cuts is also taken to include cuts from a shot of watcher to a shot of what is seen from his point-of-view, as this seems to be the usual editor's attitude to the definition') and provides percentages of the occurrence of such cuts based on a corpus of some two hundred films from the 'twenties to the present day, concluding that 'the bulk of films continue to have 30–40% reverse angle cuts, as they have had since the thirties'. On the basis of his findings, Salt criticizes Dayan for claiming that the majority of cuts in classical cinema are according to a shot/reverse shot pattern and then develops that criticism into what he regards as a fundamental objection: 'Apart from the fact that in the vast majority of films such cuts form a minority, there is no doubt that films without them can work powerfully on the audience; e.g. *Birth of a Nation*. And further, if the device is so powerful, why is it not pushed to extremes (say 70%) in *all* commercial films, rather than just a few?' Correctly, Salt identifies something of the tendency towards the equation of suture and shot/reverse shot or point-of-view cutting (the Dayan passage in question refers to the latter: 'there are also moments when the image does not represent anyone's point of view; but in the classical narrative cinema these are relatively exceptional'[25]) and indicates the failings of any simple account of classical cinema deriving from a crude literalization of that equation. In so doing, however, he remains blind to the importance of the notion of suture for understanding operations of cinematic discourse, to the possibility that the shot/reverse shot pattern might be a fundamental — but not the only — articulation of suture (the statistics then demonstrating this, showing a steady, regular maintenance of the films of classical cinema within its terms — 30–40%), that, consequently, suture is a multiple functioning of the discursive organization of any given classical cinema film.

Rothman is close to Salt at one or two points, or rather he might have added Salt's details into his questions to Dayan. Having noted that the latter equates system of suture and point-of-view cutting, Rothman further narrows the field of debate by considering Dayan to be essentially referring to a very strictly defined point-of-view shot succession (Melanie Daniels in *The Birds* is shown looking out of the boat to something we cannot see, the next shot shows us the view across Bodega Bay, what she is looking at), apparently excluding, for example, typical shot/reverse shot dialogue sequences. His major criticism is then that the point-of-view shot is part not of a two-shot but of a three-shot figure, this 'specifically reversing the Oudart—Dayan scenario': 'It is not that the viewer discovers the frame of the shot looking out across Bodega Bay (unaccountably), infers a sovereign "absent-one" and falls prey to a tyrannical system which makes him take Melanie, shown in the reverse shot, to be that absent-one. Rather, following upon the first shot of the sequence with its conventional cue that asserts its frame, the viewer perceives Melanie's absence from the next frame. Perception of this specific absence is a condition of the viewer's reading of its as a shot from her point of view. This reading is confirmed by the third shot of the sequence, with its return to Melanie.'[26] Moreover, extended series of telescoped point-of-view sequences can be constructed, the third shot in one sequence doubling as the initial shot of a second and so on.

The emphases made by Rothman are important, but their effect is not to render the concept of suture — of the suturing operation of cinematic discourse — no longer pertinent; rather, they suggest a necessary displacement, the need to move away from the simple notion of the immediate image, the symbolic apprehension, the imaginary resolution, the constant and single figure of the absent one. What is in question in both Dayan and Rothman is the organization and hold of the look and looks in film: the film goes before me, sees me (I am its address), and I can never look from where it sees me except in so far as it takes me up as the term of its shifting relation, as the term of its passage (it moves through me, the turn of its representation) and its point (it moves for me, the fiction of its unity) — a balance in which I am in together the symbolic and the imaginary, production and product. The system of the suture as described by Oudart—Dayan begins to pose the problem of this taking up but does so in a way which issues in a too readily monolithic conception — the Absent One, the concentration on shot to reverse shot point-of-view cutting — that tends to ignore the multiple layerings and times and advances, the suturing function in that multiplicity.

Take Chantal Akerman's *News from Home*: the city, images of New York, and the novelistic, by letters, a mother in Brussels writing to her far-off daughter, little incidents and appeals (always how much she is missed: 'ma petite fille, tu nous manques tellement'), read, whispered, quoted on the sound-track, over or under the noises of traffic or subway. No character, no fictioning look to be seen; the shots succeed with no other tie than the fact of that succession, until the last shot from a boat drawing away from New York, the city gradually lost in the image to the expanse of the sea, the film ending as it vanishes on the horizon. Following the Oudart—Dayan scenario, there is then no suture: the look is not appropriated into the imaginary field of the film, the Absent One is not resolved; the film has no shot/reverse shot sequence, no figuration of the images, nothing but their continual replacement. Yet the spectator is included and moved in the film, in a structure and a rhythm of lack and absence (which are not the same thing). What is the direction of these images for this voice and its story, of this voice and its story for these images? The final shot can retrospectively produce the images as those of the daughter but the film remains in its time in the lack of each image, signifiers whose representation — 'a signifier represents a subject for another signifier' — is broken, unaccomplished: effect of the relation apart of voice and seen (it is to be noted that the descriptions of the system of the suture say nothing of the importance of the ties between image and sound tracks), of the duration of the shots (the system of the suture in fact depends heavily on a relative constancy and brevity of the passage from shot to shot, on the eviction of any *margin* of the image in time), of the play within that duration on the flatness or the framing or the division of the image, a process of finding — not starting from, as in the Oudart–Dayan account — a certain multiplicity (the shot in the subway across to the platform on the far side: people waiting and moving alter perception of space and depth, point to the different frames provided by a series of pillars, with trains coming and going until, finally, a train arrives at the nearest platform and abruptly redefines appreciation of spatial disposition), of the non-emergence of any pattern of a look (other than as missing in the film, stressed by the shot in the subway train when people begin to question the look of the camera and the site of our gaze, implicating us in the failure of a binding fiction that would assume and make a sense of the images given). We are placed in the film but that place is not secured, is shifted, and turns, in the meanings the film makes in that insecurity, in those dislocations, on the construction of a central absence — the absence of the daughter, differently posited on image and sound tracks. From that absence, the film refuses to suture, to convert Other to Absent One (such a conversion near to the position of the mother in her letters), hence to resolve as the sign of something for someone, to fix a unity — 'a sign represents something for someone'. Or rather, it refinds suture effectively as a term of the logic of the signifier, poses the problem of the relations of the subject in the symbolic and the holding of those relations in the imaginary; in which problem lies the real of the film, that of feminism, and of film, that of image, voice, noise, duration, rhythm, the impossible question of a woman's desire in all that.

As Miller aims at logic of the signifier, so Oudart aims at a logic of the cinematic, of cinema articulated as discourse. Oudart cannot but come after Miller: the spectator of a film is always already in the symbolic, on the stage of the two fundamental operations, in a production of suture; he or she solicits the image as much as it does him or her, there is no initial outside of the symbolic at the cinema, in cinema, no immediate coming in the image which is always instituted as such, image for, a film image. *News from Home produces* a displacement of established junctions of symbolic and imaginary, of the terms of identification — and *that* is its 'immediacy'.

What one has are films, discursive organizations, implications of spectating (the last formulation in order to avoid 'a spectator' with its idea of a necessary unity, to stress the activity of looking . . . and hearing). It is possible and crucial to describe the limits, constraints, effects of the machine cinema, pose, for example, its reality as 'imaginary signifier', but a logic of the cinematic in the sense of the articulation of cinema as discourse is at once a logic of the cinematographic, the form of a particular mode of the organization of signification, such as the Oudart—Dayan system of the suture. To say that the system of the suture is a particular logic, a writing, is not, however, to say that cinema could be articulated as discourse outside of any suture. Which is to return to the difficulties of the concept and of its translation from Miller to Oudart. At one extreme, suture then becomes a term for any continuity join, for the matches of classical editing; thus Bonitzer can write: 'The door is a nodal object of classic narrative cinema . . . what Bazin called "door-knob cinema"; a usable object in that it allows transition from one shot to another, point of suture of the syntagmatic caesura. . . .'[27] Less simply, and more generally, it is equated with the system based on shot/reverse shot patterns of 'filling in' across and for the spectator from image to image; hence Oudart's assertion that *Au hasard, Balthazar* does not suture. What was emphasized above in connection with *News from Home*, however, was not that the film did not suture but that it did not suture in the way of the system, that it posed differently — indeed posed the problem of — the functioning of suture, the junction of symbolic and imaginary (which is what is in question with the concept of suture). No discourse without suture (as described by Miller, element of a general logic of the signifier) but, equally, no suture which is not from the beginning specifically defined within a particular system which gives it form (the effective lesson of Oudart's description of cinematic as cinematographic); and which is not, moreover, directly political to the extent of its relation of the subject in specific positions of unity and meaning — the very demonstration of *News from Home*, the recognition of Miller's momentary reference to 'a subject, therefore, defined by attributes whose other side is political . . . '.

III

'Whose other side is political. . . . '[28] From that other side, as it were, psychoanalysis has been increasingly called upon as having a specific and necessary contribution to make to a materialist understanding of the operation of the ideological in its relations of subject positions of meaning. Thus, for example, Pierre Raymond in his *Matérialisme dialectique et logique*: 'A number of philosophers insist on the relationship between linguistic systems and the unconscious. This relationship is of particular interest to Marxists, who see that language and unconscious have in common with ideologies the staging of the subject. Which does not mean that the relationship is easy to establish. . . . '[29] Or again, Michel Pêcheux in *Les Vérités de La Palice*, a book which attempts to suggest something of the bases for a theory of discourse within an Althusserian perspective: 'There is no hiding with stock formulations the heavy absence of a conceptual articulation elaborated between *ideology* and *unconscious*.'[30]

It is discourse for Pêcheux which makes the heavy absence felt, gives the area where the articulation must be developed. Against an integrally linguistic conception, he wishes to describe discourse with reference to the mechanisms of the setting in position of its subjects, such a description cutting across traditional oppositions of the *langue/parole* variety for which discourse becomes simply the concrete acts of the use by

individuals of an abstract language system (it was seen above
how psychoanlaysis is involved in a similar displacement).
The aim, evidently, is to reappropriate the linguistic into the
social without denying its specificity and to pose the question
of the ideological to language accordingly, to work through
the notion of *discursive formation*: 'We shall call *discursive
formation* that which in a given ideological formation, that is,
from a given position in a given conjuncture determined by
the state of the class-struggle, determines "what can and must
be said . . . ". This comes down to saying that words, expressions, propositions, etc. receive their meaning from the discursive formation in which they are produced . . . individuals
are "interpellated" as speaking-subjects (as subjects of *their*
discourse) by discursive formations which represent "in
language" corresponding ideological formations.'[31] A discursive formation, that is, exists as a component of an ideological formation itself based in particular conditions of
production (ideological state apparatuses) and the terms of
the discursive formation/ideological formation relation are
those of subject and interpellation. Individuals are constituted as subjects through the discursive formation, a process
of subjection in which the individual is identified as subject
with the discursive formation in a structure of miscognition
(the subject thus presented as the source of the meanings of
which it is an effect). Interpellation names the mechanism of
this structure of miscognition, effectively the term of the
subject in the discursive and the ideological, the point of
their correspondence: 'We shall not here solve the problem of
the nature of this correspondence. Let us merely say that it
cannot be a question either of a pure equivalence (ideology =
discourse) or of a simple distribution of functions ("discursive
practice"/non-discursive practice). It would be better to talk
of an "intrication" of the discursive formations in the ideological formations, an intrication whose principle would
reside precisely in "interpellation".'[32] What Pêcheux wants
is then to give this intrication some descriptive substance by
providing a non-subjective theory of the constitution of the
subject in its situation of enouncer (how does the subject
have the meanings it has and how does it have those meanings
as subject?).

Interpellation, however, taken over from Althusser's well-known essay on 'Ideology and Ideological State Apparatuses',[33] raises serious difficulties that have been demonstrated at length by Paul Q. Hirst and that centre, for present purposes, on the way in which the recognition demanded by the mechanism of interpellation would presuppose the subject the mechanism is said to constitute: 'Recognition, the crucial moment of the constitution (activation) of the subject, presupposes a point of cognition prior to the recognition. Something must recognise that which it is to be. . . . The social function of ideology is to constitute concrete individuals (not-yet-subjects) as subjects. The concrete individual is "abstract", it is not yet the subject it will be. It is, however, *already* a subject in the sense of the subject which supports the process of recognition. Thus something which is not a subject must already have the faculties necessary to support the *recognition* which will constitute it as a subject. It must have a *cognitive* capacity as a prior condition of its place in the process of recognition. Hence the necessity of the distinction of the concrete individual and the concrete subject, a distinction in which the faculties of the latter are supposed already in the former (unless of course cognition be considered a "natural" human faculty).'[34] The criticism is correct in so far as it indicates that interpellation can in no way be the key either to ideology or to subjectivity (the fact of the individual as subject), the two being held as interdependent. One solution then proposed – cursorily taken up by Althusser in the use of the individual/subject distinction and the vague emergence of a reference to Lacan at points in his essay – is to separate out a number of instances in the construction-constitution of a subject, with psychoanalysis the available account of one of these specific areas: *(subject-)support*, biological individuality of individuals as material base from which they are brought to function in social relations; *ideological subject*, place in the operation of discursive/idelogical formations, constitutive of these, assuring the entry of (subject-)supports into the different social processes; *psychoanalytic subject*, position in the relations of the signifier, produced in the (subject-)support, effect of its structuration by the signifying chain.[35] Psychoanalysis thus becomes,

within historical materialism, the description of the constitution of the individual (subject-)support as subject for interpellation in discursive formations as ideological subject;
which is a role that psychoanalysis finds little difficulty in
accommodating, standing as the truth of the individual
subject, abstract from social process, ideological formation —
the political over on the other side.

Yet it is quite the contrary that should be the case. Exactly
in so far as psychoanalysis is directed against any idea of
there being a set of contents of the unconscious, makes of
the unconscious a term of subject-division in the signifier, an
action in the speaking-being, so it is involved, always and
immediately, in the social relations of language as discourse
(and not in absolutes, archetypes, essential meanings or
whatever). In this respect, Lacan's teaching has a double
edge, leads two ways: on the one hand, nothing but discourse,
discourse then taken as the sole province of truth, the
analyst (Lacan, lone bearer of a word 'without equal') its
Master ('women do not know what they are saying, which is
all the difference between them and me' *SXX*, 68); on the
other, nothing but discourse, hence no transhistorical finality
of truth, hence the possibility of a radical practice and transformation of the whole history of the subject. The same kind
of double-edgedness can be traced at many points in psychoanalysis: the analytic situation itself, for instance, which is at
once the provision of an effective space for the apprehension
of the series of fantasies in which the analysand's history of
the subject is held and the establishment of the position of
the analyst's mastery with the rituals of a profession, a class,
a certain balance of power of discourse; or again, the notion
of interminability in analysis, giving both the stress on the
production of the subject in language, against any final or
original truth, and something of an imaginary of analysis, a
confirming concept of its maintenance away from the other
side, closed to social process and any question of the transformation — 'termination' — of the subject in its history
there. Psychoanalysis is thus available for the call that is
made upon it, but not simply; and the difficulties emerge,
continuing to emerge with the separation-of-the-subject-into-
instances solution, as those of an articulation, Pêcheux's

'articulation elaborated between *ideology* and *unconscious*', which is perhaps itself too rigid and fixed a conception for what is at stake.

For Pêcheux, interpellation is in conjunction with identification, that conjunction, of course, representing part of his appeal to the psychoanalytic: 'the interpellation of the individual as subject of its discourse is effected by the identification of the subject with the discursive formation that dominates it'.[36] Quoting from Althusser, Pêcheux offers the following summary of his articulation of ideology and unconscious in these terms: ' "The individual is interpellated as (free) subject in order that it freely submit to the commandments of the Subject, in order that it (freely) accept its subjection." If one adds, first, that this subject with a capital S — absolute and universal subject — is precisely what Lacan designates as the Other with a capital O and, second, that, still according to Lacan, "the unconscious is the discourse of the Other", one can see how *unconscious repression* and *ideological subjection*, while not the same, are materially linked in what may be called *the process of the signifier in interpellation and identification. . . .* '[37]

In fact, that summary only states the problem (and Pêcheux's own problems: with interpellation, with the material link between repression and subjection), in connection with which it is perhaps worth setting out one or two simple theses to clarify something of the intermesh of terms such as *ideology, imaginary, symbolic, unconscious*: 1) the ideological is not reducible to the imaginary (which is part of the difficulty of the account of interpellation in the 'Ideology and Ideological State Apparatuses' paper, as again in Pêcheux); the ideological always involves a relation of symbolic and imaginary (the imaginary is a specific fiction of the subject in the symbolic); 2) the symbolic is not reducible to the ideological; there is no ideological operation which does not involve a symbolic construction, a production of the subject in meaning, but the symbolic is always more than the effect of such operations (language is not exhausted by the ideological); 3) the symbolic is never simply not ideological; psycho-analysis, and this is its force, has never encountered some pure symbolic, is always engaged with a specific history of the subject (language is not exhausted by the ideological but is never met other than as discourse, within a discursive formation productive of subject relations in ideology); 4) the unconscious is not reducible to the ideological; it is a division of the subject with the Other, a history of the subject on which the ideological constantly turns but which it in no way resumes. In short, a materialist theory of the constitution-construction of the subject cannot be developed in abstraction from the discursive and the ideological but, equally, cannot be developed as an account of interpellation which effectively takes the subject as given and not in effect of the signifier. The mesh of the various instances, tightening together, is difficult and crucial; suture could well be defined as the term of that crucial difficulty.

In this respect, moreover, it is necessary to remember that the very concept of the subject itself derives from a secondary and linguistic perspective and tends constantly towards the imaginary (as in Althusser, who reproduces the subject as a kind of essence of ideology). What 'subject' designates is not a unity, not even a unity of division, but a construction and a process, a heterogeneity, an intersection. Lacan's version of the causation of the subject and the very introduction of suture are indicative here: the subject is minus one, the real of castration; plus one, the resolution of that real in the imaginary; a movement in the symbolic — 'gaping, flickering, alternating suction'. Suture names the relation of the subject in the symbolic which is its join in the chain, its representation from signifier to signifier ('a signifier represents a subject for another signifier') and its identification as one in the fiction of the sign ('a sign represents something for someone'). The division-separation causation of the subject describes this process, the subject always returning in its implication in the desire of the Other — 'what does it want?' and 'who wants?': questions in which the subject always fails (comes back to the fact of its process, its division) and is always found again (its separation, its procuration from that division), taken up immediately in meanings and their production in discursive formations. A theory of ideology must then begin not from the subject but as an account of suturing effects, the effecting of the join of the subject in structures of meaning; which account would thus involve an attention to the whole history of the subject, the interminable movement of that history, and not its simple equation with ideology.

IV

The realization of cinema as discourse is the production at every moment through the film of a subject-address, the specification of the play of incompleteness-completion. That emphasis, given above, must be maintained, but also extended a little. A film operates with a number of matters of expression, a variety of codes, both cinematic and non-cinematic; meaning is not just constructed 'in' the particular film, meanings circulate between social formation, spectator and film; a film is a series of acts of meaning, the spectator is there in a multiplicity of times. In this connection, one might distinguish in the relation of the spectator as subject in the film *preconstruction*, *construction*, (or *reconstruction*) and *passage*. Preconstruction involves the ready-made positions of meaning that a film may adopt, not merely large categories of definition, political arguments, thematic boundaries, and so on, but equally, for example, the signs and orders of language itself, the existing social conventions of colour, the available ideas of film (genre is a major factor of preconstruction). Construction is the totalizing of a more or less coherent subject position in the film as its end, its direction, the overall fiction of the subject related. Passage is the performance of the film, the movement of the spectator making the film, taken up as subject. The ideological achievement of any film is not merely in one or the other of these instances, it is first and foremost in its hold of the three: the appropriation of preconstruction in reconstruction (the film's construction effectively reconstructs from its different materials) and the process of that appropriation. The term of that hold in the classic fiction feature film is narrativization, the constant conversion to narrative, catching up the spectator as subject in the image of the narrative and in the film as its narration. The system of the suture described by Oudart—Dayan is one of the modes of this narrativization (others, also suturing, still need to be examined, notably those working between image and sound tracks).

Very rarely do we say that a film is 'contemporary', unless, remaining within the area of preconstruction, by reference to the 'urgency' of its theme. It is, however, fairly common for a film to be characterized as 'dated', with the reference here being to the signs of the representation *recognized as such*, to a certain loss in the fine balance of enunciation and enounced which is contained as historical in the crude sense of 'their past' versus 'our present', the particular film then declared 'interesting' and/or 'amusing' for the spectator today (this is especially evident with television's presentation-consumption of films). The non- 'dated' film is thus *close*, its discursive ordering pulling the image towards unity for *us*, its activity of meaning transposed into the coherence of a near-ness; we enter the structure of address, join the film; the spectator is recast as the subject of the film's relations of the symbolic and the imaginary together, its suturing. Which, moreover, is very much a question of time; there are multiple times between spectator and film (Oudart's accounts of the experience of film images can perhaps best be read in this stress) but the film, classically, is always brought into time with its significant flow, its balance, its narrativization; producing thereby its essential contemporariness — constantly with you for you, moving you with it in its narrative image.

Lacan talks of the 'in some sort *pulsatory* function of the unconscious': 'whatever, an instant, appears in its opening is seemingly destined . . . to disappear again' (*SXI*, 44/43). Behind that formulation lies the idea of the *defile* of consciousness developed by Freud in the *Studies on Hysteria*, published in 1895. Freud writes of a kind of narrow passage (*Engpass*) or narrow cleft (*enge Spalte*) 'in front of the patient's consciousness', an aperture in which memories appear during analytic treatment in a stop—go movement; the problem being the lack of regularity in the movement, the passage continually blocked by this or that memory, like 'a picture that refuses to disappear': 'There is some justification for speaking of the "defile" of consciousness. . . . Only a single memory at a time can enter ego-consciousness. A patient who is occupied in working through such a memory sees nothing of what is pushing after it and forgets what has already pushed its way through. If there are difficulties in the way of mastering this single pathogenic memory — as, for instance, if the patient does not relax his resistance against it, if he tries to repress or mutilate it — then the defile is, so to speak, blocked. The work is at a standstill, nothing more can appear, and the single memory which is in process of breaking through remains in front of the patient until he has taken it up into the breadth of his ego. The whole spatially extended mass of psychogenic material is in this way drawn through a narrow cleft and thus arrives in consciousness cut up, as it were, into pieces or strips. It is the psychotherapist's business to put these together once more into the organization which he presumes to have existed.'[38] It is as though, at the very moment of its birth, Freud is describing the cinematic apparatus, with the difference that that apparatus is constructed to ensure the constancy of the flow of images, a unity of presentation, a stable memory.

Which last brings us back to narrativization: the economy of the film's flow in a binding coherence, its remembering, the realization of a single forward time within which multiple times can be given play and held. The system of suture, be it noted, breaks as soon as the time of the shot hesitates beyond the time of its narrative specifications (demonstrated throughout Benoît Jacquot's *L'Assassin musicien*).

The subject of a film is the play between its multiple elements, including the social formation in which it finds its existence, and the spectator; no film which does not grasp the spectator in terms of that heterogeneity, which does not shift the spectator in ties, joins, relations, movements of the symbolic and the imaginary, with the real a constant and impossible limit (impossible *for the film*, involving a transformation *that would have to include the film*). A film may also — will also? — project a subject, some unity of the play produced; most constrainingly, a narrative image. Suture, finally, names the dual process of multiplication and projection, the conjunction of the spectator as subject with the film — which conjunction is always the terrain of any specific ideological operation of a film.

Questions of Cinema

Notes

Published as 'Notes on Suture' in *Screen* vol. 18 no. 4 (Winter 1977/8) pp. 48—76.

1. Jacques-Alain Miller, 'La suture', *Cahiers pour l'analyse* no. 1 (1966) pp. 39—51; translation, 'Suture', *Screen* vol. 18 no. 4 (Winter 1977/8) pp. 24—34. Two discussions of the paper in the same year and context were also published in *Cahiers pour l'analyse*: S. Leclaire, 'L'analyste à sa place?', no. 1 (1966) pp. 50—2 A. Green, 'L'objet(a) de J. Lacan, sa logique et la théorie freudienne', no. 3 (1966) pp. 15—37.

2. In order not to encumber this piece with reference notes, the following conventions are here adopted for works by Jacques Lacan: *É = Écrits* (Paris: Seuil, 1966); *SXI = Le Séminaire livre XI* (Paris: Seuil, 1973); *SXX = Le Séminaire livre XX* (Paris: Seuil, 1975). Translations of the first two of these exist as: *Écrits: A Selection* (London: Tavistock, 1977); *The Four Fundamental Concepts of Psycho-Analysis* (London: Hogarth Press, 1977). Reference is given in the text to the French and then to the translation where possible (note that 'Positions de l'inconscient' is not included in the English selection from *Écrits*).

3. J. Lacan, 'Conference aux États-Unis', *Scilicet* no. 6—7 (1977) p. 49.

4. See, for example, S. Freud, 'The Unconscious' (1915), *The Standard Edition of the Complete Psychological Works* vol. XIV (London: Hogarth Press, 1957) p. 201; and discussion below, pp. 203—4.

5. Demonstrated by Metz in the course of his detailed consideration of the psychoanalytic possibility of the figures metaphor and metonymy; C. Metz, *Le Signifiant imaginaire* (Paris: Union Générale d'Éditions, 1977) pp. 251—340.

6. J. Lacan, *L'Identification* (Paris: 1977; pirate edition of the 1962 seminar) p. 24.

7. S. Leclaire, 'L'analyste à sa place?', p. 51.

8. J.-C. Milner, 'L'amour de la langue', *Ornicar?* no. 6 (1976) p. 43.

9. Jean-Pierre Oudart, 'La suture', *Cahiers du cinéma* no. 211 (April 1969) pp. 36—9, and no. 212 (May 1969) pp. 50—5; translation, 'Cinema and Suture', *Screen* vol. 18 no. 4 (Winter 1977/8) pp. 35—47.

10. See especially (all references are to issues of *Cahiers du cinéma*): 'Bresson et la vérité', no. 216 (October 1969) pp. 53—6; 'Travail, lecture, jouissance' (with Serge Daney), no. 222 (July 1970) pp. 39—50; 'L'effet de réel', no. 228 (March—April 1971) pp. 19—26; 'Notes pour une théorie de la représentation' (I), no. 229 (May—June 1971) 43—5; 'Notes . . . (II), no. 230 (July 1971) pp. 43—5; 'Un discours en défaut' (I), no. 232 (October 1971) pp. 4—12; 'Un discours . . . ' (II), no. 233 (November 1971) pp. 23—6.

11. See, for example, Pascal Bonitzer, *Le Regard et la voix* (Paris: Union Générale d'Éditions, 1976) pp. 17, 31, 47—8, 105, 130, 140—1.

12. Daniel Dayan, 'The Tutor-Code of Classical Cinema', *Film Quarterly* (Fall 1974) pp. 22—31. Criticism of Dayan's article is to be found in

William Rothman, 'Against the System of the Suture', *Film Quarterly* (Fall 1975) pp. 45–50. (These two pieces are included in Bill Nichols (ed.), *Movies and Methods* (Berkeley and Los Angeles: University of California Press, 1976) pp. 438–59; references here will be to these reprintings.)

13. Both 'cinematic subject' and 'filmic subject' occur in Oudart; the latter in so far as he is describing the process of reading a film, the former in so far as that description is given in the context of how film works discursively, of cinematic discourse.

14. Oudart, 'Travail, lecture, jouissance', pp. 45–6.

15. Hence a difficulty in the translation of the Oudart article: the term *cinématographique* is translated as 'cinematic', thus in accordance with its use in Metz and rendering a descriptive generality; equally, however, and more appropriately, it might be given as 'cinematographic', the *logique du cinématographe* being the logic of a writing, the definition of *a* cinematic discourse, thus in accordance with Bresson, who opposes theatrical cinema with *le cinématographe*, 'writing in sounds and images which forms a visual and auditory text' (see *Notes sur le cinématographe* (Paris: Gallimard, 1975; translation, *Notes on Cinematography*, New York: Urizen Books, 1977)).

16. Dayan, 'The Tutor-Code of Classical Cinema', p. 450.

17. Ibid. p. 439.

18. Ibid. p. 451.

19. Rothman, 'Against the System of the Suture', p. 454.

20. C. Metz, *Essais sur la signification au cinéma* I (Paris: Klincksieck, 1968) p. 72; translation, *Film Language* (New York and London: Oxford U.P., 1974) p. 67.

21. 'The Tutor-Code of Classical Cinema', pp. 439, 449, 450; 'Against the System of the Suture', p. 457.

22. R. Jakobson, 'Entretien sur le cinéma', in *Cinéma Théories Lectures* (special issue of the *Revue d'esthétique*) (Paris: Klincksieck, 1973) p. 66.

23. 'The Tutor-Code of Classical Cinema', p. 449.

24. Barry Salt, 'Film Style and Technology in the Forties', *Film Quarterly* (Fall 1977) pp. 46–57; quotations pp. 50–2.

25. 'The Tutor-Code of Classical Cinema', p. 447.

26. 'Against the System of the Suture', p. 455.

27. Bonitzer, op. cit. p. 105.

28. Some of the emphases briefly made in this section are developed further in S. Heath, *The Turn of the Subject* (London: Macmillan, 1981).

29. P. Raymond, *Matérialisme dialectique et logique* (Paris: Maspero, 1977) p. 57n.

30. M. Pêcheux, *Les Vérités de La Palice* (Paris: Maspero, 1975) p. 136.

31. Ibid. pp. 144–5.

32. Ibid. p. 145n.

33. Louis Althusser, 'Idéologie et appareils idéologiques d'État', *La Pensée* (June 1970); reprinted in a collection of Althusser's essays

entitled *Positions* (Paris: Éditions sociales, 1976) pp. 67–125; translation, 'Ideology and Ideological State Apparatuses', in *Lenin and Philosophy and Other Essays* (London: New Left Books, 1971) pp. 121–73.

34. Paul Q. Hirst, 'Althusser's Theory of Ideology', *Economy and Society* vol. 5 no. 4 (November 1976) pp. 404–5.

35. Cf. M. Tort, 'La psychanalyse dans le matérialisme historique', *Nouvelle Revue de Psychanalyse* no. 1 (Spring 1970) p. 154.

36. Pêcheux, op. cit. p. 148.

37. Ibid. pp. 122–3.

38. S. Freud, *Studies on Hysteria* (1895), *The Standard Edition of the Complete Psychological Works* vol. II (London: Hogarth Press, 1955) pp. 291, 296.

Chapter 4

Film Performance

A story by Apollinaire from 1907 (subsequently included in the 1910 volume *L'Hérésiarque et Cie*, the original title for which had been *Phantasmes*): 'Un beau film'.[1] The narrator, the Baron d'Ormesan, tells how he and a group of friends founded the Cinematographic International Company — 'which for short we called the CIC'! — and sought to obtain films 'of great interest' for exhibition in the principal towns of Europe and America. A number of such films were procured but the Company 'lacked the representation of a crime'. The Baron and his friends thus decide to remedy that lack by organizing their own crime for the screen: a courting couple is captured in the streets of Paris one night, then a gentleman on his way to a gambling club; preparations are made in a specially rented house — 'our photographer set us his apparatus, saw to the appropriate lighting, and stood ready to record the crime' — and the gentleman is forced, under threat of himself being killed, to murder the young lovers. The crime is sensational (the victims prove to have been minor foreign nobility), the film a spectacular box-office draw: 'You can imagine our success. The police did not for a moment suppose that we were offering the reality of the murder of the day, though we took great pains to announce that that was indeed just what we were doing. The public made no mistake. It gave us an enthusiastic reception. . . . ' Later, an innocent person is arrested and executed for the killing, the Company duly recording the execution to be added as a conclusion to its film. The Baron simply ends his narrative with an estimate of the amount of money he gained from his excursion into the commerce of cinematography.

Un beau film: the crime of the good film is the film itself, its time and its performance — its *performing of time*. It is not by chance that Apollinaire's fascination with the new medium is immediately in 1907 the story of a murder, the relation of cinema and crime: film is exactly a putting to death, the demonstration of 'death at work' (Cocteau's 'la mort au travail'[2]). Made of a series of stops in time, the timed stops of the discrete frames, film depends on that constant stopping for its possibility of reconstituting a moving reality — a reality which is thus, in the very moment of appearance on screen, as the frames succeed one another, perpetually flickered by the fading of its present presence, filled with the *artifice* of its continuity and coherence. Every film a fiction film: at once in this reconstitution of the scene of its crime — the practice of division and articulation — as the impression of 'reality itself', the scene intact, unviolated; and in the distance on which it nevertheless plays for its mode of solicitation as spectacle, the mode of presence in absence, a real time there on film but not that same real time which is shown on film gone for ever. Hence the Baron's spectators have no problem ('the public made no mistake'): they know that they are really and not really seeing the crime; they are securely in *the fiction of reality* (and the crime, precisely, is in the film). This is the context of what has been described as the cinematic regime of pure memory: 'everything is absent, everything is *recorded*, as a memory trace which is instantaneously so, without previously being something else'.[3] Record and reality are together as a system of traces present always as the term of an absence: film's fiction as 'the record of reality', the whole imaginary signifier of cinema as *memory-spectacle*.

Cinema is founded as the memory of reality, the spectacle of reality captured and presented. All presentation, however, is representation — a production, a construction of positions and effects — and all representation is performance — the time of that production and construction, of the realization of the positions and effects. Which is why, to anticipate an emphasis that will be made later, an avant-garde — and political — practice of film is involved necessarily at least in an attention to the real functioning of representation and is involved directly thereby in a problematic of performance, of film performance; attention and problematic that pose the limits of the 'good film', of the cinematic institution.

In its classic forms in our 'advanced societies', representation is the achievement and operation of systems of coherence, of unity, which make up for the process of their structuration with strategies of completion that mask the heterogeneity — movement, difference, contradiction, fading — they effectively serve to contain, to *figure out*. The pole — or horizon — of such systems is the innocence of a realism given as re-presentation, the simple transmission of life recorded, imprinted: 'photographic realism' as the nineteenth-century expression for this horizon would significantly have it; 'significantly' because of the power here of the imagination of the camera (the reference it becomes, the terms of its exploitation) and of everything bound up with it (film included, of course). That realism, however, is precisely a horizon, wanted and envisaged — believed in — as a kind of potential of quotation (the photograph can indeed be quickly developed in the nineteenth century as a market in tokens of reality-itself-in-its-absolute-identity), a kind of basic currency of the real (thus the photograph becomes the very money of reality which in turn is its guarantee and standard), but as potential and a currency *to be used*, to be invested — and, in fact, realized — in specific projects. In other words, that realism is never the end of and could never exhaust representation, the systematic production of coherence and unity, the construction of the positions and effects of a 'subject' and a 'reality'. Realism is only ever, and above all in its innocent proposals as straight transmission, an image — the final figure — of the representation system in which it is engaged; a system which, positioning and effecting, is a ceaseless performance *of the subject in time for the reality given, of subject-time.*

The performance of subject-time is itself a complex time, phasing between two constant moments that — these remarks concern classic narrative cinema, the commercial exploitation of film — are layered together: the subject-reflection and the subject-process (the layering and balance of the two being the film's performance of subject-time). The subject-reflection is a narrative effect (or series of effects): in the movement of the chain of differences — the flow of multiple intensities of image and sound — the narrative defines terms for the movement of the chain, specifies relations and reflects a subject as the direction of those relations, produces the coherence of view and viewer. Effected by the narrative, the subject-reflection is in the order of the vraisemblable, the fantasy order of an achieved unity of relations on the subject confirmed as sufficient centre ('fantasy founds the vraisemblable', writes Lacan in one of his rare considerations of film[4]); the film thereby proposed for the subject it *includes* and *creates* in a scenario of desire fulfilled, a subject bound up in the consistance of the imaginary. Going along with the subject-reflection, the subject-process is just that: the *process*, all the elements of the system in its production-performance, the whole apparatus of the representation; is a *multiple circulation*, the perpetual movement of difference, the insistence of the symbolic against any imaginary centre. The close of the circulation is the subject-reflection — the very fiction of 'the subject' — but that circulation is always more than the closure it can realize: the subject-process is the 'more'.

The two moments of subject-process and subject-reflection are, it was said above, in a *phasing*. In physics, a phase is a

particular change or point in a recurring sequence of movements or changes; as, for example, a vibration or an undulation.
What is at stake in the establishment of a system of representation with narrative film is the constant shifting together of
those two moments or phases, their recurrent balancing out:
they system achieves a reflection, images of unity, but, as
production, is in excess of those images, that reflection, in
which nevertheless the narrative offers to contain its production. The effective hold of representation lies in the *mise en
scène* of circulation and fixity: the performance of the spectator as subject over the two as process-and-reflection, each
maintained — the phasing, the balance — in terms of the
other.

The function and functioning of the performance of
representation can be grasped more readily in the light of
insights from analytic work on the relations of the individual
as subject to meaning in language. Such work — stemming
above all from a linguistics responsive to the problems raised
by psychoanalysis — recognizes an important distinction
between the *subject of the enounced* and the *subject of the
enunciation*, between the subject in the proposition or statement made and the subject of the making of the proposition
or statement. Thus, a classic paradoxical example, in the
utterance 'I am lying', it is evident that the subject of the
proposition enounced is not one with the subject of the
enunciation of the proposition — the 'I' cannot 'lie' on both
planes at once: there is a division of the 'I' necessary for the
utterance to mean. Freud himself alludes to this splitting of
the subject in language in his comparisons of the multiple
appearance of the ego in dreams with the common fact of
anaphoric pronominalization in sentences of the kind 'When
I think what a healthy child *I* was' and more recently the
psychoanalytic theory of Lacan has been concerned with the
enounced/enunciation distinction in its descriptions of the
constitution and process of subjectivity.[5] The passage into
and in language divides and *in that division effects* the individual as subject: 'The cause is the signifier without which

there would be no subject in the real.'[6] The subject, that is, is not the beginning but the result of a structure of difference, of the symbolic order, and that result indexes a lack — the division — which is the constant 'drama of the subject in language', the inscription of desire and the elaboration of an imaginary order of wholeness, a set of images in which the ego seeks resolution as totality: 'it is because it fends off this moment of lack that an image takes up the position of bearing the whole cost of desire: projection, function of the imaginary . . . '.[7] The construction of the identity of the subject is a movement of exchange, a movement ceaselessly for balance between subject of enounced and subject of enunciation, symbolic and imaginary. In short, there is a permanent performance of the subject in language itself; permanent *and interminable*, never finished, the passage into and in language without end and hence the point of highly developed forms of social attention and regulation, the determination of institutions to play out the drama of meaning, to repeat the production of cohesion and identity, to provide fictions and images, to *make sense*.

Institutions such as cinema: in this context the description of the performance of the subject in film begun above can be given further formulation, coming back on the two moments of subject-reflection and subject-process. In narrative films, the products of the institution cinema, there is an achieved activity of creation and return: movement and play are set going and yet always returned to a hold on the spectator, with the hold defined across that very movement and play. *On the one hand*, the film opens up a flow and circulation, is a symbolic production in which unity and position are ever slipping away, lacking — deferred and lost in the gap of the present, 'death at work' (every film is potentially a danger). *On the other*, the film is figured out by its narrative as a totality, the imaginary relation of the spectator to an undivided present full of images of the accomplishment of desire (liking a film, the people in it, the things seen), of fictions of wholeness (including that of 'the film', the object mastered by the spectator); exactly a memory-spectacle in which the elements of production are bound up and resolved; the representation of unity and the unity of representation. The first is at the loss of the subject of the enounced, retraced in the tensions of desire, put into process; the second is the negation of the subject of the enunciation, the stasis of reflection. What is crucial is not one or the other but *the operation of the two together* (the layering, the phasing). Narrative makes the join, the suture, relating the film and giving it as that relation; not simply specifying the imaginary but setting equally the limits of the symbolic, the play allowed. Film is to remember for you, remember you: to remember *bearably* — the point of the narrative — the drama of meaning and identity. It is this that is the function and the functioning of the operation.

How then does narrative film work in its performance of representation and subject? The attempt here to begin to reply to that question will involve consideration of three factors: i) the basic apparatus of identification; ii) narrativization, the elaboration of narrative in film and the terms of memory and spectacle proposed; iii) the novelistic, the ideological category of the narrative elaborated.

To describe the basic apparatus of identification exploited in narrative film is to start from the importance of the look. Classically, cinema turns on a series of 'looks' which join, cross through and relay one another. Thus: 1) the camera looks (a metaphor assumed by this cinema) . . . at someone, something: the profilmic; 2) the spectator looks . . . at — or on — the film; 3) each of the characters in the film looks . . . at other characters, things: the intradiegetic. This series possesses a certain reversibility: on the one hand, the camera looks, the spectator looks at what the camera looks at and thereby sees characters in the film looking; on the other, the spectator sees characters in the film looking, which is to look at the film, which is to find the camera's looking, its 'having looked' (the presence in absence). The first and second looks, moreover, are in a perpetual interchange of 'priority', of 'origination': the camera's look is found only by looking at the film but the former is the condition — one of the conditions — of the latter.

It is this series of looks which provides the framework in turn for a pattern of multiply relaying identifications (a term that would need to be carefully specified in each case; what is important now is merely to stress the multiplicity). The shift between the first and second looks sets up the spectator's identification with the camera (rigorously constructed, placing heavy constraints, for example, on camera movement). The look at the film is an involvement in identifying relations of the spectator to the photographic image (the particular terms of position required by the fact of the photograph itself), to the human figure presented in image (the enticement and the necessity of a human presence 'on the screen'), to the narrative which gives the sense of the flow of photographic images (the guide-line for the spectator through the film, the ground that must be adopted for its intelligible reception). Finally, the looks of the characters allow for the establishment of the various 'point of view' identifications (the spectator looking with a character, from near to the position of his or her look, or as a character, the image marked in some way as 'subjective').

The power of such an apparatus is in the play it both incites and controls: a certain mobility is given — across the different levels, the various relays (with genres as specific versions of that mobility) — but followed out — effectively *relayed* — as the possibility of a constant hold on the spectator, as the bind of a coherence of vision, of, exactly, 'a vision'. Remember Bazin's fascination with a shot of Yvonne de Bray in Cocteau's *Les Parents terribles*: 'the object of the shot is not what she is looking at, not even her look; it is: *looking at her looking*'.[8] The apparatus of look and identification as the machinery for the fiction of such a position, cinema's institution of a film's view and viewer (the point of that view) in the totalizing security of 'looking at looking'. Play then, but a play *for*: taken up in the film, the spectator is dispersed to be re-established in mastery — the apparatus is the availability of film's subject vision.

That subject vision, moreover, is the impossibility for a film to be *heard*. The regime of the 'talking picture' is one of the containment of sound as the safe space of the narrative voice, its securing in and for the apparatus. There is a significant hierarchical tourniquet in this respect: the image is all-powerful (the essence of cinema; people pay to *see* a film), the sound-track a supplement (often regarded historically as a potential threat to the luminous clarity of the image); at the same time, however, that the sound-track as voice, as dialogues, is dominant, arranging the images in scenes (which avoid the threat) — the film comes to a stop when it runs out of words, nothing left it but the words of 'The End'. Which is why work on the sound of a film has become so fundamental a problem and concern of avant-garde practice: from — citing European examples only — Godard ('the struggle of an image against a sound and of a sound against an image') to Straub–Huillet (shooting with direct sound against the arrangements, the scenes, of commercial production), to Duras (the voice pulled away from its 'abject proximity' to the image; the creation of a plural space of voices over the silence of the images). To disturb the achieved relations of sound and image in the apparatus is to disturb the performance, to break the whole coherence of vision.

The apparatus thus described is a basis remade and confirmed in every classic narrative film, its levels welded together as such as the elaboration of the narrative catches up and closes the film.

'Let's go and see . . . No, I've already seen it.' The problem of 'already' — in this sense of 'once', 'one time' — is the problem of films in so far as they are caught up and closed as narrative (outside the terms of commercial production and consciously against classic narrative forms, independent cinema will achieve films that it is impossible to have 'seen once'). Narrative contains a film's multiple articulations as a single articulation, its images as a single image (the 'narrative image', which is a film's presence, how it can be talked about, what it can be sold and bought on, itself represented as — in the production stills displayed outside a cinema, for example), its sounds as a single register of the image (hence the avant-garde question of hearing a film). In order to see the film again, you need to forget it so as to have once more — so as once more directly to be — the memory it constructs you. The final time of film as narrative is that of identity, centre perspective, oneness, the vision of the unified and unifying subject, the reflection of that.

Narrative makes the join of symbolic and imaginary, process and reflection. That making, the elaboration of the narrative, may be called narrativization: the narrative is the close, the fiction of the film ultimately rendered; narrativization is the rendering, the movement to the narrative in the film, of the film to the narrative. Narrativization is the complex operation of the film as narrative and the setting of the spectator as subject *in the operation*: the spectator is placed as subject for the narrative relations and constituted in their reflection, but placing, relations, constitution are a process in which, equally, the spectator is entertained as subject — countenanced and occupied, kept going, held in (the etymology of 'entertainment'). As subject, in other words, the spectator comes all over the film, and comes together; narrativization is the guarantee of the 'all over together'. A film is thus more than the narrative problem of 'already', 'once', previously mentioned. To see a film again you need to forget it, but you always need the film again (this film or another, the return to the cinema), the process, exactly the time of its performance, its performance of you — subject — in time.

Performance as a remembering, the production of a memory. To stress this is not, in the first instance at least, to insist on the degree to which memory, symptomatically, has been so crucial a topic in film — think of *Secret Beyond the Door* or *Pursued* or *Marnie*, of *Letter from an Unknown Woman*, entirely organized as a remembering, or *Suspicion*, where the intrigue turns on the absence of any memory of Johnnie (Cary Grant) and the accumulation for Lina (Joan Fontaine) of memory fragments that can never be resolved but in suspicion, the psychological category that fixes the film for the spectator. Nor is it to insist again on cinema itself as a specific memory system, memory traces instantaneously so. Rather, it is a matter of indicating the memory force of the elaboration of narrative through the film. In classic cinema, there is free play within the frame — the set — of the narrative, the elaboration of which edges the ramifying flow of images in a direction, constructs a legality (what is to be seen and heard, what is to be related, a context of rightness), regulates a point of view. Narrativization is the mode, that is, of a continuous memory, the spectator as though 'remembered' in position, in subject unity, throughout the film (which is why, within this process, images of dismemberment provide such a powerful and lucrative theme, as witness *Jaws*); with that remembering a pressure at every moment of the film, dispersion and binding up a constantly simultaneous movement (hence the possibility of the emergence of dismemberment as a safely pleasurable theme), a subject circulating and a subject fixed from that circulation — the pleasure of the film in the layering together, the balance, the performance, the remembering and the memory.

In psychoanalytic terms, the narrative, with the apparatus ensuring its ground, retains the film in a play of castration known and denied: a process of difference and the symbolic, the object lost, and the conversion of the process into the reflection of a fixed memory, an invulnerable imaginary, the object — and with it the mastery of the subject — regained. Near in this to that of fetishism, the structure of the memory-spectacle of film is the perpetual story of a 'one time', a discovery perpetually remade with safe fictions. It is not by chance that classic narrative films should be so often arrested in the fascination of 'the scene', a theatrical moment of the highlighted perfect image, and the image of 'the woman' ('looking at *her* looking'): the illuminated body of Lisa (Joan Fontaine) modelling in *Letter from an Unknown Woman*, the first cabaret appearance of Amy Jolly (Marlene Dietrich) in *Morocco*, not to mention the explicit treatment of scene, image, the cinematic theatre of fetishism in a film like *Sylvia Scarlett*; examples, moreover, which should not be allowed to overshadow the ordinary inevitablity of scene and image, momentarily found in so many films.

Perpetual, the story of the 'one time', the found image, is repeated, in film after film, the steady production of the industry; the remembering takes place again and again, a constant return. A classic narrative film works with a particular economy of repetition. The coherence of any text depends on a sustained equilibrium of new informations, points of advance, and anaphoric recalls, ties that make fast, hold together.

One part of the particular economy is the exploitation of
narrative in film in the interests of an extreme tendency
towards coalescence, a tightness of totalization; the film is
gathered up in a whole series of rhymes in which elements —
of both 'form' and 'content' — are reproduced, shifted, and
turned back symmetrically, as in a mirror; in *Touch of Evil*,
for instance, the two Quinlan (Orson Welles)/Tanya (Marlene
Dietrich) sequences which answer one another at the beginning and the end of the film, the second bringing back and
reversing the elements of the first, the film looping round on
itself at its close. Yet this symmetry, the fascination of the
film itself as flawless scene, is an effect of the elaboration of the
narrative which gives at the same time the necessary advance,
an order. Absolutely, repetition is an absence of direction, a
failure of coherence: the return to the same in order to
abolish the difficult time of desire, it produces in that very
moment the resurgence of inescapable difference, produces
indeed the poles of 'same' and 'different'; its edge, its final
horizon, is thus death, the ultimate collapse of same and different, pure totality of indifference. Remember how Freud can
see repetition as the essence of drive and accord the death drives
the fundamental place — beyond the pleasure principle — in his
later accounts of physical functioning. The narrative join of a
film recasts repetition — difference, the interminable flux of
desire, the horizon of death — into the balance of a fiction
(an integrity of recall and progression), thus maintains the
historical function of the subject ('the death drive expresses
essentially the limit of the historical function of the subject'[9]).
A contrario, certain developments of repetition away from
the classic narrative order in avant-garde film entail a threat
to that function; a threat translated in the common reactions
of 'boredom', the irritation of 'nothing happens' — a great
deal does happen, of course, but not the performance of 'the
subject'.

'When the bourgeoisie had to find something else besides
painting and the novel to disguise the real to the masses, to
invent, that is, the ideology of the new mass communications,
its name was the photograph.'[10] Godard's remark serves to
emphasize this at least: the film is developed and exploited

from the photograph as an alternative and successor to the novel for the production-reproduction of the *novelistic*; the novelistic is the ideological category of the narrative elaborated in film, as it is of that in the novel. The title of the novelistic is *Family Romance* (or *Family Plot*, as the recent Hitchcock film would have it); the problem it addresses is that of the definition of forms of individual meaning within the limits of existing social representations and their determining social relations, the provision and maintenance of fictions of the individual; the historical reality it encounters a permanent crisis of identity that must be permanently resolved by remembering the history of the individual-subject. Narrative lays out — lays down as law — a film memory from the novelistic as the re-imaging of the individual as subject, the very representation of identity as the coherence of a past safely negotiated and reappropriated — the past *'in'* the film (once again, the thematic routines: memory itself; childhood, *Citizen Kane*; nostalgia, *Meet me in St. Louis*; and, infallibly, the *Oedipus* — a film about possession by the devil? *The Exorcist* cannot but fold in the question as to the possessed girl's missing father) and *'of'* the film (the sequential and consequential join of the images from beginning to end, the holding of the spectator as the unifying position — the subject — of their relation in time).

It is to Freud that we owe the expression 'family romance' (an essay published in 1909 is devoted to 'Der Familienroman der Neurotiker') and this is in no way fortuitous: effectively, psychoanalysis is the novelistic from the other side, the development in and against it of a critical knowledge of its terms, its instances, its movements, its reasons. The Dora, Rat Man or Wolf Man case histories as Freud writes them are exactly novels overturned, monuments in the *demonstration* of the novelistic.

In no way fortuitous; but that necessity often remains unseen, and unseen by psychoanalysis itself. There is no subject outside of a social formation, outside of social processes which include and define positions of meaning, which specify ideological places. Yet this inclusion, definition and specification does not exhaust the individual subject: at once because it says nothing concerning practice and also because it says nothing about the concrete history of the construction of the individual for such inclusion, definition and specification. It is this latter area that psychoanalysis identified and opened up (the 'new continent' discovered by Freud), that it takes as its province. Yet, to turn back round again, the real history with which psychoanalysis thus deals is still directly and immediately social, not 'before' or 'underneath' or 'elsewhere' to social processes, ideological places. There is a material history of the construction of the individual as subject and that history is also the social construction of the subject; it is not, in other words, that there is first of all the construction of a subject for social/ideological formations and then the placing of that constructed subject-support in those formations, it is that the two processes are one, in a kind of necessary simultaneity — like the recto and verso of a piece of paper. It is to the implications of such a simultaneity that psychoanalysis has found it difficult to respond: it describes an area that is absolutely specific but its encounter with that area, hence the terms of its descriptions, is always specifically social, within specific social formations; psychoanalysis is itself historical and a fully historical science.

Historical too in another sense, a corollary of the necessary simultaneity. As was said earlier, the construction of the subject is never finished, is interminable (psychoanalysis is not just to do with the first three or four years in the life of an individual); entry into language, for example, crucial in psychoanalysis's account of the construction and a point of the individual/social articulation, is not 'once and for all': the individual is always entering, emerging as a subject in language (the lapsus for Freud was an explosive indication); the process of representation is permanently remade in language at that point of individual-social articulation (the complex process in which 'a signifier represents a subject for another signifier' and 'a sign represents something for someone',[11] of the movement from production to product together). The individual is always a subject in society, the place of social and ideological formations, but is more than simply the figure of that representation, is in excess of such placing formations. An important — determining — part of ideological systems is then the achievement of a number of machines (institutions) that can *move* the individual as subject, shifting and tying desire, realigning excess and contradiction, in a perpetual retotalization — a remembering — of the imaginary in which the individual-subject is grasped as identity. It is in terms of this 'double bind' — the statement of social meanings and the holding of the individual to those meanings, the suturing of the enounced and the enunciation, what was called above 'the vision of the subject', that the institution of cinema can be understood. In this context, the force of psychoanalysis lies in the breaking it provokes of that vision, its attention to the limit and excess of the function of the subject and, from there, the questions it poses with regard to the whole subject performance repeated in those specially developed social machines.

The problem addressed by the novelistic — what its fictions are to resolve — is that of the relation of individual meaning and social determination as an identity, of the realization of subject coherence; a problem, quite simply, in a world in which the social struggle of men and women in history has become the effective arena of value, of providing regulatory modes of 'talking about oneself', 'imaginations of life', 'self representations', 'your images'. This operation of the novelistic, however, is not merely in the representation (what is represented, the content, the image); it is equally, as has been the stress here throughout, in the performance of the representation (the performance — of the subject — the representation is); and because there is no immediately given and constituted subject to which representations have, as it were, only to be presented for assent: representation and subject are produced in the performance, which is thus involved in the multiple stratifications of the necessary simultaneity, the multiple times of the history of the construction of the subject and its representations. What is a film, in fact, but an elaborate time-machine, a tangle of memories and times successfully rewound in the narrative as the order of the continous time of the film?

In its films, cinema reproduces and produces the novelistic: it occupies the individual as subject in the terms of the existing social representations and it constructs the individual as subject in the process, in the balancing out of symbolic and imaginary, circulation for fixity. The real of a film is complex, mobile, historically plural at the point of the function of the subject, mesh of determinations which interest both psychoanalysis and historical materialism. The 'achievement' of the institution cinema in film — the apparatus of identifications, the narrative space of look and voice — is the construction-occupation as filling-in, the *completion* of the subject, the translation of plurality into a *certain* history, the single vision.

There is a crime in Michael Snow's *Wavelength*: the noise of breaking glass, the man who enters the room and falls out of frame to the floor, the woman who finds the body and telephones a man named Richard. There is also the crime of the film itself: against the certain history, the single vision, the *beau film*. At so many stages in the previous discussion, reference could have been made to the contrary practice of Snow's film, its dissociation from the classic terms of film performance.

Wavelength is produced as a complex of differing times: fragments of a narrative time, little quotations of narrative stereotypes drifting in on image — the fall, the telephoning — or sound — the crash of glass, a siren — tracks; the existence in time of the loft traversed in the film; a kind of encoding time, elements — colour and light-value changes, for instance — make various micro-systems through the film; the time of the continuous forty-five minute zoom from its widest to its smallest field; the times of the sound track, not simply the rising sine-wave that couples with the movement of the zoom-in but comprising a host of brief dispersed moments, as with the shutting of the window and the play with the noise 'outside' or with the 'Strawberry Fields' song over the radio; and so on. No production of any simple memory: the film plays with and on memory — as in the superimpositions: the room, the film suddenly posed in a past or a future to the present moment of the zoom — but the play is never unified in a pattern, a figure of desire realized in totality. In short, no *identification*, the apparatus pulls apart. Hence, probably, the common reactions to *Wavelength* as 'tragic' (the response of Ihab Hassan, for example, finding himself 'thinking of death' when watching Snow's work[12]). In their way, the reactions acknowledge the difficulty of times, the difference of the film: a film progression but in jerks, breakings, dissociations; a film without any subject performance, or rather a performance only in the difficulty, the difference, outside of *a* time, *a* vision. Despite the lack of any evident political signified (as though such an 'evidence' could furnish criteria), Snow's films are politically insistent in their question of the cinematic institution of the subject in film, their question of another subjectivity — material, heterogeneous, in process — , of a film that *makes a body*.

'We are never quite contemporary with our present. History goes forward masked, is inscribed on the screen with the mask of the previous sequence and we no longer recognize anything in the film.'[13] The 'making a body' is there: recognizing in film, a subject splitting in the multiple contradictions of a present that includes those of the work of the film itself, such a history. The quotation, however, is from the sound track of *Vent d'est*. A provocation to bring together *Wavelength* and the Groupe Dziga Vertov? Simply the quick notattion of the actuality and importance of the problem of film performance in these terms. The Baron d'Ormesan's public made no mistake in the secure illusion of the good film; the task now is to make new relations of film performance.

Notes

Address given at the conference on 'Performance: Film/Theater/Video', Center for Twentieth Century Studies, University of Milwaukee— Wisconsin, February 1977; published in *Ciné-tracts* no. 2 (Summer 1977) pp. 7–17.

1. Guillaume Apollinaire, 'Un beau film', in M. Décaudin (ed.), *Œuvres complètes de Guillaume Apollinaire* vol. 1 (Paris: A. Balland et J. Lecat, 1965) pp. 206–8.

2. A phrase cited and developed by Straub; 'Entretien avec Jean-Marie Straub et Danièle Huillet', *Cahiers du cinéma* no. 223 (August 1970) pp. 53–5.

3. Christian Metz, 'Le signifiant imaginaire', *Communications* no. 23 (1975) p. 31; translation, 'The Imaginary Signifier', *Screen* vol. 16 no. 2 (Summer 1975) p. 47.

4. Jacques Lacan, 'Faire mouche', *Nouvel Observateur* no. 594 (29 March—4 April 1976) p. 64.

5. For examples of Freud's comparisons, see *The Standard Edition of the Complete Psychological Works* (London: Hogarth Press, 1953—66) vol. IV p. 323; vol. XIX p. 120. Lacan has a particularly clear discussion of the distinction in *Le Séminaire livre XI* (Paris: Seuil, 1973) pp. 127—30; translation, *The Four Fundamental Concepts of Psycho-Analysis* (London: Hogarth Press, 1977) pp. 138—42.

6. J. Lacan, *Écrits* (Paris: Seuil, 1966) p. 835.

7. Ibid. p. 655.

8. André Bazin, 'Théâtre et cinéma', *Qu'est-ce que le cinéma?* vol. II (Paris: Cerf, 1959) p. 87.

9. Lacan, *Écrits*, p. 318; translation, *Écrits: A Selection* (London: Tavistock, 1977) p. 103.

10. Jean-Luc Godard, 'Premiers sons anglais', *Cinéthique* no. 5 (1969) p. 14.

11. Lacan, *Écrits*, pp. 835, 840.

12. Comments during an open discussion with Snow in the context of the 'Performance: Film/Theater/Video' conference.

13. '*Vent d'est* (bande paroles)', *Cahiers du cinéma* no. 240 (July—August 1972) p. 35.

Chapter 5

Film, System, Narrative

'Every film shows us the cinema, and is also its death.' Here is that *singularity* of a textual system on which Metz has laid so much stress. Operation, displacement (if merely by virtue of the inevitable shifting of codes into action), a film — any film — goes along with the cinema that it continually and simultaneously recasts. If 'the study of a singular filmic system is never the study of cinematic specificity' (and this is the very reason of *Langage et cinéma*, Metz's attempt rigorously to define and separate the terms of the filmic and the cinematic), it is indeed that the film is on the side of the heterogeneous, that its work cannot be grasped by a simple listing of codes, that it poses for analysis new tasks, a new object: 'the only principle of pertinence capable now of defining the semiology of film — other than its application to the filmic rather than to the cinematic fact — is the will to treat films as *texts*, as units of discourse, thus putting oneself under the obligation of looking for the different systems (whether or not they be codes) which inform and are implicated in them.'[1]

System, systems. Developed in *Langage et cinéma* as 'ultimate (or initial?) principle of unification and intelligibility', with a certain accompanying plurality if need be (the various overall — and rival — descriptions that might be given of a film), the notion of a textual system is subsequently adapted in the interests of an increasingly supple systematizing account: a film is conceived and approached not as *one* system, a unity of its organization, nor even as *several* systems, the sum of its different readings, but as *involving* system, systematic activity, 'something of a structural and relational (but not necessarily exhaustible) order'. Henceforth, it is such a *movement* of relations that will be characterized as a 'textual system'.

This adaptation should be given all its importance, finding the film as it does in a certain originality of system (already suggested, though limited, by the 'singularity' of *Langage et cinéma*: 'if a film is "invention" or "creation", it is solely inasmuch as it is an *operation*, as it adds something to the pre-existing codes, brings with it new structural configurations unforeseen by any of them'); an originality which reflects exactly the heterogeneity of a film, what it marshals each time for that death of cinema. Thus the question of the 'object' becomes fundamental. To approach a film from the standpoint of an idea of code is to circumscribe it in terms of structure and coherence — the object is considered as a kind of almost-code: 'it is a system but it is not exactly a code'. To grasp it in its operation, its unsettling movement (since it picks up and breaks the unity of codes, 'deforming each of them through the presence of the others, contaminating them with one another, replacing in the process one code by another'), is to return the film to the terms of its economy — the object then as the space of a force of relations (their circulation-distribution) that it is essential — the task of analysis — to demonstrate in its logic, to bring out the positions it takes on and constructs with the systems it implicates. The effect of Metz's rethinking of the notion of a textual system is to change the object 'film' in the direction of such a demonstration: analysis no longer seeks to propose a single organization, to discover an ultimate principle of unification, but to pose the work, the process of the film, to give onto the moving surface of its 'indefinite thickness'; a semiology, therefore, of the enunciation as much as of the enounced, of discourse as much as of narrative, of production and not of the product alone, in short, of the *actuality* of a text.

How then is analysis to proceed? 'What gives us the most central access to the textual system is no doubt the relation between the cinematic elements and the script elements, and not the ones nor the others, nor their addition.' The proposition is both strong, a crucial recognition for any study of a textual system, and difficult to maintain: does the work of a film pass *simply* through a distinction between cinematic and script (narrative, 'the manifest thematic complex')? Through a clarity of their 'relation'? The idea of a 'central access'?

In the margins of these questions, of their discussion, I want to inscribe a few difficulties met with in the course of a long analysis of a film directed by Orson Welles, *Touch of Evil* (1957–8), difficulties which bear evidently — and despite the fragmentary presentation they will here receive — on the relations between system and narrative in the fiction film, and which seem to indicate that it is through an attention paid to the putting in order of the narrative, to the figures of narrative balance, that such an analysis must envisage its object. If the fiction film works to produce a homogeneity, works to flatten out contradiction, that homogeneity is only ever the *product* of the film; in no way can it exhaust the textual system — the filmic process, the relational movement — which is precisely the term of its production. Haunting obsession of the film which renders the heterogeneous in the very terms in which it represses it, finds itself caught up in a material outside that it *expresses* — that it signifies even as it forces it out — under the advance of the narrative; tension and twist of the practice of the system into narrative, figures of its gaps and divergences.

It is as though the film — a film — presented itself in the form of a *narrative image*, a kind of static portrait in which it comes together, on the basis of which it is talked about (the production stills displayed outside a cinema are so many incitements to such an image). 'Unity', 'work', the fiction film is defined by its closure: the consistency (this is well and truly the realm of the imaginary) or again the coalescence (the signified which fills the signifier) of this image which is in fact the film's currency, that on which it can be bought and sold, marketed (by criticism, for instance). This being so, the detail of the film — the possible chance of the signifier — matters little. Sure enough (but the observation is no doubt banal), working 'in detail' on *Touch of Evil*. I have often been confronted by critical summaries that are unashamedly false to the manifest discourse — the body — of the film ('series of images, sounds and words in a certain order capable of being *attested*') but which none the less (and it is this that is significant) answer exactly to the narrative image, to the negotiable meaning: errors then, but correct errors, perfectly in accordance with the hold of the film, helping it to achieve and sustain consistency, coalescence.

The film must hang together; the narrative, therefore, must work. Hence the requirement of practicability so constantly held to by the unfolding — the resolving progress — of the narrative film. Every element introduced must be practicable in the development of the narrative, must be taken up again and be 'finished off' as an evident function in its progress, its resolution (the fiction film follows very much an order of *evidence*). While talking on the telephone, Vargas (Charlton Heston), the hero of *Touch of Evil*, opens his briefcase, takes out a gun and checks that it is in good working condition; later, he finds the briefcase, entrusted to his wife who has been kidnapped, opens it and discovers the gun to be missing; the gun finally reappears in the hands of his enemy. The example is typical of this 'taking up again', this 'finishing off': the gun was not introduced for nothing, is *of use*. The narrative, that is, strives to gather up the elements it puts forward in order with them to go forward *evidently*.

This, however, is never simple, never without slippage: the narrative cannot contain *everything*. Except by resorting to a scrupulous — 'abstract' — construction of profilmic space (in the manner of the scene in Ichikawa's *An Actor's Revenge* which utilizes only three actors, a tree and a rope against a black backcloth, but this is a very different economy to that of the films of the dominant Western cinema), the narrative film can only seek to maintain a tight balance between the photographic image as a reproduction of reality and the narrative as the sense, the intelligibility, of that reality (a balance which is the ideological good fortune of the fiction film, simultaneously sense and reality, naturalizing the one from the other). The film picks up — indicating by framing, shot angle, lighting, dialogue mention, musical underscoring, and so on — the notable elements (to be noted in and for the progress of the narrative which in return defines their notability) without for all that giving up what is thus left aside and which it seeks to retain — something of an available reserve of insignificant material — in order precisely to ring 'true', true *to reality*. In short, the film-narrative is a *regulated* loss, that loss becoming the *sign* of the real.

Yet it happens too that this regulation runs into its own loss, goes off in evasions and abandonments. Abandonment: taken to a hotel on the promise of information concerning her husband, Susan (Janet Leigh), Vargas's wife, is tricked into having her photograph taken in front of the entrance with a young Mexican, the start perhaps of a plan to blackmail or compromise her in some way; but though she is later sent the photo, nothing comes of it, it has no finish; the narrative lets it drop, abandons. Evasion: near the beginning and near the end of the film are two great scenes between Quinlan (Orson Welles), an unscrupulous cop ready for any kind of deal or scheme that will enable him to convict a suspect and who is being pursued by Vargas for just such a frame-up (I am borrowing here from the version of the narrative image provided by André Bazin[2]), and Tanya (Marlene Dietrich), owner of a *maison close* that Quinlan used to visit in days long gone; scenes that are oblique to the line of the narrative, that do not have its sense, its direction; scenes that stop, evade the action of the film, and that bring with them moreover a whole mythology or nostalgia of the past: of Quinlan and Tanya, of Welles and Dietrich (*Follow the Boys*, the film-review in which they played together in 1944), of cinema (the richly Sternbergian décor of Tanya—Dietrich's house); scenes in which the narrative slips, drifts.

'That festival of affects that is called a film', writes Barthes.[3] The narrative takes care of this affectivity (which it thus also sets out), places it (comes to an end of the free circulation, constructs positions for the subject). Finally, the narrative is the very triumph of *framing* (the links between conventions of framing and the demands of the narrative have often been stressed); the frame is what holds tight against movement and slippage, cuts short the interminable play of the signifier, the subject in process, imposes a coherence and a continuity of representation.

Simple definition: a narrative action is a series of elements held in a relation of transformation such that their consecution — the movement of the transformation from the ones to the others — determines a state S' different to an initial state S. Clearly the action includes S and S' that it specifies as such — beginning and end are grasped from this action, within the relations it sustains; the fiction of the film is its 'unity', that of the narrative. A beginning, therefore, is always a violence, the interruption of the homogeneity of S (once again, the homogeneity — S itself — being recognized in retrospect from that violence, that interruption); in *Touch of Evil*, this is literal: the explosion of a bomb-planted car, killing the two passengers. The task of the narrative — the point of the transformation — is to resolve the violence, to replace it in a new homogeneity. 'Replace' here, it must be noted, has a double edge: on the one hand, the narrative produces something new, replaces S with S'; on the other, this production is the return of the same, S' replaces S, is the reinvestment of its elements. Hence the constraint of the need for exhaustion, the requirement of practicability: every element presented must be used up in the resolution, the dispersion provoked by the violence must be turned into a reconvergence. Ideally, a narrative would be the perfect symmetry of this movement: the kiss the explosion postpones is resumed in the kiss of the close of the film as Susan is reunited with Vargas — the same kiss, but delayed, set into a narrative.

Let us agree, and this is the thesis of structural analysis, that every narrative depends on a process of transformation. It remains nevertheless that the coherence of the transformation — with at the end of the film the narrative image — brings into play determinations that are fully cultural and ideological. The fiction film, the product of classic cinema, knows a quite specific economy of narrative (though tributary of the novel: how many films, still today, that are not first of all novels?): the elements are multiplied — photographic reproduction looks after this — in the name of a realism, a faithfulness to life, while at the same time there is an increasing pressure for their unification into a sense, their ordering into a constant and intelligible position. It is on this position that hinges the ideological and economic speculation in narrative from novel to film: the crux is the maintenance of a violence, a heterogeneity, from the position of a subject unity. The position of realism is the position of intelligibility and the guarantee of intelligibility is the stability, the unity, of the subject; thus narrative, dispersion and convergence, becomes the fiction of reality and of the reality of the film, its coherence; thus narrative appears as an obliteration or covering over of division, symbolic process: 'what distinguishes fiction films is not the "absence" of a special work of the signifier, but its presence in the mode of denegation, and it is well known that this type of presence is one of the strongest there are'.[4] This 'presence' is the paradox — or better the tourniquet — of the narrative: denegation, it brings with it, states, the heterogeneity and process it seeks to contain. What has to be understood as the textual system is exactly this *friction* of the narrative film.

The transformation of the narrative elements, their reinvestment, goes by patterns of exchange at the centre of which is the object to be restored (the narrative here is that space where things circulate *a little*; there is a free play *within its frame*). The explosion of the car interrupts the kiss between Susan and Vargas, separates them; henceforth, Vargas's action as hero of the narrative is the desire to get things back into place: re-establish Law in the light of Justice (defeat Quinlan); have his wife returned to him 'clean' (as a result of Quinlan's schemes, she has been arrested on drugs and murder charges).

This action is accomplished in the exchange of Menzies
(Joseph Calleia), who passes from Quinlan, whose devoted
associate he had been until then, to Vargas, whom he helps to
reveal the truth. The exchange is stressed: Menzies, who
lovingly finds his identity in Quinlan *becomes* Mike Vargas,
the instrument — the 'mike' — with which the latter records
the confessions of the unscrupulous cop; moreover, this
transference has its 'magic' token: Menzies gives Vargas
Quinlan's stick — the rod of power and the key to the crime,
to Quinlan's guilt.

What the action restores, what the exchanges are for, is
Susan, *the woman*, the very object of the Law. Logic of the
narrative (of *Touch of Evil*): the Law is out of order, *therefore*
the woman is no longer there, in her place; or again, the
woman is a heat, a fire, a conflagration (this is the guiding
metaphor of the film), *therefore* the Law is no longer assured,
in order; this being the 'evil' of the title, as well as the task of
the narrative: find the woman, the (legal) place of desire.
The narrative allows the problem to be posed in terms of
images of the Law (Vargas against Quinlan, Vargas as representative of a just — 'democratic' — law) in order to resolve
thereby the excess of desire (Vargas as husband, the right
limit — equally 'democratic' — of sexuality); the first serves as
a cover for the second which is called upon to resorb itself in
it. Indeed, following that psychology vaguely coloured with
'psychoanalyticity' — or 'traumaticity', since it is a matter of
bringing everything down to an explanatory trauma — of
which the American cinema has been so fond, if Quinlan is
crooked, it is because the murderer of his own wife escaped
justice and punishment; thus if the Law is out of order, it is
finally a personal problem (a drama), in no way implicating
the question of the Law itself.

The woman must be restored, but the woman as good object,
that is to say, as object, which is to say in turn — and the
circle is closed — as 'the woman', Vargas's woman, his wife.
Blind spot of the film, the woman is put for an impossible
pleasure, in violation of the order: on the one hand, the

woman as focus of desire; on the other, the desire to know nothing of that desire, to wipe it out as the memory of a different economy, that of sexual *contradiction*, of a sexuality in excess of its established reduction to a simple genitality, the order of the phallus: a body crossed with differences, a subject divided, not 'one', in process. Turned towards restoration, the film, in the very development of its narrative (the woman set aside: expelled from the main action until she can be brought back into place), goes through the figures of the repression it operates, swerves to systems — fragments of systematicity — that do not *quite* fit into the narrative unity, its direction of the film. This gives, for example, simultaneous with the wish to restore Susan as good object, the necessity of demonstrating her, the woman, as *bad* object: object of panic (the scene in the motel between Susan and the 'Night Man', a hysterical neurotic, jumpy at her body, her presence as other); object of assault (captured by a gang of youths, target of Quinlan's hatred and attacks); fetish object (Susan is at one point caught as she is undressing in the beam of light from the torch of an aggressor, is held there, stripteased). It gives too, in a kind of symbolic discrepancy from this demonstration, a whole mass of 'propositions' — stirrings of stories, of other exchanges — constantly running out of phase with the narrative purpose: thus, where the psychologizing explanation has it that Quinlan's wife was strangled long ago by a killer who evaded the police and that therefore Quinlan will stop at nothing in his pursuit of those whom he takes to be guilty of crimes, the film — the twist of its relations — says clearly that the killer can only be Quinlan himself; he who strangles Grandi (Akim Tamiroff, the head of a local mafia, presented as an intolerable sexual confusion, another transgression of the Law) over Susan's body stretched out on a huge hotel bed: frenzied music, neon lights flashing on and off outside, rapid cutting from Quinlan pulling tight to Susan moaning, everything coming to a frantic climax.

These propositions, these returns on the sense of the narrative, work over different matters of expression, straddling them

like so many shifters from code to code; which makes the
analysis of the textual system difficult in the perspective of a
simple fidelity to an opposition between the cinematic and
the filmic. A quick example: in the car explosion, Zita (Joi
Lansing), the woman passenger, is burnt alive; in front of the
cabaret where she was employed as a striptease dancer, a sign
announces 'Twenty Sizzling Strippers'; while following
Quinlan at the beginning of the investigation of the explosion,
Vargas is intercepted by one of Grandi's 'nephews' who aims
a bottle of vitriol at him, misses his target (or hits it, the
narrative miss made good in the mesh of the symbolic) and
splatters a photo of Zita on a poster that is held for a moment
in close shot: Zita burns a second time, with, on the sound-
track, the sizzling of the vitriol over the poster. Thus is set
going a chain which mobilizes writing, the photographic
image and recorded sound, specific cinematic codes (the car
blows up in a violet rhythm created by a pattern of cutting
and shifts in framing) and codes that are not specifically
cinematic (the English language — 'sizzling').

That chain set going touches on what is at issue in the textual
system, condensed in an alternative the terms of which,
although not the sole property of film (they are found elsewhere) are figures that are filmic properties — a whole
'cinema'. As was said, the narrative must serve to restore the
woman as good object (the narrative image depends on this);
which obliges it to envisage her as bad object (the other side
of the restoration that it seeks to accomplish). Given which,
there are two resources: either the woman truly posed as an
object in order that sexuality be put at her distance as such —
this is the woman stripteased, Susan fixed as spectacle under
the beam of light (Still 1), or again the pin-up, the star (always
the essential luminosity), Susan as Janet Leigh, the only way
known *to the narrative* to admit desire (Still 2); or the woman
obliterated, extinguished (like a fire) — captured by the
Grandi gang, nothing happens to Susan, simply she is faded
out (Stills 3A and B); recourses that the chain ceaselessly
picks up to mark the points of their excess, the terms they

1

2

3A

3B

4

5

engage. It is as though the film – the textual system – followed *literally* the stereotype-metaphor of an 'explosive' sexuality, the woman as 'dynamite'.

Here are two empty frames, images of emptiness, that cut across this alternating play of light and dark (Stills 3 and 4). The first is the absence of the object, is thus a pregnant emptiness, eroticized but uncertain – Susan remains out of frame, the beam (of the torch, of the projector) is dispersed, wasted. The second is the presence of the object but undercut, tipped into absence still: at the moment of the restoration, Susan and Vargas kiss in the front seat of a car; the same circle of light, fringed with darkness, the film cannot – even as it does – bring Susan fully back in the light of the narrative; she comes back in the chain at once to figure her absence. All this, these figuring moments, are seen only in single frames, when one slows or stops the film; they elude – *precisely* – the steady, continuous time of the narrative.

Barthes: 'As fiction, the Oedipus complex served at least some purpose: that of producing good novels, of telling good stories (this is written after having seen Murnau's *City Girl*).'[5] Is it conceivable that the film narrative will always provide the clues of this fiction? The fact remains that I note in the course of Welles's film the scattered signs of its oedipal logic: the swollen foot (Quinlan hobbles along as a result of his 'gammy' leg), the stick of the riddle (the key to the crime), the man who uncovers the truth of himself as the criminal (Quinlan ends up a murderer), the theme of blindness (wanting to phone Susan, Vargas enters a shop kept by a blind woman), the baby left to die (Susan lets herself be photographed because a baby is suddenly held up in front of her and which she turns to admire: it is the symbolic that reasserts its dominance in this abandonment of the narrative, the baby that is given no life in its development: before he enters the blind woman's shop, Vargas finds another baby in his path – he puts on dark glasses, refuses to see clearly).

Ceaselessly, the film puts off 'something else' into the past, makes a screen against it; the indefinite memory of a far-off time, the *novel* of Quinlan: murder of the woman, his wife, *and* fairy universe — a cinematic dream (a dream of cinema) of Tanya (Ti*tania*, the Queen of the Fairies in *A Midsummer-Night's Dream*, this in a film which multiplies Shakespearian references). Something else outside the narrative which, from its order, its sense, can see it only as death, as the image of a paradise lost; an image to which criticism does not fail to respond: 'Tanya's piano, the only pure rhythm in this syncopated film, like a heart still beating in an agonising organism, is the last burst of life, an unbearable tenderness in the face of death . . . the momentary appearance of the lost happiness that music alone is capable of depicting on the threshold of hell.'[6] A perfect response to the mode of the narrative — the Law is established, stands against the horizon of an inevitably *tragic* sexuality. Simply, something else comes too, another return through the narrative sense, the chain continues: from Tanya to Zita (Zi-ta-nya) to Susan — what wipes out, again, here too at the end, the honeymoon kiss (Still 5), figures emptiness in Susan's expected place, is Tanya, the fantasy of this 'past', the shadow-mother of the 'something else'.

The something else, the other film of which this film says everywhere the slips and slides: the narrative of the film and the history of that narrative, the economy of its narrative production, its logic. To approach, to experience the textual system can only be to pull the film onto this double scene, this process of its order and of the material that order contains, of the narrative produced and of the terms of its production. Analysis must come to deal with this work of the film, in which it is, exactly, the death — itself the disturbance — of any *given* cinema.

NOTES

Written and published in French as 'Système-récit', *Ça* no. 7/8 'Hommage à Christian Metz' (May 1975) pp. 8—17; this translation previously unpublished. The long analysis of *Touch of Evil*, to which reference is briefly made, is 'Film and System: Terms of Analysis', *Screen* vol. 16 no. 1 (Spring 1975) pp. 7–77 and vol. 16 no. 2 (Summer 1975) pp. 91–113; additional note, '*Touch of Evil* – the long version', *Screen* vol. 17 no. 1 (Spring 1976) pp. 115–17.

1. This and subsequent paragraphs draw on discussions of the concept of 'textual system' in the following two works by Metz: *Langage et cinéma* (Paris: Larousse, 1971) pp. 14, 46–7, 72–9; translation, *Language and Cinema* (The Hague and Paris: Mouton, 1974) pp. 21, 62–4, 96–105; 'Le signifiant imaginaire', *Communications* no. 23 (1975) pp. 21–6; translation, 'The Imaginary Signifier', *Screen* vol. 16 no. 2 (Summer 1975) pp. 35–41.

2. André Bazin, *Orson Welles* (Paris: Cerf, 1972) pp. 115–16.

3. Roland Barthes, 'En sortant du cinéma', *Communications* no. 23 (1975) p. 104.

4. Metz, 'Le signifiant imaginaire', p. 29; translation, p. 39.

5. Roland Barthes, *Le Plaisir du texte* (Paris: Seuil, 1973) p. 76; translation, *The Pleasure of the Text* (London: Cape, 1976) p. 47.

6. Jean Collet, '*La Soif du mal*', *Études cinématographiques* no. 24–5 (1963) p. 116.

Chapter 6

The Question Oshima

The night of 25/26 February 1936. Tokyo under a layer of snow. A reception takes place at the American Embassy in honour of Viscount Saito Makoto, recently Prime Minister and now something like Lord Privy Seal. As a treat, Ambassador Joseph C. Grew has had a copy of *Naughty Marietta* — the Van Dyke musical starring Nelson Eddy and Jeannette MacDonald — brought over from Hollywood. Will Saito like it? He stays, delighted, to the end of his first sound film, leaves later than expected, full of gratitude. In the early morning, he is assassinated by a group of young officers in the course of an abortive putsch, part of the history of the growth of Japanese militarism in the 1930s.

Empire of the Senses (*Ai no corrida* — Oshima Nagisa, 1976) opens in snow-layered Tokyo, takes up a newspaper story of 1936, poses a critical question to cinema. That question lies in the articulation of the sexual, the political and the cinematic, and in the impossibilities discovered in the process of such an articulation. Briefly, the following notes work out from the problem of the cinematic institution — 'the imaginary signifier' — in an attempt to refind a little of the impossible of Oshima's film, of its experience of limits, to demonstrate the effective terms of its question, more important than the film itself, or, rather, the very point of its importance.

Consider a film such as *Letter from an Unknown Woman*
(Max Ophuls, 1948), a film of which from one perspective —
that of the question to cinema — *Empire of the Senses* is the
direct and ruinous remake. At the centre of *Letter from*, a
classic Hollywood narrative film with genre specificities (the
'woman's film') and stylistic markings ('Ophuls' as the name
for 'extensive use of music, long elaborate takes with flowing
camera movement', etc.), is the full image, sexuality as look,
the *looked-for image*. Lisa (Joan Fontaine) models and is *the
model*: radiantly dressed and lit, she circles for the gaze of
prospective clients at the fashionable dress-shop where she
earns her living and at the same time for that of the spectator
who has paid to *see* the film. Twice, as she does so, men,
spectators in the film, respond to the perfection of the flawless — *whole* — body, to the image of a female beauty, of the
female *as beauty*, which holds the sexual cinematically as just
that: the desired and untouchable image, an endless *vision*.
As always, however, the centred image mirrors a structure
that is in excess of its effect of containment, that bears the
traces of the heterogeneity — the trouble — it is produced to
contain: sexuality here is also the 'more' that the look elides,
that is elided from the look, and that returns, constantly in
the figures of its absence. After the first modelling scenes,
Lisa spends one night with Stefan (Louis Jourdan), the man
she has loved and worshipped in silence since childhood; as
they begin to kiss, the image fades, the screen is left black
with nothing to see. Evidently, this is convention, its context
the Hays Code, the awareness of what can and cannot be
shown. But convention is never simply a fact outside a film:
what can and cannot be shown, the determining confines of
image and look, is *in Letter from*, is part of its film action
and meaning. The fade, the image absent, is *Letters from*'s
momentary and fundamental figure, comprising in its elision
the time of acknowledgement and consequent guilt (Lisa is
caught up in the more than the image, the one night makes
her pregnant, detailing her suffering the film details her
punishment for transgression) *and* of denial and consequent
innocence (the unshown leaves Lisa pure, intact as image, still
perfect; she is only ever daughter or sister and then mother to
Stefan, never — the exact function of the fade, the meaning

of the convention in the film — a sexual lover). Immediately afterwards, the film goes back to the image of Lisa modelling, now for Stefan, and continues with its drama of vision, the image that Stefan has lost and the images that he remembers as Lisa remembers in her letter, as we remember through the narrative which orders our memory of the film, *our* vision.

Centred image, drama of vision, space of the look, towards a coherence of vision of us: classically, narrative cinema operates on a very powerful apparatus of 'looks' which join, cross through, and relay one another. Thus: 1) the camera looks (a metaphor assumed by this cinema) . . . at someone, something: the profilmic; 2) the spectator looks . . . at, or on, the film; 3) each of the characters in the film looks . . . at other characters, things: the intradiegetic. This series possesses a certain reversibility: on the one hand, the camera looks, the spectator looks at what the camera looks at and thereby sees characters in the film looking; on the other, and equally, the spectator sees characters in the film looking, which is to look at the film, which is to find the camera's looking, its 'having looked' (the mode of presence in absence on which cinema is here founded). The first and second looks, moreover, are in a perpetual interchange of 'priority', of 'origination': the camera's look is found only by looking at the film but the former is the condition — one of the conditions — of the latter. The series of looks is then the basis in turn for a pattern of multiply relaying identifications (a term that would need to be carefully specified in each case): the turn between the first and second looks sets up the spectator's identification with the camera (rigorously constructed, with heavy constraints on, for example, camera movement); the look at the film is involved in identifying relations of the spectator to the photographic image and its movement, to the human figure presented in image, to the narrative which gives the sense of the flow of images, acts as guide-line; the looks of the characters allow for the establishment of the various 'point-of-view' identifications.

The power of such an apparatus is in the play it both proposes and controls: a certain mobility is given but followed out — relayed — as the possibility of a constant hold on the spectator, as the bind of a coherence of vision, of, exactly, *a vision.* Remembering Bazin's fascination with the shot of Yvonne de Bray in Cocteau's *Les Parents terribles* (1948): 'the object of the shot is not what she is looking at, not even her look: it is *looking at her looking*'.[1] The apparatus is the machinery for the fiction of such a position, for the totalizing security of 'looking at looking' — and at 'her'. No surprise, therefore, that the achievement of that security, the institution of cinema in film, becomes the actual narrative of so many films, their relentless concern. Years after her single night of love, Lisa encounters Stefan once more at a performance of *The Magic Flute*: as Papageno sings 'A maiden or a woman' (if a feminine mouth will kiss me, I'll soon be well again'), Stefan turns in his seat trying to seek out Lisa's face, the face of the woman who now — as always — is gone; an extreme close-up, pulling free in its extremeness from any simple assignation of a time and place in the diegesis, as much an index of the film's organizing activity, shows the seeking eyes, with Lisa commenting in her voice-over letter-narration that 'somewhere out there were your eyes and I knew I couldn't escape them'; he follows her down into the foyer, 'I've seen you somewhere, I know'; and so it goes on, the entire film a problem of seeing and knowing, of the image glimpsed and lost and remembered — as of *the* woman, the mother (Lisa is always in Stefan's past, the time of his — and the film's — desire), the goddess ('the Greeks built a statue to a god they didn't know but hoped some day would come to them; mine happens to be a goddess').

Empire of the Senses produces and breaks the apparatus of look and identification; it does so by describing — in the geometrical acceptation of the word: by *marking out* — the problematic of that apparatus; hence its drama is not merely 'of vision' but, undercutting that classic narrative transposition, of the relations of the cinema's vision and of the demonstration of the terms — including, above all, the woman — of those relations.

Throughout, the film is engaged with an organization and movement of the intradiegetic look. The very first shot after the credits is a tight close-up of Sada (Matsuda Eiko) lying down, eyes wide open, gazing out off at the space 'in front of' the confines of the frame, at the camera, at the viewer-spectator; in the very last shot camera and spectator suddenly hold a position outside the character/space system previously established in the final scene and look down on Sada lying beside the dead Kichi (Fuji Tatsuya), her eyes open towards him, our eyes faced with the characters traced in red — in the blood of his severed genitals — on his body ('Sada, Kichi: together the two of us only'), while a voice-over, Oshima's voice, gives the news incident aftermath (Sada wanders through Tokyo for four days, her case inspires a strange sympathy) and the date (this happened in 1936). Between the unresolved initial look from the screen, out of the image, and the abruptly found distance and voice of the close, it is the look that orders the sexual space of the film; with the narrative, as it were, the narrative of that ordering (and not of 'the incident'). From the start, the sexual is given in the image of the look (the assumption of the apparatus, thus of a film such as *Letter from an Unknown Woman*) but the look is then also given against the image, out of its 'truth', its mode of 'knowledge' (the apparatus discontinued, its coherence of a vision in pieces).

In the first shot, Sada gazes out; cut to a brief shot of another woman of the house who takes off outer clothing; cut back to Sada's gaze — from the opposite side of the 180-degree line, a peculiar and untied reversal of her position in frame — with the second woman beginning to caress her and, when Sada fails to respond, whispering 'you'll see'; cut to the two of them crossing an inner courtyard, snow falling, until they come to a room and crouch down to look in; cut not to what they see but to them seen seeing, to them seen from inside looking in, framed in the crack of the slightly opened partition, looking out at camera and spectator — a shot that occurs five times as they watch Kichi and his wife and that receives all the precedence of the scene. Thus, with a play on 'looking at looking', is set up a constant figure for the film: the sexual is seen and seen seeing; when Kichi and Sada make love, the look is passed elsewhere, to geishas, servants, always women.

   This order of the look in the work of the film is neither the
thematics of voyeurism (note already the displacement of the
look's subject from men to women) nor the binding structure
of a classic narrative disposition (where character look is an
element at once of the form of content, the definition of the
action in the movement of looks exchanged, and of the form
of expression, the composition of the images and their
arrangement together, their 'match'). Its register is not that of
the 'out of frame', the *hors-champ* to be recaptured in the
film by the spatially suturing process of 'folding over' of
which field/reverse-field is the most obvious device, but that
of the edging of every frame, of every shot, towards a *problem*
of 'seeing' *for the spectator*. '*Anata mo*' ('and you too . . . '):
the closing words of *Death by Hanging* (*Koshikei*, 1968),
themselves abruptly spoken in voice-over by Oshima, form
equally the question of *Empire of Senses* — where are *you* in
this film and what is this film for you to be *there*? The earlier
formulation in connection with the play on 'looking at looking'
can be completed: the sexual is seen and seen seeing and the
spectator seen in that seeing (there is a little précis of such a
passage in the scene when Kichi and Sada make love in a
Japanese garden while a woman near by brushes the sand: as
Sada sits down on Kichi the screen is filled entirely with the
red of her kimono, over which image she comments 'someone
is looking'); what is it to be the *viewer* of a film, to have its
view? and with this film now?
   The apparatus of look and identification is cinema's institution of a film's view and viewer (the point of that view), is the
system of a film's *available* vision. Oshima's film finds the
apparatus and its terms of vision as problem, as a specific
construction (not a natural reproduction, a simple reflection),
and does so exactly in so far as it poses radically — *absolutely*
(an emphasis that will need to be taken up later) — the sexual
in cinema and film. Inevitably characterized as the film in
which 'everything can be seen', *Empire of the Senses* is acutely
the film of the impossibility of 'the seen', haunted not by a
space 'off' that must and can be unceasingly caught up into a
unity, the position of a view for the viewer, but by a 'nothing
seen' that drains the images of any full presence, of any adequate view: everything and nothing, the film is perpetually

splitting, the division of the place of the spectator as subject
in the troubling of sight and look. The most visible instances
in the film (the paradox of 'the most visible' here is a version
of the splitting, of the everything and nothing) are the shots
outside the lovers' room on the two occasions on which one
of them has just returned after an absence: the shots hold a
partition wall (and in one case the empty corridor) through
the thin material of which can be made out areas of colour
and the human forms. No tease of erotic suspense: everything
has been seen but there is something else to be seen, *nothing*,
a more than seen, perhaps to be heard (Kichi's account of
entering Sada: 'darkness . . . seeing nothing . . . water flowing
. . . blood, not blood, little red insects, in my eyes, nose,
mouth . . . see nothing more . . . pleasure'), perhaps to be
there as colour (the red that makes the surface of the film,
colour is always potentially in excess of 'the seen', a threat to
the 'objective' image and its clear subject). By contrast, it can
be noted that the sole moments of the full image are precisely
given as those of fantasy (a fantasy is an imaginary scenario
in which a subject's desire is figured fulfilled) – Sada's picture of Kichi running on the hill as she sits in the train.
Fantasy is the very regime of the image as totality, the inclu-
sive coherence of the looked-for proffered as realized. Moreover, as Lacan remarks in his brief appreciation of Benoît
Jacquot's *L'Assassin musicien*, 'fantasy founds the vraisemblable';[2] a film such as *Letter from an Unknown Woman*
providing a sufficiently typical example of the foundation:
the apparatus assumed as the establishment of a subject-vision
(a vision of the subject) for the film which then thematically
reflects and 'works over' in its narrative the terms of that
fiction of vision, of that fixed image-relation.

In Oshima's film, the splitting of 'the seen' turns on the
development of a divided inclusion of the spectator. Thus the
look out of the image already mentioned: a 'fourth look'
which sends back and loosens the relay circuit of camera-
viewer-character, the security of 'looking at looking'. Thus
too the particular use of character look in the spatial organization of the film, the construction of its scenes. Consider in
this respect the 'wedding night': after the supper and the
toasts, Kichi and Sada are encouraged by the geishas sitting

round in front of them to consummate the 'marriage'; there begins a movement of cutting across the room between the couple and geishas along the line of a look off into camera (Kichi's as he lies on top of Sada who this time experiences no pleasure, the geishas' as they watch), the movement continuing 'autonomously' when the geishas set up a separate action of their own involving a young geisha aroused by what she sees and whom they penetrate with a dildo in the form of a long-tailed bird. On the one hand, everything, a space filled sexually, both sides of the room held together for a total scene, nothing not seen; on the other, that space broken in the very moment it is filled, the scene's total divided and the spectator's view given in that division, the repeated irruption of a nothing seen (and produced in the seen in the circulation and loss of the sexual and pleasure). One filmic figure of sexploitation is the pan, figure of the integral more, the *partouze* (the camera for the viewer *partout*, everywhere, an order of culminating plenitude); that of Oshima's film is this cutting as division, the summing of a space that always joins apart, elsewhere.

Empire of the Senses, moreover, has a scene in which the same figure operates, that has a structural and thematic equivalence to the opera encounter in *Letter from an Unknown Woman* (one of the points of ruinous remake). Fairly late on in the film, Kichi and Sada start to make love watched by an elderly geisha who admires their potency; Sada suggests that she would like Kichi; he touches the woman and moves on top of her to make love. The initial admiration-and-suggestion is shot from inside the lovers' room looking towards the geisha sitting in the doorway. Once the donation has been agreed, the scene pivots with a transition shot taken from one end of the corridor outside the room and showing Kichi squatting in the doorway to touch the old woman, who is lying down facing away from the camera (Sada being off-screen, inside the room). The next shot complets a 180-degree turn, showing Sada in the room seen through the doorway from the corridor across the legs of Kichi and the geisha. The love-making is then given in a series of some ten shots which cut between Sada and the geisha's face and between Sada and the interlaced bodies with Kichi looking round off into camera (at Sada; as in the 'wedding-night' scene, on top of Sada, he looks off at the geishas); until the climax which cuts from an extreme close-up of Sada's lips to the old woman's face, eyes closed, false hair awry, to return to the angle and framing of the first shot of Sada from across the legs. The scene 'incompletes': from Stefan's image of the woman past, film's cinematic bind on the look, to an exchange — the two women, Kichi, and the absence, the other side — which terminates each image, the image, poses the problem — and the history — of the look in film, in cinema; the mother is dead (Kichi 'embracing my mother's corpse'), a flow of excrement, the looks fall off the screen, the film's space parts irreparably on the spectator; Stefan's seeking eyes, mirror for the spectator-viewer on whom film's narrative movement has been developed to insist, have been displaced as Sada's lips, the wound in the sequence, destroying the balance of the cutting on the look (itself already used to divide); Oshima talks of wanting 'to pass a shadow of death through the film'.[3]

What is at stake in all this? What is being described here? With difficulty and uncertainty, it is a matter of trying to grasp in Oshima's film something of a real problematization of the apparatus of cinema which engages immediately — indeed begins from — the various interlocking factors in the order that apparatus functions to obtain and maintain: image, look, their relation of the sexual. Bazin's 'looking at her looking' formula has been several times referred to; the same Bazin also talked, however, of cinema's potential for a 'quasi-obscenity of seeing'. The register of *Empire of the Senses* lies effectively *in the disphasure of look and sight*: the apparatus is pulled out of true, its guarantee of vision; the look divides and the spectator loses *the* view of the film, the simple position of viewer; a question then not of watching (watching is the mode of look and identification) but of what it is to *be seeing* the film. Such a question politically occupied Vertov, wishing to produce the disalignment of camera-eye and human-eye in order to displace the subject-eye of the social individual into an operational — transforming — relation to his or her reality; but it is decisive too, evident at least in the first five or ten minutes, in a film like Brakhage's *The Act of Seeing with One's Own Eyes* (1973) with its pervasive pressure of invasion, the look invaded by seeing: show what cannot be watched at once in the shown (the morgue, the dissection, 'I couldn't look') and in the showing (the absence of any position of a look, the camera disjoined — in framing, height, movement — from the construction of a sense), remove — *dismember* — the coherence of a unified subject-vision.

It is not by chance that, after years of the history of the 'theatrical cinema' Vertov foresaw and loathed, the Brakhage film, like the Oshima, should be involved directly with death; the 'quasi-obscenity of seeing' is a profound connection of death and the sexual (the latter equally directly marked in *The Act of Seeing*: the fragmented male body). That connection is known in classic cinema but exactly as the violence and dispersion which apparatus and narrative are there to contain, and to contain on the image: the image, finally, of the women: 'looking at her looking'. Think again of *Letter from an Unknown Woman* and its arresting gaze on the illuminated body of Lisa/Joan Fontaine, the film the theatre of that. The image for such a gaze is the centre and determination of the suspended scenario of narrative film, its constantly desired primal scene. With the apparatus securing its ground, the narrative plays, that is, on castration known and denied, a movement of difference and the symbolic, the object lost, and the conversion of that movement into the terms of a fixed memory, an invulnerable imaginary, the object — and with it the mastery, the unity of the subject — regained. Like fetishism, narrative film is the structure of a *memory-spectacle*, the perpetual story of a 'one time', a discovery perpetually remade with safe fictions.

This is the context of the particular economy of repetition in classic cinema where narrative is in fact the order of a *bearable* repetition. The coherence of any text depends on a sustained equilibrium of new informations, points of advance and anaphoric recalls, ties that make fast, hold together. One part of the particularity of classic cinema is its exploitation of narrative in the interests of an extreme tendency towards coalescence, an economic tightness of totalization; the film is gathered up in a whole series of rhymes in which elements — of both 'form' and 'content' — are found, shifted, and turned back symmetrically, as in a mirror; the most simply obvious instances in *Letter from* include the café scenes (Stefan entering with Lisa to cancel a previous rendezvous/ Lisa entering alone to look for Stefan), the train departures (Lisa bidding farewell to Stefan, her one-night lover, for 'two weeks'/Lisa bidding farewell to Stefan, her son from that night, for 'two weeks'), the views from the staircase (as Stefan brings up first one of his many women-friends and then Lisa), and, of course, the carriage scenes which open and close the film, looping it round on itself. Engaged with narrative, deciding a narrative, *Empire of the Senses* has something of this patterning out: elements are given for narrative investment, to be related — used up — across the film (the knives that appear from the very first meeting of Kichi and Sada — 'you should have something other than a knife in your hand'), rhymes are produced between scenes and scraps of scenes (the scene with the elderly geisha echoes and answers the scene earlier with the servant woman in the garden, just as it returns on the scene at the beginning with the old man who wants to but cannot make love to Sada). The notion of rhyme, however, already becomes rather uneasy, the possible examples lack the clarity — the evidence — of those that make up *Letter from*. In fact, what is in question is an economy that disperses the rhymes it half suggests into chains of elements — a shadow of death passing from the old man's unerect penis to Sada's face on the pillow next to that of her 'serious' town councillor, to the proprietor of the drink stall ('for a long time now it has only served me to urinate with'), to the black-shirted councillor again, to the elderly geisha, the maternal corpse — and brief starts of chains — from the bird-dildo inserted between the lips of the young geisha's sex to the mute old man, who executes a bird-like dance, to Sada's lips pressed against Kichi's penis — that run on the surface of the film, freed from any articulation of 'form' and 'content' as a structure of obsession. Repetition in *Empire of the Senses* is consequently left as either abrupt or crude. The first mode is that of the organization of the scenes in a succession in which they go repeating one another

but without the derivation of any unifying memory from
their succession, with no *narrative* pattern of recall, advance,
resolution (hence, indicatively, the lack of transitional pas-
sages: a hand suddenly reaches out to seize a foot on the stairs
or a carriage is suddenly seen crossing from left to right on
the opposite bank of a river and a new scene is begun). The
second, the final order of the film as it progresses, is that at
work in the scenes of strangulation. Three times, and at length,
Sada strangles Kichi; the repetition is crude in that each time
brings no new information, brings only — precisely — death:
the death finally of Kichi, and the fading of the subject, of
the subject erect through a text, the given vision, the *direction*
of and for meaning (thus the reaction of 'boredom': the loss
of the narrative pact of purpose in time, of making sense,
reaching a view).

Repetition is the return to the same in order to abolish the
difficult time of desire and the resurgence in that very
moment of inescapable difference. The edge of repetition —
its horizon of abolition, the ultimate collapse of same and
different — is then death; Freud can see repetition as the
essence of drive and accord the death drives the fundamental
place — beyond the pleasure principle — in his later accounts
of psychical functioning. Relevantly for the present discussion,
the implications of those accounts are brought out by Lacan
in his 'Fonction et champ de la parole et du langage en
psychanalyse': desire is interminable, finds itself in a repetition
that poses the limit of death as the 'absolutely own possibility'
of the historically defined subject: 'a limit that is there at
every instant in what that history has of completion; it represents the past under its real form; that is, not the physical
past whose existence is gone, nor the epic past as rounded off
in the work of memory, nor the historical past from which
men and women derive the guarantee of their future, but the
past which manifests itself overturned in repetition'; in short,
'the death drive expresses essentially the limit of the historical
function of the subject'.[4] *Empire of the Senses* comes near
that limit of the subject, and, exactly, by repetition as loss of
function, an absolute past to the subject forgotten in the
subject-positions — with their own pasts (epic, historical, etc.)
— erected thereon; but it can do so — a question in return to

the frequent blindness of psychoanalysis — only historically, in the demonstration of a history, and a history of which here the institution of cinema is a part.

In its films, classic cinema is a certain balance of repetition: a movement of difference and the achievement in that movement of recurring images — for example, the woman as 'the same', a unity constantly refound. Narrativization, the process of the production of the film as narrative, is the operation of the balance, tying up the multiple elements — the whole festival of potential affects, rhythms, intensities, times, differences — into a line of coherence (advance and recall), a finality for the repetition.

The realized narrative, the term of the process, is historically specific, is a mapping of the *novelistic* for the reproduction of which the cinematic institution is developed and exploited; the novelistic, that is, is the category of the specification of narrative in film, as in the novel to which cinema is made to furnish a successor. The title of the novelistic is *Family Romance* (or, a recent avatar, *Family Plot*); the problem it addresses is that of the definition of forms of individual meaning within the limits of existing social representations and their determining social relations, the provision and maintenance of fictions of the individual; the reality it encounters a permanent crisis of identity that must be permanently resolved by remembering the history of the individual-subject. Narrative lays out — lays down as law — a memory in film from the novelistic as the reimaging of the individual as subject, the very representation of identity as the coherence of a past safely negotiated and reappropriated — the past 'in' the film (*Letter from an Unknown Woman* with its overall theme of remembering within which a whole family romance can be carried along in fragmentary mnemic traces of a sexual history known and denied by its knowledge in these representations) and 'of' the film (*Letter from* with its direction, its rhymes, its constant images, its positioning of view for viewer, its unifying relations of the subject watching). Coming near to the limit of the historical function of the subject, *Empire of the Senses* is thus involved in and against the novelistic, in and against the cinematic institution as industry of the novelistic — which involvement is what the analysis of the film offered here has tried to suggest.

Kichi and Sada are the obsolete, the anachronism of the Akasaka section of Tokyo, the world of the geisha houses, the gay quarters. The film aims at the past which manifests itself turned over in repetition, its point is the sexual absolutely (as in the room, the closed world of the lovers able, says Oshima, 'to pursue their own pleasures'); but that 'absolutely' is historical, the limit of the historical function of the subject, of the institutions, cinema included, which serve to define the subject-function, and political, the social relations in which function, subject, institutions are in the last instance determined. It is the articulation of the sexual, the cinematic and the political that, finally, makes the question of the film.

The political is insistent in the film, the punctuation of an outside, elsewhere to the room: children with flags — the *hinomaru*, the 'round sun', emblem of pre-war militarism — jabbing at an old man, the black-shirted councillor refusing to leave with Sada against a background of flying kites indicating the national Boys' Day celebrations, soldiers marching through the streets watched by crowds of children again with flags, the voice-over at the end: 'this happened in 1936'; the year of that attempted February putsch, the stirrings of the movement towards military-dominated government. The political is in the film, insistent in these punctuations, in brief echoes, touches — the snow at the beginning, the room and Kichi's account of being shut inside Sada (*Hakko Ichui*, the whole world under one roof, a nationalist slogan of the thirties) — but as the *outside*, the voice with the date still abrupt at the end, a sudden distance back over the film, as though to state the necessity of an articulation between the sexual and the political and at the same time its impossibility, literally unthinkable.

Unless . . . unless one were to start from the very apparatuses of the establishment of the possible and the thinkable, the apparatuses of representation and ideological formation, machines such as cinema itself. Hence the sexual, the political *and* the cinematic. Hence *Empire of the Senses* as a film not 'about' Kichi and Sada, not 'about' 1936, but as a film working on a problem, in an attempt to pose the relations of the sexual and the political in cinema, the sexual politics of film. The voice at the close is not that of the documenting of a historical past but that of the demonstration of a complex historical present; the question of a history that is *on* the subject *between* the sexual and the political, *cinematically*; the demonstration then near enough in its effects to what Marx envisaged at the beginning of *The Eighteenth Brumaire* when he talked of a content that 'goes beyond the phrase', of a radically new that breaks the fixed frames of the 'form'/ 'content' distinction itself. Cinema is much more than an object of study (psychoanalytic included), the political cannot be contained in its recognized instances (must change any 'recognized'); and both draw on the sexual which displaces them in their turn: this being that complex present — the question — of Oshima's film. To argue over difficult scenes (the rape of the middle-aged geisha, the egg), over the positive or negative aspects in the depiction of Sada, is in this context to miss the critical force of the question, which is a question not about this or that representation, but about the fact of representation, the fact of representation in cinema, this constantly throwing up difficulties, terms for argument. Remember perhaps that *Empire of the Senses* is not *simply* far from *Letter from an Unknown Woman*.

Let us come back to the anecdote with which we began: Saito, the reception, the assassination, the abortive putsch. Yes, of course, *Naughty Marietta* has nothing to do with all that, is only, precisely, pure anecdote. And yet . . . It is quoted here in the perspective of *Empire of the Senses*, a film which deals in the past — incidents, historical incidents — in order to accomplish a work on what has to be called the distance and the presence of cinema: the cinema distant, of small importance, and nevertheless essential, very close to 'us' (the spectacle of myself, images for me). *Naughty Marietta*, Saito, *Empire of the Senses*, Japan today (the contemporariness of which is none other for Oshima than that of the resurgence of imperialism) — the real of Oshima is somewhere there and in what can be done with it between a film and its spectator. What is the institution of cinema in film? The terms of its production of images? Its operation of you, 'you too' '*anata mo*'? That history? The question Oshima.

Postscript

'I look elsewhere and differently, there where there is no spectacle.'   Hélène Cixous[5]

Reading this piece again, after a year or more, it seems to me that its main failing, the result perhaps of the extreme closeness of the film at the time of writing, lies in a certain lack of directness in the way in which the question of *Empire of the Senses*, 'the question Oshima', is finally engaged. What is at stake throughout, that is, is evidently (but with great difficulty) the whole problem of representation and sexual difference in cinema, the problem posed acutely by Oshima's film, this being its interest and its urgency (to stress which is to try to indicate something of its value for use, not at all to acclaim it as 'a good film', the latter notion very precisely challenged by the question of this film to film, to cinema). Reactions, moreover, have been to that acuteness, the film equally rejected and assumed as important by feminists, and often becoming a point of reference by woman (women not necessarily feminists) in those places where it has been commercially exhibited.[6]

Discussing *Letter from an Unknown Woman*, the piece attempts to bring out in its analysis that the sole imaginary of the film is '*the* woman', the sole signifier the look as phallus, as order, as the very apparatus of the film — and of film produced as that cinema of relaying looks — which serves endlessly to remake the scene viewed, the theatre of the woman for the male gaze, the total spectacle. *Sole* imaginary, *sole* signifier? 'Sole' says merely that any difference is caught up in that structured disposition, that fixed relation in which the film is centred and held, to which the times and movements and excesses of its symbolic tissues and its narrative drama of vision are bound. The crucial issue in this context then becomes that of the place of women in that relation, the place of the look for women, an issue that has frequently been considered in terms of an emphasis on a lack of investment in the look by women; as Irigaray puts it: 'Investment in the look is not privileged in women as in men. More than the other senses, the eye objectifies and masters. It sets at a distance, maintains the distance. In our culture, the predominance of the look over smell, taste, touch, hearing has brought an impoverishment of bodily relations. It has contributed to disembodying sexuality. The moment the look dominates, the body loses in materiality. It is perceived above all externally and the sexual becomes much more a matter of organs that are highly circumscribed and separable from the site of their assembly in a living whole. The male sex becomes *the* sex because it is very visible, the erection is spectacular. . . . '[7]

What the piece seeks to demonstrate and specify as the question Oshima has its force here. *Empire of the Senses*, as the conclusion stresses, is not *simply* far from *Letter from an Unknown Woman*, is not outside the problematic of the Ophuls film, is rather its crisis discovered in a kind of radical proximity, pushing to limits, to limits of cinema and to the problem of representation and sexual difference in its field, in its very disposition. For a woman to take place in a film like *Letter from* is for her to represent male desire (to stand as the term of a social representing of desire determined by and redetermining a structure of division — the social operation of 'male'/'female', 'man'/'woman' — and oppression on the basis of that division — the difference assigned functioning as the inevitability, the 'right', of the domination of the one category by the other). Equally, however, Oshima, in his own somewhat symptomatic fashion, says much the same thing of *Empire of the Senses*: 'When I write a script, I depict women, but when it comes to the filming, I end up centrally depicting men.'[8] Oshima's film does trouble, is effectively disturbing in the ways the piece suggests, yet constantly rejoins *Letter from* on the very grounds of that trouble and disturbance — *cinema*. The question is finally that of the fact of cinema, of this late-nineteenth-century machine (contemporary with psychoanalysis, itself perpetually worrying over what Freud calls 'the riddle of the nature of femininity') and its intrication in a specific representing function, a specific construction of a male desire (so too psychoanalysis? is the nature of those decisive encounters in its history — Breuer, Freud and Anna O, Freud and Dora . . . Lacan and Aimée — quite by chance?). Yes, of course, the question is crude, simplistic, not allowing for the diversity of cinematic practices (as is that parenthetically addressed to psychoanalysis) but it remains nevertheless important, must inform any alternative practice, whether attempting to evict any scene and to grasp film in the process of its material effects (the 'structural/materialist' strategy) or to produce a different scene, a new relation for women (the 'new language' envisaged by the Musidora group, for example, throughout their anthology *Paroles . . . elles tournent!*[9]); and this today above all when it is clear that images of women as woman's image have become a major focus of deliberate ideological concern in dominant cinema, from *Three Women* to *The Turning Point*, from *The Goodbye Girl* to *Coma*. What the piece wishes to stress in the movement of its analysis from *Letter from* to *Empire of the Senses* is that that is precisely again the question Oshima, the interest and urgency of his film.

Interest and urgency that can go beyond the particular context of cinema. Something of the terms of the piece's account of Oshima's film are echoed, for example, in a passage in which Irigaray develops the idea of women's non-investment in the look: 'The possibility that a nothing seen, that a not masterable by the look, by specula(risa)tion, may have some reality would indeed be intolerable to man, since threatening his theory and practice of representation. . . . '[10] *Empire of the Senses* is crossed by that possibility of a nothing seen, which is its very trouble of representation, but that possibility is not posed, as it were, from some outside; on the contrary, it is produced as a contradiction within the given system of representation, the given machine. The problem is one of a specific institution of positions and relations of meaning, not one of an essence to be recovered, and the nothing seen is grasped as such from within that institution, as a point of and against its particular structure of repression, its particular construction (just as the 'invisibility' of the sex of the woman to which Irigaray refers is only a figure of an order that defines woman from man and sets her as the scene of his representation and power). Thus cinema divides not in any immediate sense on men and women but on these positions and relations of meaning of 'man' and 'woman' in its representations and its production of those representations, the subjectivity it engages; with the lack of investment in the look by women realized *there*, ideologically, not from something originally wanting in woman, women then being returned to a kind of archaic sensuality (a place in which they have been accommodated historically by men).

Occupied, even if in a provisional and limited way, with these issues of cinema, representation, sexual difference, the piece is little occupied with *Letter from an Unknown Woman* a film by Max Ophuls (is an interest in 'the work of Max Ophuls' today anything more than academic, the province of film studies and criticism?). That 'Ophuls' is the name for a certain exasperation of the standard Hollywood production of his time is no doubt the case, as it is too that that exasperation is a veritable mannerism of vision, and of vision of the woman — with the masquerade become the very surface of the text, laid out, *exposed*: the masquerade of 'the woman' (the luxurious feminine of jewellery, furs, mirrors . . .), the masquerade of 'the woman in film', cinema's object, pursuit-and-goal (the ceaseless enunciation of the ceaseless fascination of the ceaseless tracking of the woman for the gaze, the look, of her spectacle, of the desire to come there in a ceaseless momentum of appropriation which, in its extreme in *Madame de . . .* , is near itself to the impossibility known, half-seen). A Hollywood film, an Ophuls film, *Letter from an Unknown Woman* is exemplary for the piece, not typical, in its demonstration of the relations sustained in cinema, as cinema, of woman and look and narrative and scene, is itself, in that, not simply far from *Empire of the Senses*.

Notes

First published in *Wide Angle* vol. 2 no. 1 (1977) pp. 48—57; rewritten in French in a new version and published as 'D'un regard l'autre', *Ça* no. 15 (1978) pp. 9—23; given here in the original version but with some change in the beginning and ending. The 'Postscript' was written for a reprinting of the piece in a booklet to accompany a retrospective of the films of Max Ophuls at the 1978 Edinburgh Film Festival; Paul Willemen (ed.), *Ophuls* (London: British Film Institute, 1978) pp. 85—7. The issues of sexual representation raised in this 'Postscript' are discussed at length in 'Difference', *Screen* vol. 19 no. 3 (Autumn 1978) pp. 51—112.

1. André Bazin, 'Théâtre et cinéma', *Qu'est-ce que le cinéma?* vol. II (Paris: Cerf, 1959) p. 87.

2. Jacques Lacan, 'Faire mouche', *Nouvel Observateur* no. 594 (29 March—4 April 1976) p. 64.

3. Oshima, Interview, *Cinéaste* vol. VII no. 4 (1977) p. 35.

4. J. Lacan, *Écrits* (Paris: Seuil, 1966) p. 318; translation, *Écrits: A Selection* (London: Tavistock, 1977) p. 103.

5. Hélène Cixous, 'Entretien avec Françoise van Rossum-Guyon', *Revue des sciences humaines* no. 168 (1977) p. 487.

6. For the assumption of importance see, as examples, the reviews of the film by Ruth McCormick, in *Cinéaste* vol. VII no. 4 (1977), and Françoise Collin, in *Les Cahiers du GRIF* no. 13 (October 1976); for the constant reference to the film, see the volume of interviews and testimonies edited by Marie-Françoise Hans and Gilles Lapouge as *Les Femmes, la pornographie, l'érotisme* (Paris: Seuil, 1978).

7. Luce Irigaray, in *Les Femmes, la pornographie, l'érotisme*, p. 50.

8. Oshima, quoted in *Cahiers du cinéma* no. 285 (February 1978) p. 72.

9. Des femmes de Musidora, *Paroles ... elles tournent!* (Paris: des femmes, 1976).

10. L. Irigaray, *Speculum: de l'autre femme* (Paris: Minuit, 1974) p. 57.

Chapter 7

Repetition Time
Notes Around 'Structural/materialist Film'

The term 'materialist' in the expression 'structural/materialist film' used to characterize a certain development of work in avant-garde independent film-making[1] has to be understood away from any simple reference to the physical materiality of film. 'Materialist' stresses process, a film in its process of production of images, sounds, times, meanings, the transformations effected on the basis of the specific properties of film in the relation of a viewing and listening situation. It is that situation which is, finally, the point of 'structural/ materialist film', its fundamental operation, the *experience* of film, and the experience *of film*.

Any film is the fact of a process, whether it be *Hall* (Gidal, 1968) or Welles's *Touch of Evil*. The practice of 'structural/ materialist film' is defined in the *presentation* of a film's process, 'the presentation of the material construction of film'; process, construction are displayed reflexively, not displaced uniformly into the pattern of a narrative, bound up for the stable subject-centred image.

Important to presentation of process is an attention to temporality (time is 'film's primary dimension'), duration ('how

long something lasts'). It is usual in this connection to begin
by adducing the exposition of the possible one-to-one relationship between shooting time and reading time, equivalence
between the duration of the event recorded and the duration
of the film representation of that event; a film such as *Couch*
(Warhol, 1964) providing a stock example, with its takes the
length of single rolls of film that are then joined together in
sequence, this giving 'a "shallow" time which permits a
credible relationship between the time of interior action and
the physical experience of the film as a material presentation . . . Warhol's most significant innovation'. That quotation
is from Le Grice, for whom durational equivalence often
seems to be something of a primary ethic of film-making, in
the light of which Snow's *Wavelength* (1967), for instance,
can be found seriously wanting: 'One-to-one relationship
between the projection duration and the shooting duration is
lost through breaks in the shooting not made clear in the
form of the film. By utilizing a contrived continuity to parallel
the implied time of its narrative, the film is in some ways a
retrograde step in cinematic form.' Durational equivalence,
however, is itself a turning back in cinema's history (accepting
for a moment the idea of a progressive development), right
back to the practice of the films screened by Lumière in the
Grand Café; which is to say that it is not necessarily the realization of the physical experience of the film as a material
presentation: on the contrary, it can function perfectly well,
as with the historical reception of the Lumière films, as a
foundation of the supreme illusion of the real, the actual
'before one's eyes', the vision of 'nature caught in the act'
(the excited comment of one of the first spectators). So that,
in fact, much more is at stake in 'structural/materialist film',
in the films themselves: Le Grice's own *White Field Duration*
(1973), for example, aiming to establish the length of projection time as a material experience by exposing the viewer to a
white screen, or Snow's *One Second in Montreal* (1969), a
film which Le Grice praises and which holds still images for
increasing and decreasing periods of time, patterning durational
experience of the film for the viewer.

   Any film works with time and duration; Indeed, narrative
cinema classically depends on the systematic exploitation of

a multiplicity of times: the time of the narrative action but equally the time of the elaboration of the narrative, which brings into play a whole number of figures, rhymes, movements that cut across the film in differing rhythms, shifting the spectator in their relations. Simply, the exploitation is systematic, in final time with the elaborated narrative, the achievement of that (so the film 'goes quickly'); the multiplicity is constantly tied down to the narrative which gives purpose and direction to the film, is its principle of homogeneity. Nor is narrative the only mode of binding time. Consider Bruce Baillie's *All My Life* (1966): the single-shot three-minute pan — sky, hedge, flowers — traces a duration which is held in time with the song on the sound-track, the song closing camera movement, colour, screen duration into the unity of its time and significance. The contrary practice of 'structural/materialist film' is to break given terms of unity, to explore the heterogeneity of film in process. Snow's *Standard Time* (1967), for instance, cites one reference (one standard) for time on the sound-track, a morning radio broadcast, another on the image-track, an extremely elliptical human presence which conventionally serves as the centre for the elision of the process of film production, and then works over an eight-minute duration of film with an unbound series of pans and tilts that ceaselessly pose the question of viewing time.

The disunity, the disjunction, of 'structural/materialist film' is, exactly, the spectator. What is intended, what the practice addresses, is not a spectator as unified subject, timed by a narrative action, making the relations the film makes to be made, coming in the pleasure of the mastery of those relations, of the positioned view they offer, but a spectator, a spectating activity, at the limit of any fixed subjectivity, materially inconstant, dispersed in process, beyond the accommodation of reality and pleasure principles. 'Boredom' is a word which is sometimes assumed by the film-makers with regard to their films, the boredom which is the loss of the imaginary unity of the subject-ego and the very grain of drive against that coherent fiction, the boredom which Barthes sees close to *jouissance* ('it is *jouissance* seen from the shores of pleasure'[2]).

A specific strategy for the tension of duration set up by 'structural/materialist film' is that of repetition, at its simplest in the use of 'loops'. Gidal's work, for instance, has made particular and complex use of repetition: *Hall* with its pattern of long-to-medium-to-close shot movements from the view of the hall into the various objects seen at its far end, then repeated over again; *Room Film 1973* (1973) with its five-second units each shown twice in succession; *Condition of Illusion* (1975) with its repetition of the camera's mobile angling focusing course over the surfaces of a room.

In Freud, repetition can go two ways, comes round with both a 'positive' and a 'negative' inflection. The compulsion to repeat is a way of remembering, resistant, symptomatic, difficult, that the analysis needs to shift towards a different engagement of the patient to its meaning, rendering the repetition *'useful'*. Thinking outside the analytic situation, Freud also ascribes to repetition a pleasure of remembering which he illustrates interestingly by reference to rhyme in poetry, the coherence of a formal organization that maps out paths of recognition, of the known. Repetition is in function with the binding – *Bindung* – that Freud describes as co-extensive with the unity of the ego, the maintenance of relatively constant forms within which the free flow of energy is channelled and so contained. As against all of which, or more precisely going along with all of which, repetition is also and increasingly recognized by Freud as the very type of the resistance characteristic of the unconscious, a compulsion that can be rendered useful but that is first and foremost a threat to ego coherence, as the very essence of drive, tending beyond the pleasure principle to absolute discharge, to the total dispersal of unity; Lacan talks of 'the more radical diversity constituted by repetition in itself'.[3]

The economy of repetition in classic narrative cinema is an economy of maintenance, towards a definite unity of the spectator as subject; systems of repetition are tightly established but on the line of a narrative action that holds the repetitions as a term of its coherence and advances with them, across them, its sense of difference, of change, of the new. The practice of 'structural/materialist film' is another economy; the spectator is confronted with a repetition that is 'in itself', not subsumed by a narrative and its coherence, that is literal, not caught up in the rhymes that habitually serve to figure out the narrative film. The spectator is produced by the film as subject in process, in the process of demonstration of the film, with the repetition an intensification of that process, the production of a certain freedom or randomness of energy, of no one memory: in *Condition of Illusion*, the return of an impossible openness of the film as object of desire, flashes of memories, this statuette, this rapid zoom in and out, this white surface, this pulling of focus, a network in which the vision of the I, the ego, is no longer confirmed as the master view. Literal repetition is the radical new that *jouissance* demands; Lacan again; 'Everything which varies, modulates in repetition is only an alienation of its meaning.'[4]

Perhaps paradoxically at first consideration, the strategy of repetition in 'structural/materialist film' breaks identification. In *Condition of Illusion*, which involves the instability of possibilities of recognition (speed of camera movement, use of focus, proximity, angle, etc., leaving only a few objects and places in the room identifiable according to the norms of photographic reproduction), the repetition suggests a possibility of 'catching up', 'making sure', 'verifying' which in fact remains unexploitable, ineffective (one never sees 'more'), resistant in the very literalness of the repetition (no variation, modulation, no 'new angle'). In *Hall* something of the reverse procedure arrives, via the repetition, at something of the same kind of break: extremely stable, normally reproduced objects are given clear from the beginning, the editing moreover reducing the distance from which they are seen, cutting in to show and detail them, repetition then undercutting their simple identification; the second time round, the bowl of fruit cannot be seen as a bowl of fruit, must be seen as an image in a film process, detached from any unproblematic illusion of presence, as a production in the film, a mark of the presence of that.

Discussion of identification in film, of course, is not habitually concerned with this identifying of (objects, what is shown) but rather with identifying into (the film's narrative movement), identifying with (the characters of the narrative, 'the people in the film'). 'Structural/materialist film' works counter to these appropriations, by the elimination of narrative action and agents (*Condition of Illusion*), by their extreme marginalization as a kind of legibly illegible disjunct (Gidal's *Silent Partner*, 1977, with its fragments of noise of conversation, glimpse of legs, person whistling on the soundtrack, very title), by their derisively obvious quotation (as sometimes in Snow's films, *Wavelength* or *Back and Forth*, 1968–9), by their strictly measured delimitation for the demonstration of the film process (the picnic in Le Grice's multi-projection *After Manet*, 1975, or the repeated phone-ringing incident in *Blackbird Descending*, 1977, picnic and incident given as functions in transformation, notions such as 'record' and 'actuality' displaced from the reproduction of life to the production of film reality). The spectator is to be held at a distance, but at the distance of the presentation of material construction, is to be held to that.

Identification is the hold of the image, from the initial assumption of significance, identifying of, to its ultimate confirmation by narrative order, identifying into and with. Certain films refuse the very image itself or reduce it to the very limits of its physical supports — light and screen in *White Field Duration* — but in general, 'structural/materialist films' are engaged with images, assume the fact of their production, often attempt to move in the time of that production — an effect of *Condition of Illusion* where camera focus and pace seem frequently to be hesitating just on the boundary of stability and recognition. Which is to say that they begin at least, like any other type of film, from the primary identification that Metz sees as constitutive in the cinematic apparatus itself: 'the spectator identifies with him/herself, with him/herself as a pure act of perception (as wakefulness, alertness): as condition of possibility of the perceived and hence as a kind of transcendental subject . . . as he/she identifies with him/herself as look, the spectator can do no other than identify with the camera too, which has looked before at what is now being looked at . . . '.[5] They begin from but end against the solicitation of the unity of the look that the apparatus offers for exploitation (is developed to exploit): the all-perceiving subject free in the instrumentality of the camera that serves to relay and reproduce at every moment the power of that central vision. 'Structural/material-ist film' has no *place* for the look, ceaselessly displaced, outphased, a problem of seeing; it is anti-voyeuristic.

What is thus at stake is a practice towards 'a deliberate exterior reflexiveness of the audience': 'the viewer is forming an equal and possibly more or less opposite "film" in her/his head, constantly anticipating, correcting, re-correcting — constantly intervening in the arena of confrontation with the given reality, i.e. the isolated chosen area of each film's work, of each film's production'.

If the figure of memory is metaphor (one signifier for another which, absent, repressed, is consequently retained nevertheless in a certain effect of signification), then the project of 'structural/materialist film' is non-metaphorical: a film must not substitute for its process (and reproduce the spectator in the image of that substitution); must not substi-tute narrative, the predominant metaphor in cinema, onto the order of which the process of filmic production is trans-ferred (the Greek *metaphora* means transference), this nar-rativization containing the heterogeneous elements and fixing a memory of the film, making it coherently available as a sure progress of meaning. Without narrative, the memory of a film fails. Simple test: after a viewing of *Condition of Illusion*, the account given will be extremely 'subjective' (particular traces of desiring relation: liking-remembering this or that moment, wanting it in the repetition) or extremely 'objective' (towards a description of the film's construction, its use of repetition, camera mobility, and so on), the two, exactly at their extreme, joining up with one another; what is missing is the habitual common ground, the narrative metaphor or transference or model of the film, its memory for the spectator placed as its subject, bound and centred on its terms of meaning. Or rather, the spectator as subject-ego (the ego is the place of the imaginary identifications of the subject), the maintained illusion of coherence (derived in film from the maintained coherence of the illusion); but the subject is always more than the ego, the 'more' that 'structural/materialist film' seeks to open out in its demonstration of process: the subject-circulation in the symbolic with its chains of signifying elements, unity overturned in the other memory of repetition.

'There can be no radical narrative film.' This basic tenet of 'structural/materialist film' (narrative is the culminating order of illusionism, identification, subject unity, etc.) is at the same time a continual point of debate and doubt. Le Grice can find himself 'not convinced that illusion and narrative are excluded as elements of the "structural/materialist" problematic'; Gidal even can talk of 'the narrative of a black labourer building a window frame and pane' in his *C/O/N/S/T/R/U/C/T* (1974, a film that depends on multiple superimposition of almost identical images). The difficulty is the very term 'narrative' which tends to be used with an absolute imprecision: what is the historical force of the statement that there can be no radical narrative film? Arguments the other way, however, are often equally imprecise, themselves avoiding effective historical questions and appealing to a kind of inevitable-presence-of-narrative schema, narrative as inescapable in film construction.

Take *Condition of Illusion*: no agents of action are given in the film; agency is with the camera, its movement over and focusing of the room's surfaces, which agency itself is tensed into (taken up in the tension and the time of) the structural functioning of the film's duration with its pattern of repetition. It is sometimes said that the film is the narrative of the progress round the room, a notion that transfers the identification of surfaces and objects in a temporal succession to the agency of the camera as narrating source, as narrator, the seen film thus held together as the narrative product of that agency-narrator. What is interesting here is to grasp the extent to which narration is in our imaginary of film as important as, and, in fact, more important than, narrative: film, that imaginary has it (supported by the conventional systems of address in narrative cinema), must be representation for, in order, directed towards something for someone (narrative as the common ground of film and spectator). Thus with *Condition of Illusion*, the power of the response against the film to find an order of narration, a direction; 'against the film', since what such a response has to ignore, impossible in the experience of the film, is, once again, the repetition, the disturbing return of the signifier across the signs of any narration (where 'a sign represents something for someone', 'a signifier represents a subject for another signifier'[6]).

In the expression 'structural/materialist film', 'structural' stands in some sense as the term of the eviction of narrative which it thus also serves to replace, taking over the problem of relations in film, referring to aspects such as the use of repetition. At the same time, however, it can be seen as covering over questions of history, of the history of the subject.

Three instances can be distinguished in the relation of the spectator as subject in a film: *preconstruction, construction* (or *reconstruction*) and *passage*. Preconstruction involves the ready-made positions of meaning that a film may adopt, not simply large categories of definition, political arguments, thematic boundaries, and so on, but equally, for example, the codes and orders of language itself, the existing social conventions of colour, the available ideas of film (genre is a major factor of preconstruction). Construction is the totalizing of a more or less coherent subject position in the film as its end, its purpose, the overall fiction of the subject related. Passage is the performance of the film, the movement of the spectator making the film, taken up as subject in its process. The ideological achievement of any film is not merely in one or the other of these instances, it is first and foremost in its hold of the three: the appropriation of preconstruction in reconstruction (the film's construction effectively reconstructs from its different materials) and the process of that appropriation. As has been said, the operation of that hold in the classic narrative film is exactly the narrativization, the constant conversion of process to narrative, catching up the spectator as subject in the image of the narrative, the narrative images, and in the film as its/their narration.

'Structural/materialist film' is posed entirely in terms of the instance of passage, its area of work the presentation of the process of film (so that 'passage' becomes a misleading term: there is no simple movement 'through' the film); which is to say that it minimalizes construction-reconstruction, by the eviction of narrative, and preconstruction, by the reduction as far as possible of given signifieds. The latter strategy is theorized by recourse to a conception of relative potency: there are potent and less potent signifiers, representations: 'the image of a pregnant woman, for example, is locked into a signification so ideologically overdetermining that no kind of other operation affecting the editing, zooming, focusing, camera work, subject position behind the camera, off-screen space or sound, can subvert, attack or deny its meaning; it remains culturally enclosed'; other images are less enclosed, objects in a hall, say, or a room; the minimal level of potency allows for the attention to the *film*'s process, *its* construction. Yet, in fact, not merely is minimalization not meaninglessness, so that the objects continue to bring significations into play in the film (Gidal later finds it necessary to dissociate himself from *Hall* inasmuch as 'utilizing potent – signifying, overloaded – representations'), but the minimalization itself begins to create a veritable intensity of meaning (the statuette in *Condition of Illusion*, for example, becomes charged with a focus and importance and beauty and force).

The idea of minimal potency 'forgets' preconstruction and construction-reconstruction, the historical problem of meaning and subject position, in the interests of stressing the experience of the process of film in the viewing situation which is then given a sufficiency and, in the end, an existence outside contradiction, the concern with 'materiality' becoming a defined and limited project with its confirmed audience – and its own cultural trap. 'Structural' is again the symptomatic term of this, as though it could *simply* be a question of opposing 'non-narrative' to 'narrative', 'signifier' to 'signified'.

Repetition Time

Generally, avant-garde independent film-making has suffered from being provided with a history of its own (Le Grice's *Abstract Film and Beyond* is not really any advance in this respect). What we need most is a quite different history, radically theoretical, something like *Towards a Political Economy of Film Meaning-Production and Use*. 'Structural/ materialist film' would have its urgency in such a history, a history that the films, and this is their radical, political actuality, ceaselessly suggest in the scope — and from the limits — of their practice.

Note

Published in *Wide Angle* vol. 2 no. 3 (1978) pp. 4—11. Further consideration of Gidal's theory of 'structural/materialist' practice can be found in my 'Afterword' to his essay 'The Anti-narrative': *Screen* vol. 20 no. 2 (1979) pp. 93—9.

1. See Peter Gidal (ed.) *Structural Film Anthology* (London: British Film Institute, 1976) and Malcolm Le Grice, *Abstract Film and Beyond* (London: Studio Vista, 1977); unattributed quotations in the present text are either from those sources or from various unpublished pieces of writing by Gidal and are taken as representative of emphases constantly made. 'Structural/materialist film' is an indication of a certain practice and a rough grouping accordingly, not 'a movement'; it would include works by the following (amongst others): Gidal, Le Grice, Michael Snow, Peter Kubelka, Kurt Kren, William Raban, Gill Eatherley, David Crosswaite, Fred Drummond.
2. Roland Barthes, *Le Plaisir du texte* (Paris: Seuil, 1973) p. 43; translation, *The Pleasure of the Text* (London: Cape, 1976) p. 26.
3. Jacques Lacan, *Le Séminaire livre XI* (Paris: Seuil, 1973) p. 60; translation, *The Four Fundamental Concepts of Psycho-Analysis* (London: Hogarth Press, 1977) p. 61.
4. Ibid.
5. Christian Metz, 'Le signifiant imaginaire', *Communications* no. 23 (1975) pp. 34—5; translation, 'The imaginary signifier', *Screen* vol. 16 no. 2 (Summer 1975) pp. 51—2.
6. Jacques Lacan, *Écrits* (Paris: Seuil, 1966) p. 840.

Chapter 8

Body, Voice

The term 'auditor' for hearing does not correspond with the term *voyeur* for seeing: on the one hand, the person engaged in what has usually been described as perverse activity; on the other, the ordinary hearer or listener, the simple unproblematic activity of listening. Typically, and influentially, Freud, in the *Three Essays on the Theory of Sexuality* has a fair amount to say on scopophilia — pleasure in seeing — and voyeurism, nothing on whatever the equivalent would be for pleasure and fixation in listening (precisely the word is missing, does not come easily to mind as 'voyeurism' does). As against which, one might recall Sade's comment that, for the true libertine, it is 'the sensations communicated by the organ of hearing which are the more gratifying and whose impressions are the keenest'[1] (thus his libertines listen to long narratives, construct machines to amplify sound, achieve orgasm on hearing cries). As against which too, perhaps, seen through the door of a London sex-shop close to the offices of *Screen*, a notice advertising 'Films now showing: silent £1, sound £1.50'.

There is a kind of paradoxical turn here. In Western societies today, sexuality is heavily defined in and from image and imaging (in discussions of pornography, symptomatically, reference is immediately and automatically made to images, to modes of exhibition and showing). Hence voyeurism is maintained and accepted as the common register of sexual being, the term itself extended from its designation of a specific perversion to the characterization of a general attitude, with, of course, a steady market potential (the basis of the realization of sexuality as a commodity). Simultaneously, hearing drops at once to a level of the unperceived, taken for granted, exactly out of sight ('sex in the cinema', yes, but who would think of discussing, as an issue, 'sex on the radio'?), and at the same time pushes to a level of the extreme, the barely conceivable (with voyeurism the standard of sexuality, the sexual investment of sound, listening, is out of order, really perverse). Which is to say that hearing is difficult, a little *impossible* in its relations of sexuality, its heterogeneity to the smooth finish of the image, the achieved vision of the body. No doubt in the London sex-shop notice, the higher price reflects the notion of a 'gain in realism' — you pay more for more 'reality', sight *and* sound. But it is enough to think of certain contemporary film works to grasp the extreme resistance that can be set up in the 'addition' of sound to image (resistance marks what is left over, in excess, from the position of 'the subject' proposed): for example, *Le Regard* by Marcel Hanoun, for the most part an 'art'-alibi repetition of conventional terms of 'sex in the cinema', or *Je tu il elle* by Chantal Akerman, a critically developed essay in the terms of cinema and the subjectivity it engages, where in both cases, though differently, the love-making scenes are disturbed for a *viewer*, the spectator-subject as voyeur, in the rasp — something of an *acuteness* of presence — of the sounds: embarrassing, irritating, contracting, jarring, any response indicating division from a coherent view of the image. Hegel, summing up the history of aesthetic progress, regarded hearing with seeing as rational senses, senses of the distance of subject to object; the social multiplication of images and privileging of vision, however, has left hearing always potentially *near*, a displacement — out of the place — of the unity of the seen, the friction of a certain grain (as Barthes speaks of 'the grain of the voice').[2]

From the perspective of psychoanalysis, Lacan insists on the 'total distinction' between the scopic register and the invocatory field, the latter being nearest to the experience of the unconscious (the invocatory drive is 'not able to close':

eyes shut but not ears).[3] Thus is given the need for the ceaseless social institution, through the production and distribution
of representations, of relations of sound to image, to the
seen, of unities of positioned intelligibility. The whole history
of sound cinema is the most evident demonstration: what has
to be developed is an '*optical* sound', sound as first and foremost dialogue, the clear sense – the *word* – of the image,
sound hierarchized and classified for and from the image
(sound in so many relay 'functions': articulation of space;
description; decoration; continuity; intensification; metaphor;
evocation; comment; parallelism; counterpoint[4]). Thus, in
opposition, the recognition of an 'other scene', the work of
psychoanalysis is to break the subject contract of sight and
sound, to produce the maximum 'listen', a theatre of the
heterogeneity of the subject-body-in-meaning (that psychoanalysis is *also* locked into a *vision* of meaning – the phallus
as the law of the speaking subject, the universal privileged
signifier, 'something the symbolic use of which is possible
because it can be seen'[5] – is the contradiction of its constantly
untheorized historical place). Which work is pre-eminently
one of silence, silence as an acute moment of sound and
hearing (what is striking in the final scene of *Je tu il elle* is
that: the heard silence – tense, aggravated – of its sounds).
From hypnosis and suggestion and the laying on of hands,
Freud passes to the analytic situation and its absence of
cinema and vision, intervening less and less, letting voice and
body intersect in gaps and hesitations; the law of the subject
cut into and across and disrupted in the listened flow of an
individual speech. The displacement is there, in this realization
of silence, of silences in the given meanings, the defined
orders. Films too, a critical practice, can find a project in
such a realization, a certain silence of 'cinema': the necessity
to work – with sound and image, body and voice – for
different conditions of presence.

Films are full of people, but what is this 'fullness' of people
in films? The regime of the film as cinema is the narrative
fiction film in relation to which the presence of people can

be broken down analytically into the following instances or categories:

agent — An animated entity defined in respect of the assumption of a narrative predicate, as the agent of an action. Every action in a film has its agent but this is not to say that the agent must necessarily be 'shown' (for example, action and agent may be given linguistically in dialogue or narration over); nor need the agent be a human being, hence the barbarous but in this context usefully neutral 'animated entity' (for example, animals are often agents in films; Rin-Tin-Tin and his successor Lassie are simply the most obvious cases in point). Structural analysis was much concerned with the delimitation of patterns of narrative agency, basic sets of narrative roles. Greimas, in his work towards 'a narrative grammar independent of discursive manifestations', arrived at a model comprising six fundamental roles organized in three pairs of oppositions: subject/object, sender/receiver, helper/opponent. One role or agency may be realized in a narrative by several different actors (in the sense of 'animated entities): for example, a series of individuals who help the subject-hero; and equally, one actor may syncretize more than one role: for example, helper and opponent may be brought together 'in' one individual as a 'struggle' or as a shift in the course of the narrative (thus Menzies in *Touch of Evil* who both opposes and finally helps Vargas, the subject-hero).[6]

character — An agent of a series of narrative predicates more or less individualized in relation and in addition to their accomplishment, 'more' being the extension of this individualization into characterization as commonly understood: the demonstration of the individual in respect of a set of 'qualities', some meaningful unity, most often 'psychological' (here, as subsequently, consideration of non-human animated entities is left aside, though this would only lengthen rather than change these remarks — Rin-Tin-Tin and Lassie are, after all, anthropomorphically individualized, produced as characters). Common sense suggests that characters are always also agents and this is right (it is difficult to keep the introduction of a character free from the specification of any narrative predicate) but it remains the case that characters are encountered whose whole discursive existence is bound into their characterization, outside the assumption of any of the major articulations of the narrative action. Such characters, often with a certain comic effect (a factor of their narrative irresponsibility?), are 'turns' in the theatrical sense of the word, are 'anecdotal', detached from the movement of the narrative in something of a little narrative of themselves, which may then, of course, have thematic or symbolic or symptomatic resonances for the film overall (the motel Night Man in *Touch of Evil* is an example: a whole act in himself, with his appearance and expressions, his nervous jigging up and down, his stuttering and so on, and a moment in the representation of sexuality that the film carries along with its narrative, his panic at Susan, her body, the words 'bed' and 'sheets'). The common-sense suggestion can be reversed too into an opposite question: are agents always characters? Extension of individualization into characterization is variable. The very realization of an agent involves a beginning of individualization (though an agent can also be a group) but that individualization may remain at this minimum level (a car door is opened for the hero to get out: someone opens it but the specification of the agent may go no further than the 'some one', there may be no identification of particularity; except that in a film, very different in this to the novel where it is possible to say 'someone' or 'the chauffeur', the one doing the action will be an individual, will come with some particularities).

person — The individual ('person' as the dictionary's 'the living body of a human being') who actualizes — is the support for, plays, represents — agent and character; in the cinema of the narrative fictional film this individual is almost invariably an actor or actress. (Again, a film is different here to a novel: in the latter, agent and character are stated entirely linguistically, are not 'in-personated'.) It may be agreed that 'the professional actor is someone who possesses the technique of emptying his or her body to fill it with meaning',[7] that the actor thus absents him or herself and 'becomes' the agent-character, though this is a rather simplistic view of acting, but

nevertheless he or she will do so with their person, the continuing presence and fact of the body, this individual. Godard
makes the point after a certain fashion at the beginning of
Deux ou trois choses que je sais d'elle, talking over the shot
of a woman: 'Elle, c'est Marina Vlady . . . Elle, c'est Juliette
Janson . . . ', she the person, she the character.

Films play between character and person with a variety of
emphases which would require an analysis capable of dealing
carefully with what is often the circularity of these shifts
from the one ot the other. Make-up, costume and so on are
ways of absorbing face and body into character significance
(of helping to empty the body so as to fill it with wanted
meanings) but have been used in response to the closeness of
range allowed by cinema (compare conventional theatre) in
order to bring out face and body in their 'natural' expressivity.
Type-casting seems to refer to a placing of the person totally
in terms of the character, yet it is the insistence of the face
and the body that justifies the type, the typing; as, for
instance, with an actor like Elisha Cook Jr, Wilmer in *The
Maltese Falcon*, or an actress like Margaret Dumont, Groucho's
dignified and long-suffering foil in a number of the Marx
Brothers' films. A very different emphasis, apparently at least,
is the focus on the person over the character and the agent:
Zsa Zsa Gabor plays the Madame of a striptease cabaret bar
in *Touch of Evil* but appears very much as herself, as Zsa Zsa
Gabor; Julie Christie is introduced into *Nashville* as Julie
Christie. As these examples make clear, however, what is in
question is so often the person as persona, the person as image,
as – precisely – cinema; the living body of the human being
exhausted in, converted to that.

image – The person, the body, in its conversion into the
luminous sense of its film presence, its cinema. The high point
of the image is the *star*; it is as such that Gabor is used in
Touch of Evil: an appearance of a few seconds, highlighted
on the stairs that sweep down into the cabaret, picked out in
a theatrical space with men gazing up at her – and with a
chandelier in the form of a star hanging down beside her as a
kind of literalized metaphor, a token of her image-status, the
perfection of its achievement. The image can determine the

narrative construction of a film: Hitchcock is obliged to end *Suspicion* in a way commensurate with the image of Cary Grant; films are developed as 'vehicles', 'showcases' for this or that star. Equally, the image can be taken up in a film in a play from character to image, drawing the narrative into the spectacle of its impersonation, resolving there: think, in this respect, of *The Towering Inferno* with its clash of architect and fireman and simultaneously of Paul Newman and Steve McQueen, who come together in the end — watched by the crooked and the ordinary, the cowardly and the powerless — as a god letting flow the waters from on high, a pact of the stars much more than of characters, and effective, providing a resolution for the narrative, as such.

   figure — The circulation between agent, character, person and image, none of which is able simply and uniquely to contain, to *settle* that circulation, the figure it makes in a film. What obtain are specific regimes of the articulation of the different instances, particular versions of coherence, of the balancing out of the circulation; whether, as is most often the case by a hierarchization in the interests of character or by some pattern of movement between character and image. The articulation can fail to balance, slip into an overlayering that does not simply cohere. In *Touch of Evil*, the scenes between Quinlan and Tanya, Orson Welles and Marlene Dietrich, make up a complex figure that comes to resist unification into any clear position of reading: a minimum of narrative agency; little establishment of character for Tanya who appears only in these self-enclosed, set-off scenes; powerful images, the two stars, Dietrich almost quoted here from a von Sternberg movie, hung with ornament and jewellery; two bodies, persons with a history which is also that of cinema and other films, *Touch of Evil* as Welles's return to Hollywood, Welles and Dietrich together again now in a memory of the past, their 1944 duo in *Follow the Boys*, that is taken up into a resonance of the narrative and its system in this film, a mythical other sexuality, archaic, different, somewhere else (other to Vargas and Susan, as Dietrich is here another image to Gabor).

The limitations of this analysis of the instances of the presence of people in films are those of the cinema it describes. Thus, for example, more generally, it would need to be developed to take account of the use of people in films as ideas, elements in an intellectual argument rather than in a narrative; one might think of Eisenstein's 'typage' (a form of type-casting but using non-actors and functioning much more in terms of idea than of character, social exposition rather than psychological revelation) or of Godard's strategy of personification, people presented and deployed in a film for typicality, an entirely social or social-sexual recognition (throughout *Deux ou trois choses que je sais d'elle*, 'Mademoiselle 19 ans' in *Masculin-féminin*, the married woman of *Une Femme mariée*[8]).

In addition, however, there are limitations to the analysis in these terms even in respect of the cinema described, limitations that are those principally of the way in which it subsumes the question of the presentation and effects of the body under the heading of the person. The body in films is also moments, intensities, outside a simple constant unity of the body as a whole, the property of a some *one*; films are full of fragments, bits of bodies, gestures, desirable traces, fetish points — if we take fetishism here as investment in a bit, a fragment, for its own sake, as the end of the accomplishment of a desire. This presence of the body is evident in pornographic films, with the penis as the determining investment, the close-up of the vision (for Freud, 'the normal prototype of fetishes is a man's penis'[9]), but is equally insistent in mainstream Hollywood cinema, from the stressed attraction of a star in this or that part of the body (legs or breasts or hair or eyes . . .) to more random elements that exist for me, that I catch as a trace of my history (the curve of an eyebrow, the fall of a neck, the mometary sweep of an arm . . .), and including too — fetishes exactly — the 'attributes' of bodies (the colour of a dress, the knot of a scarf, a hat . . .).

Finally, the analysis is only a beginning, no more than an initial heuristic suggestion. What importance it has lies above all indeed in the emphasis put on analysis, on the need to explore conditions of presence, since understanding in this area has important implications for alternative practices of cinema. How far can alternatives be envisaged? How can people be differently in films, how can these conditions of presence be transformed? People in films are always in systems of representation, are always part of an enunciation, *for* that and never 'immediate' or 'themselves'; it is the analysis of those systems, of the problems of *imaging* in every sense of the word, that is crucial.

> 'Mr Griffith turned to a young actor ... "Let's see some distrust on your face."
>
> The actor obliged.
>
> "That's good!", Griffith exclaimed. "Everyone will understand it."
>
> Billy Bitzer objected, as he was to do often when Griffith attempted something new: "But he's too far away from the camera. His expression won't show up on the film."
>
> "Let's get closer to him then. Let's move the camera."
>
> "Mr Griffith, that's impossible! Believe me, you can't move the camera. You'll cut off his feet — and the background will be out of focus."
>
> "Get it, Billy", Griffith ordered ...
>
> After the rushes were viewed, Griffith was summoned to the front office. Henry Marvin was furious. "We pay for the whole actor, Mr Griffith. We want to see *all of him.*" '10

What matters in this anecdote, the famous story of 'how Griffith invented the close-up', is not its historical veracity so much as its symbolic truth. Cinema can and does fragment the body (hands moving over a piano in *Letter from an Unknown Woman*, the movement up over a woman's body, from feet to face, at the beginning of *Suspicion*) but the human person, the total image of the body seen, is always the pay-off (as the examples indicate: the hands express the pianist Stefan that Louis Jourdan plays; the movement up is the appraising rhythm of the male gaze, Johnnie—Cary Grant fixing the woman, Lisa—Joan Fontaine, for the film, as its centre, its focus). And yet, again, cinema does fragment, plays — within the limits of the narrative and its meanings and resolution — on the passage between fragmented body and the image possession of the body whole, in order ('We pay for the whole actor, Mr Griffith.'). Yet then again, another twist, wanting to 'see all' extends not just into the appropriation of wholeness and unity but also into the desire for *everything*, all of the body, every bit: cinema plays on the

hidden visible to be suggested, glimpsed, revealed, plays on
the shown and the limits of the shown and the expectations
and pleasures produced in the displacement and use of those
limits. At the end of cinema is the pornographic film sold on
'showing everything', *the* act, *the* scene, and hence 'more and
more', which is the determinant of a constant repetition, an
order of the same (significantly, the pornographic film comes
back to something of the terms of the commercialization of
cinema in the very first years of the cinematic apparatus:
rapid production of more or less interchangeable films cal-
culated quantitatively — so many feet, so many reels, so
many actors/actresses, so many permutations — and with
little or no particular narrative image differentiation; products
to satisfy a similar curiosity of cinema, of films, as seeing).
The pornographic film, in fact, is that fundamental moment
of discovery of the absence of the body in film, of a sole
order of representation, the limit of the phallus, cinema come
to that — where its narratives, its strategies, its voices, its
complications of the shown had, while it held in that order,
to that limit, engaged other possibilities, contradictions, a
certain plurality of positions and readings and effects.

   At the same time today that pornography has become one
of the most commercially viable sectors of film-making, the
Hollywood feature film, cinema, has involved itself increasingly in a violence of the body in film: the body cut, sawn,
rent, dismembered. Take *Jaws*, from the girl who runs into
the ocean ahead of her boyfriend at the beach-party beginning
and is ripped by the shark from below to Captain Quint bitten
in half, or *Alien*, with the monstrous organism bursting out
of a crew-member's stomach. In a way too this violence was
always there in cinema, in the mainstream of its history. We
are close to it, for example, in *Suspicion*, in the scene on the
wind-battered heath when Johnnie tries to touch Lisa, pulls
her hair about, jabs at her, calls her 'monkey-face' . . .

   In the case of *Suspicion*, the woman is the object of the
violence; in *Alien*, the woman is the one member of the
spaceship's crew who survives, remains intact; but, of course,
Joan Fontaine is simultaneously aggressed and admired, posed
in her image at the centre of the film, the point of its gaze;
just as Sigourney Weaver is intact only by surviving the
aggression, the violence to which *Alien* builds for its climax,
she alone, stripping for bed, when the organism makes its final

assault. This pattern of attack and protection around the bodies of women as 'the woman' is a constant in cinema (with variations and a history that could be studied). Take *Halloween*: three high-school girls (and a boyfriend) stabbed, bodies slashed, one — the heroine, the main focus — survives; the girls are killed close to a context of nudity and sexual activity (wearing only a shirt and on the way to pick up a date; in bed after intercourse; and another girl is stabbed right at the beginning of the film as she sits nude in front of a mirror, her boyfriend just gone); the survivor is the one who is not really part of the world of dates and sex, who thinks of herself as the good girl scout; and she almost gets it, is the object of the climactic aggression, the knife grazing her skin but she remaining in the end untouched.

In *After Lumière: L'Arroseur arrosé*, Malcolm Le Grice takes up the little scenario from the original Lumière film — the unsuspecting gardener, the hosepipe, the mischievous boy — and adds a woman, a moment of seduction which is here the opportunity for the boy to play his trick (in a strange doubling of the introduction of the woman, the 'boy' is just visibly played by a young girl). What Le Grice condenses is something of a history of cinema, giving a kind of instant précis of its institution since Lumière. The seduction of that cinema, to which Le Grice replies in his film, is exactly the set agreement of woman and image — representation to the full — and this through the bias of a narrative that plots and reproduces coherence, the setting, the place of the woman in image. In the play between fragment and whole, it is finally this unity that predominates, that catches up, subsumes traces, differences, the drift of intensities: the woman fixed, the same, the ideal body; the One-woman, that image, as a prime exchange-value of films in cinema.

Nietzsche provides a clear expression of the system into which this institution of cinema, its standard of representation, locks: 'Comparing man and woman in general one may say: woman would not have the genius for finery if she did not have the instinct for the secondary role.'[11] Cinema recreates, confirms the masquerade, the image of women as 'the woman'. For psychoanalysis, which is on the same side as all this (offering, as it were, a theoretical explication of Nietzsche's conventional remark), the masquerade is the assumption by the woman of a 'femininity' as the representation of desire, she playing out the economy of the phallus, becoming in a mirroring turn the signifier of the desire of the Other: 'it is in order to be the phallus, that is to say, the signifier of the desire of the Other, that a woman will reject an essential part of her femininity, namely all her attributes in the masquerade. It is for that which she is not that she wishes to be desired at the same time as loved. But she finds the signifier of her own desire in the body of him to whom her demand for love is addressed.'[12] In other words, she exchanges herself as the phallus she is for the man for the phallus she desires in the man, defined from and for his view, his look, becomes — in that 'rejection' which is the very fact of her as woman, the necessity of her existence in desire[13] — his image as her feminity, a whole cinema.

Exactly, a whole cinema. Cinema has played to the maximum the masquerade, the signs of this exchange femininity, has ceaselessly reproduced its social currency. From genre to genre, film to film, the same economy: the woman in image, the totalizing of the body, her, into unity, the sum of the gaze, the imaginary of her then as that perfect match, perfect image (and hence the violence, the aggression against women as bad, a disturbance of sexuality, as the narrative moves to establish the image, to set out its law); the man as the action of that image, the point of its rightness, the position of the film's imaginary (for women as for men, the complementarity of this double binding: she knows herself as her through him; he knows himself through his action of her). Psychoanalysis stresses that 'every identification is an identification *with a signifier*', with the phallus being the ultimate signifier.[14] Cinema, in its institution of the image of the woman, agrees: identification is with the phallus, the place given to occupy for men and women, the masquerade of cinema itself. Which is not to say, of course, that cinema is that only, even in its main historical definition, that its films are seen by spectators only in those terms; the implications of the real are multi-

farious, diverse, contradictory, films go this way and that in
their viewing, break into moments and intensities and differences for you and for me, she and he, a person here or there,
in this or that history. It is merely to acknowledge determinations, a stake, an investment of cinema.

Cinema today includes in its films nudity of the body, of the
bodies of young women — it is that that is obligatory. The
masquerade does not end here but continues: not nakedness,
which is a function of existence and history, but nudity, the
representation, the body smooth, laid for the gaze; nudity as
the image, the final adornment of the body.

What then of pornographic cinema with its extension of
nudity to the male body (an extension that has had its reflections in the commercial feature-film cinema with the beginnings of a male nudity from the end of the 1960s, from, say,
the famous wrestling scene of Russell's *Women in Love*) as
well as its fragmentation of bodies in its close-up
detailing and anonymity of parts (thus eroding something of
the *finish* of nudity which is always bound up with a certain
wholeness of the body imaged)? It is as though one does
indeed confront the 'explicit', the explicit *of cinema*: the
sexual economy of cinema, as it were, now shown, the narrative system of film brought down to the exposition of that
vision of sexuality that it has always carried through its stories
and plots and meanings. The scenario of the phallus now
becomes the narrative of the film as endless verification of
her pleasure from him and of his as that 'him', that 'virility'
(hence the necessity of the close-ups of ejaculation, the
visible demonstration and proof that *'it works'*), the body
given — male and female indifferently — as the sight and the
story of that (hence the compulsive repetition of sexuality as
a narrative, as 'the sexual act': encounter, preliminaries,
penetration, climax).

It must not be forgotten that a body in cinema, in a film, is
present in its absence, in the traces of an image (very different

to the body in theatre). The position of the spectator of a film is often described as 'voyeuristic' but voyeurs watch people not films, though no doubt many elements of voyeurism obtain in the pleasure-in-seeing cinema engages. In a study of theatre and illusion, the psychoanalyst Octave Mannoni notes with regard to cinema that 'it is as though the absence of the actor in his or her reality has the effect of giving the images of the ego the freedom of a greater emancipation'.[15] What is involved in cinema, as the point of its social and ideological functioning in this respect of the individual and sexuality, is a certain *imagination* of the ego, the setting of an ideal movement of desire and image, with the body for the spectator the aim — the focus and the purpose — of the ideal: the spectator 'emancipated', unhindered by the existence of bodies, mobile in his or her images, the free play of an egocentric appropriation and fantasy relation, *and* given as this flow of the film's images, placed in the cinema of their presentation, their order, their desire — their image. Cinema never shows the body you want but the body you want from cinema; you too are finally present in cinema only in your absence.

There is in pornographic cinema a constant repressed, the voice: so many bodies and bits of bodies without voices; merely, perhaps, snatches of dialogue, to get things going, and then, imperatively, a whole gamut of pants and cries, to deal with the immense and catastrophic problem — catastrophic since it threatens the very reason of this cinema — of the visibility or not of pleasure, to provide a *vocal image* to guarantee the accomplishment of pleasure, the proper working of the economy.

The voice is a moment of the body in its sense and history, a grain, a weight, an existence of the body and of me across the body (the voice is readily naked), 'the depositary of the desires and intentions of a past, which give it its singularity'.[16] The opening scene of Benoît Jacquot's *L'Assassin musicien* seems to pose the question of the voice as this in cinema. We have a soprano singing, evidently in rehearsal, a body, in medium shot, that is an image but also a voice, a physical effort of articulation and production, as though we are seeing a voice, a body in the particularity of a voice; interruption from a man, looking on from the auditorium, cutting dead, 'cette fille est nulle'; then at once the same voice, the same body, singing again against a black curtain, breaking down, crying, under the boos and catcalls of an audience out of frame. In the fiction, she, this soprano, is no good, 'nulle'; in the film, as we watch in a cinema, she, this woman, is brilliant, the shattering brilliance of the presence of a voice and a body that do not simply fit the frame, the image, the 'cinema'; in the fiction, she breaks down, is dismissed; in the film, in the cinema, she, this body-voice, troubles, disturbs, overdoes image and fiction, produces a remainder, something more, left over from the ideal of the image, exactly an existence, a singularity, and a singularity *with* the 'spectator' looking-listening caught up within this trouble.

In the work of Duras or Godard or Straub-Huillet, one finds, however differently in each case, exactly the attempt to hear the voice against the orders of cinema. For the voice is not the repressed of the pornographic cinema only; the development of sound in the commercial cinema generally was as support for a certain visible presence of the body, a certain regime of people in films: from the standardizations of the sound-track to dubbing and to the very fact of the script with its definition of dialogue scenes, what are given are so many means of keeping check of the voice, of pacifying it into film. Paradoxically perhaps on first consideration, sound cinema — the talking picture — puts an end at once to any friction of the body and to the weight of the voice as a moment of the singular history of a body. Godard—Gorin state this forcefully as follows: 'Before the talkie, the silent cinema had a materialist technical basis. The actor said: I am (filmed) therefore I think (I think at least that I am filmed), it is because I exist that I think. After the talkie, there was a New Deal between the filmed matter (the actor) and thought. The actor now began to say: I think (that I am an actor) therefore I am (filmed). It is because I think that I am . . . before the expression of the New Deal, every actor of the silent film had his or her own expression, and silent cinema had real popular bases. On the contrary, when the cinema begins to speak like the New Deal, every actor begins to speak the same thing.'[17] Evidently there is a strong homogenization and idealization of the silent cinema here that needs resisting and analyzing, but the point remains valid that the sound cinema is the development of a powerful standard of the body and of the voice as hold of the body in image, the voice literally ordered and delimited as speech for an intelligibility of the body, of people — agents and characters — fixed in the order of the narrative and its meanings, its unities and resolutions. In the silent cinema, the body is always pulling towards an emphasis, an exaggeration, a burlesque (the term of an intractable existence); in the sound cinema, the body is smoothed out, given over to that contract of thought described by Godard—Gorin, with the voice as the medium, the expression, of a homogeneous thinking subject — actor and spectator — of film.

Cinema is the machine of a certain presence, the institution of certain conditions of the body. Hence the political question, the question of any radical political practice of film: how and to what extent is it possible to transform those conditions, that presence? The question can only be answered from an initial and fundamental recognition of the problems of the *property* of the image. The image is never the property of me or of this or that person in the image; it is always an image *for* — for the film, its cinema. No referent can *guarantee* a discourse: the represented a discourse produces is grasped, realized, exists as such in the particular discursive process of representation, and it is this that needs first and foremost to be interrogated. Documentary film, however much it may be conceived as differing from the fiction feature-film, however much it may be defined in opposition to the latter, is just as fully in representation, raising still, and acutely, problems of people in films; so that the analysis into instances outlined earlier could serve again as a point of departure, a way of starting to bring out the issues even as it would need recasting. A film is always a document — a documentary — of film and cinema, never in any immediacy of people; new bodies, voices is also straightaway a work on the body and the voice in film and cinema, on the constructions of their presence there.

Notes

Written 1979 and previously unpublished, though drawing at points on material developed in parts of 'Film and System: Terms of Analysis' part II, *Screen* vol. 16 no 2 (Summer 1975) pp. 91–113, and 'Screen Images, Film Memory', *Edinburgh' 76 Magazine* (August 1976) pp. 33–43.

1. Marquis de Sade, *Les 120 Journées de Sodome* vol. 1 (Paris: Union Générale d'Éditions, 1975) p. 52.

2. Hegel's evaluation of hearing is in the *Vorlesungen über die Aesthetik, Sämtliche Werke* vol. 13 (Stuttgart: Frommans Verlag, 1927–8) p 254; translation, *Aesthetics: Lectures on Fine Art* vol. 1 (Oxford: Clarendon Press, 1975) p. 38; for Barthes on 'the grain of the voice', see 'Le grain de la voix', *Musique en jeu* no. 9 (November 1972) pp. 57–63; translation, 'The Grain of the Voice', in *Image – Music – Text* (London: Fontana, 1977) pp. 179–89. Along with the acceptance of the equation of sexual pleasure and visual gratification, the Hegelian rationalization of hearing has become a commonplace: 'the . . . ear (the least sensual of the senses)', Christopher Ricks, *Keats and Embarrassment* (London: Oxford U.P., 1976) p. 91.

3. Cf. Jacques Lacan, *Le Séminaire livre XI* (Paris: Seuil, 1973) pp. 96, 108, 182; translation, *The Four Fundamental Concepts of Psycho-Analysis* (London: Hogarth Press, 1977) pp. 104, 118, 200.

4. Lincoln F. Johnson, *Film: Space, Time, Light, and Sound* (New York: Holt, Rinehart & Winston, 1974) pp. 169–79; Johnson gives a short account of each of these 'functions of sound'.

5. Jacques Lacan, *Le Séminaire livre II* (Paris: Seuil, 1978) p. 315.

6. A. J. Greimas, *Sémantique structurale* (Paris: Larousse, 1966) pp. 172–91.

7. Sylvie Pierre, 'Éléments pour une théorie du photogramme', *Cahiers du cinéma* no. 226–7 (January–February 1971) p. 81.

8. 'You don't really have the opportunity to know married women otherwise than by the perspective of three-quarters of the images in this film. Images that date, that increasingly, I'm sure, are not very good; but all the same quite a lot of them are there, as though in a police report presented as such. Me, I'd very much like there to be at least films like that on men, for example . . . '. J.-L. Godard, *Introduction à*

une véritable histoire du cinéma vol. 1 (Paris: Albatros, 1980) p. 110.
Godard seems conscious here that it is above all women who have been
the focus of his intellectual — 'police report' — personifications.

    9. S. Freud, 'Fetishism' (1927), *The Standard Edition of the Complete Psychological Works* vol. XXI (London: Hogarth Press, 1961)
p. 157.

    10. Lillian Gish, *The Movies, Mr. Griffith, and Me* (London: W. H.
Allen, 1969) pp. 59—60.

    11. Friedrich Nietzsche, *Jenseits von Gut und Böse, Werke* vol. VI 2
(Berlin: Walter de Gruyter, 1968) p. 98; translation, *Beyond Good and
Evil* (Harmondsworth: Penguin Books, 1973) p. 84.

    12. Jacques Lacan, *Écrits* (Paris: Seuil, 1966) p. 694; translation,
Écrits: A Selection (London Tavistock, 1977) pp. 289—90.

    13. Since for the analyst the phallus is the universal signifier of desire,
any abandonment of the masquerade is supposedly the worrying
disturbance of a fundamental economy: 'When women give up the
masquerade, what do they find in bed? Women analysts, how do they
provoke erections? This difficulty is the price they pay when they leave
the masquerade.' Irène Diamantis, 'Entrevue avec Moustapha Safouan',
Ornicar? no. 9 (April 1977) p. 104. Luce Irigaray has well described the
perspective and the functioning of the trap of the masquerade and its
psychoanalytic account: 'The psychoanalysts say that the masquerade
corresponds to woman's desire. This does not seem to me to be correct.
I think it has to be understood as what women do in order to recover
something of desire, in order to participate in man's desire, but at the
cost of giving up their own. In the masquerade, they submit to the
dominant economy of desire, so as to keep themselves after all on the
"market". What do I understand by masquerade? In particular what
Freud calls "femininity". Believing, for example, that one has to *become*
a woman, and what is more a "normal" woman, whereas the man is a
man from the outset. He only has to accomplish his man-being, while
the woman has to become a normal woman, that is, to enter into the
masquerade of femininity.' *Ce Sexe qui n'en est pas un* (Paris: Minuit,
1977) pp. 131—2.

    14. M. Safouan, *La Sexualité féminine* (Paris: Seuil, 1976) p. 70.

    15. O. Mannoni, *Clefs pour l'imaginaire* (Paris: Seuil, 1969) p. 180.

    16. Guy Rosolato, 'La voix entre corps et langage', *Revue française
de Psychanalyse* 1 (1974) p. 83.

    17. Jean-Luc Godard and Jean-Pierre Gorin, 'Enquête sur une image',
Tel Quel no. 52 (Winter 1972) p. 84.

Chapter 9

Language, Sight and Sound

'Cinema and language' has been in many ways the great theoretical impetus for work on film over the last few years: the attempt to pose with regard to cinema the fact and the analogy of language, to determine similarities, connections, terms of interaction. In many ways again, we seem now to be emerging from the hold of that impetus, from the kinds of questions it produced; emerging *from* them, it should be stressed, *on the basis of* the demonstration of their limits, and then, perhaps, *against* them, with different questions, or with some of the old questions differently. What follows is a brief account of something of the present context of 'cinema and language', a consideration of one or two points that are important in its current discussion.

Fundamental to this present context is, of course, semiology and its relation to cinema in the work of Christian Metz, whose immediate question, in his initiatory 1964 essay entitled 'Le cinéma: langue ou langage?', was exactly that of how to pose and define cinema as language. Rigorously worked through, the question was answered in terms of the difficulty of the linguistic model or analogy in respect of cinema: cinema as a language without a language-system, 'un langage sans langue'.[1] Question and answer, however, at the same time that they serve to emphasize the difficulty of cinema as language and hence its difference from language, also effectively function to enclose cinema in the given assumptions of language, in the Saussurian model of *langue*, the system or code of a language, and *parole*, the instances of the use of that system or code, with *langage* as the overall term, the sum of *langue* and *parole*. Its films so many messages, cinema is clearly a kind of language but, lacking a system or code equivalent to a *langue*, is unlike language in the linguistic terms of which it is nevertheless precisely then defined, as 'un langage sans langue'. The model determines the conception and treatment of cinema.[2]

This enclosure can be readily seen in the to-and-fro of the argument of *Langage et cinéma*, the book in which Metz exhaustively explores from a linguistic perspective the notion of cinema as language. 'Cinematic language is different — rather than "distinct" — from what a language-system, a *langue*, *would be*, but takes its place (for here no *langue* exists).' The thesis of something that takes the place of a language-system gives at once a difference, 'cinematic language has neither the same cohesion nor the same precision as a *langue*', and a closeness, the very difference being within this constant exploration of cinema through the *langue/parole* model which is thus always definingly near to hand, always the analogy or framework for description; as, for example, in the distinction between film and cinema, where the former is 'on the side of the message', the latter 'on the side of the code'. While it stresses cinematic language as constituted by the combination of a number of codes, as codically heterogeneous, the argument also finds occasion in such a film/cinema distinction to adopt 'provisionally' the 'fiction' of 'a unitary system': '*cinematic language*: set of all the general and particular cinematic codes, inasmuch as one provisionally neglects the differences separating them and treats their common trunk, by fiction, as a real unitary system'; to which unitary system can then be opposed the film as message and the *langue/parole* model retained, confirmed.[3]

The 'lock' of that model is not just a problem for the semiology of cinema, for thinking about cinema as language. What is at stake in Saussure's model is the reduction of the social fact of language to a stable system of signs available for free exchange by speaking subjects in individual uses of the common, normative code for the communication of particular informations: the individual utterances, the instances of *parole*, actualize the abstract reality of language as *langue*, the system as contract or horizon or ground for every subject, a social unity. As against which can be stressed the radical necessity to pose social and individual and linguistic together in their complex process, the necessity not to abstract the social into an underlying unity of language but to reappropriate the *action* of language in and into the social; and this without denying the specificity of language, the terms of the individual in its relations, while insisting none the less on the question of the ideological to language and individual.

For cinema, that necessity can be heard today as many varied points of interrogation, grasped in the pressures making for the development of this or that new strategy and practice, touching in different ways on what is classically elided in the semiological conception of cinema and language, crossing its limits. Thus, for examples: the return of a stress on the body, on 'not moving away from the body', on engaging language in its nearness to that, the body-in-and-through-and-in-resistance-to-and-in-excess-of-language, putting *that* to cinema, 'not assigning language [or cinema with it] to a code, even if it might be agreed that it always secretes one more or less; its life has priority over its code and not the reverse';[4] the insertion of political issues of language and cinema, cinema and language, of 'analysis with image and sound';[5] the attempt to locate in cinema, *as* cinema, problems of representation and sexual difference, the question of language, for instance, in Mulvey and Wollen's film *Riddles of the Sphinx*, 'If we had a non-patriarchal symbolic order, what would the language be in that situation? What would the non-patriarchal word be?';[6] the concern, an old concern coming back anew in the context of the critique of semiology, with the idea of inner speech in respect of cinema, exploring something of the reality of Eisenstein's notion of the passage on screen, in cinema, of 'all phases and all specifics of the course of thought'[7] (it might be remembered that Eisenstein would always talk of *constructing*, and not of using, a cinematic language). These points of interrogation and pressure are cited somewhat pell-mell, so many different indications, but also as crucially important, to be taken up in what follows.

'A language is not an inert material';[8] an emphasis from the wish not to assign language to a code that is found too in the more recent, psychoanalytically referred work of Metz, running over 'the paradox of the code': 'in the final analysis, the code can owe its characteristics, and its very existence even, only to a set of symbolic operations (the code is a social *activity*), and yet is a code only in so far as it gathers up and organizes the "inert" results of those operations'.[9]

It is indeed against the 'inert' of *langue* or code that psychoanalysis has become important in current theoretical discussions of questions of cinema and language: psychoanalysis as exactly an attention to language in action and process, in its material effects and operations. It is sometimes said that Freud, unfortunately, lacked an adequate linguistics, missed what would have been the decisive support of Saussure and Jakobson ('Geneva 1910, Petrograd 1920 suffice to explain why Freud lacked this particular tool', as Lacan once put it[10]), but perhaps also it was not so unfortunate, not simply a liability to have had no equivalent to the conception of the *langue/parole* model. Freud worked more interestingly than is generally allowed with a 'linguistics' of the word as knot of meaning, semantic-affective complex, and with a specifically historical orientation, seeking to develop for psychoanalysis the thesis of the repetition by ontogeny of phylogeny, plunging into the history of the individual in the history of language to demonstrate the involvement of the unconscious in the repetition of linguistic material and effects from the origins of language to the present day (this is the purpose of such directly linguistic papers as 'The Antithetical Meaning of Primal Words'[11]). With that linguistics and concern with language as subjective process, without Saussure's model, or with Lacan's use and displacement of Saussure through Freud, psychoanalysis, the 'talking-cure', is always in language; it is there that it locates and traces the movement of desire, follows the interminable constitution of subjectivity. The discovered unconscious is not some place, some 'where', but an implication of language, language as 'the condition of the unconscious',[12] the unconscious structured as and from a language: 'it is the whole structure of language that psychoanalytic experience discovers in the unconscious'.[13]

What is significant for the moment is the way in which that experience and its theorization in these terms cut across, disturbing, the system/individual set of *langue/parole*, and Lacan has used the expression *lalangue* to specify the instance of this cutting across, this disturbance. Where *langue* is a formal system to be described and *parole* its individual uses by communicating agents, *lalangue* names the subjective activity of language, the very 'object' of psychoanalysis, near to the 'basic language', the *Grundsprache*, heard by Freud in the Schreber case-history or in that of the Rat-man;[14] *lalangue* as the articulation in the language of a given linguistic-system, in the matter of a language, of the movement and insistence of desire, with its figure (for psychoanalysis) maternal language, the mother tongue — the language *par excellence* which supports desire in its initial objects: look, voice, breast, excrement. In short, psychoanalysis comes with a whole different version of language, of what exists as 'a language': 'A singular mode for the equivocal, that is what a language is amongst other things. Thereby it becomes a collection of places, all of them singular and all of them heterogeneous; from whatever way one considers it, it is other to itself, ceaselessly heterotopical. Thereby it becomes just as well substance, possible matter for fantasies, inconsistent set of places for desire. The language is thus what the unconscious makes in and of it, lending itself to all imaginable games for truth to speak in the movement of words. *Lalangue* is all that; one grasps it negatively away from usual reference terms — *langue, langage*.'[15]

If psychoanalysis then importantly enters current discussion of cinema, it cannot be as the coherence of a new model to be applied in this specific field, though in practice the attraction of a static appeal to this or that psychoanalytic 'theme' (mirror-stage, fetishism, etc.) has been great, but as the insertion of a question, the question of language and meaning and the process of subjectivity, that breaks up some of the certainties of 'cinema and language', ramifies that 'field' in different directions, so many shifts from any given unity of description.

Take, to begin with something of a context for that insertion, elements of the idea and practice of sight and sound, instances of their opposition, cross-opposition, inversion and double inversion — inversion and inversion again — from psychoanalysis to cinema on this question of language.

Psychoanalysis has been defined here as bound up in language, its experience as an experience of language, its very situation one of the development of a veritable apparatus of language (analytic practice as a kind of optimally functioning language theatre, language given a hearing). Cinema, often, has been assumed and defined as essentially separate from language or, a different emphasis but on the same grounds, as universal language, enthusiastically ('la langue universelle est trouvée!' of the first Lumière spectators) or dismissively (Leavis's 'species of amusing and informational Esperanto'[16]): cinema as minimally linguistic, as visual, things as words (this was Freud's distrust of cinema and his wish to avoid it dealing with psychoanalysis in these terms: the simplistic visualization of a complex and highly structured linguistic process). This conception, indeed, the assurance of its ideological currency and effectivity, can be grasped in the very treatment of verbal language in the developed commercial cinema and the regulation in respect of that treatment of the multiple possibilities of sound. What determines is the standardization of the sound-track for speech for the image, with verbal language and sound reduced to that visual intelligibility; hence, *inter alia*: synchronization, mixing for the achievement of an acceptable — accepted — level of clarity of dialogue, elaboration of the sound-track in visible terms (sound 'in' or 'off'), attention to the creation of proper sound 'perspective' (sound anchored in and contributing to the maintenance of the representational space of the image), sound editing in the interests of smoothness of image flow (for example, the sound of one shot is very slightly run over the join of the next shot, hiding the interruption of the cut, preserving the illusion of an undivided presence), studio dubbing of the sounds 'in' the image (the sounds heard on the sound-track are selected in relation to their 'visibility' in the image and re-created according to codes of verisimilitude in sound recording studios), even the very *size* of the image on screen and the power of its investment over sound (compare the difference in the economy of sound and image when watching a film on television, the latter recasting sound/image 'size').

This containment of language and sound, moreover, is part of a complex and entangled history in which cinema condenses and intersects a whole series of issues of sight and sound and language. Thus, again simply citing one or two aspects of that history, sound is both very early and very late in cinema: *early*, Edison's initial interest was in moving pictures as accompaniment for his phonograph, the very first years of cinema saw a host of sound-for-film projects (the work of Eugène Lauste, for example); *late*, the well-known story of the time taken for sound to be finally developed and adopted in cinema, the delay until the mid-1920s. Sound, when it comes, loses for a while, forgoes the possibility of, mobility of camera and outdoor location shooting, a certain freedom of vision, but gains an immediate unity of the image as 'scene', a certain theatre of sight; in the balancing out of loss and gain an economy of sight and sound is founded which henceforth constrains the terms of its modification (for example, with the recovery of the mobility of the camera after the introduction of the blimp) and of its difference (alternative orders and practices of cinema, defined as other *from* that economy, that standard: for example, documentary or independent avant-garde film). Sound is intensely modern in its technical foundation, the electronics of the twentieth century, very far removed from the nineteenth-century image machinery of the film camera, and yet at the same time, given the massive modern investment in the image and its reproduction, often seemingly able to be envisaged as something more or less archaic or marginal, potentially and radically other to the current image; Eisler, in his treatise on film music, written in Hollywood, gives one symptomatic expression of this: 'The human ear has not adapted itself to the bourgeois rational and, ultimately, highly industrialized order as readily as the eye, which has become accustomed to conceiving reality as made up of separate things, commodities. . . . Ordinary listening, as compared to seeing, is "archaic"; it has not kept pace with technological progress.'[17] One catches up here a vertiginous spiral of turns and oppositions and overlaps. What sense could we give today to the idea that hearing has not progressed with technology? But then how do hearing and sight 'progress'? The point is constantly the appeal to some other to the standard of the image and its 'optical sound', which, moreover, is to cut across psychoanalysis, the notion of the archaicity of hearing finding important resonances and difficulties in respect of analytic conceptions. Lacan, for instance, stresses hearing, or more exactly the invocatory drive, as closest to the experience of the unconscious, while Freud always regards the visual as most archaic, visual imaging as the register of unconscious presentations (but then again these terms of 'archaic', 'closest', 'visual' need to be examined in their specific meanings and arguments here). In the midst of all of which, returning to film, sound determines the final *property* of cinema: the world domination achieved by the Hollywood industry and the secured relation of that industry to the sources and mechanisms of finance capital; and the law of the speaking subject, the artistic and legal fiction of the creation of a film, its very sense, the ground of its language.

Consider, following out from this context, two issues in the thinking of sight and sound that can come back on the question of cinema and language: the emphasis sometimes put, against the convention and conventions of cinema and the visual, on the voice; the distinction between 'thing' and 'word' presentations in Freudian theory and its implications with regard to the reference to psychoanalysis in current work on cinema.

The coming of sound in cinema is the coming of language through the voice, the sound-track is developed in the end for that: synchronized visible speech, dialogue that makes scenes for the order and flow of the images, to which other possibilities of sound are sacrificed or subordinated. Yet in speech, running through language, the voice is also a certain deposit of the body, a certain 'grain', something else again, in excess, which the standards of Hollywood learned to pacify (and first and foremost by the very selection of voices, voices that conformed, that 'recorded well') and in specific instances to exploit (the presentation of this or that voice, often crystallized in the theatrical staging of a song, the voice of a Marlene Dietrich or a Lauren Bacall). It is this potential excess that has become the point of emphasis, the voice used towards a heterogeneity in and against the image; the work of Straub–Huillet (*History Lessons*, *Othon*, *Moses and Aaron*, *Fortini/Cani*), its uses of reading or recitation of written literary texts or of sung diction and performance, is only the most obvious example in contemporary film practice. Equally, the voice is assumed against the visual, against the look, and in particular in feminist writing; thus Hélène Cixous: 'What is important is the vocal, the musical, the language at its most archaic and at the same time most highly wrought level.'[18] Something of which idea of language in the vocal-musical at its most archaic and simultaneously elaborate level is the practice of Marguerite Duras (*India Song*, *Son nom de Venise*). That assumption, moreover, is found again round the question of 'femininity' in psychoanalytic theory today, the thesis that 'the eroticization of the voice and the discourse it vehicules is more present in feminine sexuality': 'mythologically, there is something which links femininity with the voice'.[19] Certainly, look and voice, scopic and invocatory, are given by psychoanalysis as in 'total distinction': 'the distinction is total', comments Lacan, who goes on exactly to stress the invocatory as closest to the experience of the unconscious, the unconscious, never closed to the force of the auditory.[20] (This proximity of voice and unconscious in its descriptions would be an aspect to be taken into account in considering the effective situation for psychoanalysis of the voice/feminine conjunction — the implications of the suggested relation: feminine — unconscious — archaic.)

In fact, Freud's own formulations seem directly contrary to this (it is worth noting moreover the relative absence of treatment of voice and vocal in his extensive writings), seem directly involved — with the distinction between thing- and word-presentations — in a non-linguistic, much more visual version of the unconscious. Part of Freud's argument from that distinction is precisely that it is the visual which is more primitive, more archaic than the auditory (though both visual and auditory — Freud is very Hegelian here — are still much further advanced than the tactile, the olfactory and the gustatory). Dreams are described as essentially visual (and this, of course, is just what has led to attempts to equate cinema and dream, cinema as like dream); language found in them as speeches, utterances, is not worked up, not elaborated in the dream, but is simply reproduced from matter heard during the day, is daytime material (it *must* be this because the unconscious does not know the logic of syntax, tenses, identity, and so on, is not linguistic).[21] Yet at the same time, what has to be grasped is that the visual of dreams is thing-*presentation*: interpretation, listening to the turns of unconscious desire, does not stop on 'things' (does not *show*), it breaks up and extends these presentations (seeks to find what they *say*). The visual in any sense of some purely visual realm (itself a quite imaginary notion) is finally non-existent in the Freudian description of the unconscious; the visual is always in a production of meanings and run through by language, by a language history, which has determination in that production of visual-in-meaning. Freud's linguistics of the word is not a pre-Saussurian *pis aller* but an important focus on this mesh of meaning production that is the very definition of the unconscious; the word, to borrow from the stress of Freud's early monograph *On Aphasia*, as 'a complex presentation constituted of auditory, visual and kinaesthetic elements'.[22] The focus holds against the reduction of the operations, relations, constructions of meaning — hence against the reduction of the unconscious — to a secondary, systematized delimitation of an object 'language', exactly the level at which the *langue/parole* model is cast. Insisting on speeches in dreams as daytime material, Freud is insisting on the radical excentricity of dream productions to the stable order of subject to meaning in the given social forms of a language and its institutionalized practice; utilizing a distinction between 'words' and 'things' and assigning the former to the register of the secondary, the latter to that of the primary processes, with the emphasis then on dreams as visual, thing-presentations, Freud is resisting the linguistics idea of the word, fixed units of subject-conceptual meaning. The unconscious, and the 'visual' of dreams with it, is very much in language, on condition that language is understood in a transformation of the terms of the object 'language' of linguistics (and, for example, in the context of a history of the individual as subject in language and in which language itself is a history 'repeated now every time the development of speech has to be gone through in an individual'[23]).

Which is to come to the reason for a concept such as Lacan's *lalangue*: the unconscious is a movement, a work, a history, a repetition and so on in and through a symbolic function which, for Freud as for Lacan, is always implicated in language — neither verbal nor pre-verbal, the unconscious as a *drift* in language, in the matter of language. Thus Freud, at every moment that he operates the distinction between 'thing' and 'word', the antithesis of 'visual' and 'verbal', everywhere finds language; as though involved in a forceful resistance to and reassessment of Wittgenstein's note that 'what *can* be shown, *cannot* be said',[24] resistance and reassessment around the whole idea of 'language', 'meaning', 'saying'.

It is in relation to these problems of thing and word and saying that Freud looked from the beginning towards the development of a conception of inner speech, near to what Eisenstein would call 'the quivering inner words that correspond with the visual images'.[25] In the course of his work on aphasia, Freud had come to posit that 'understanding of

spoken words is probably not to be regarded as simple transmission from the acoustic elements to the object associations;
it rather seems that in listening to speech with understanding
the function of verbal association is stimulated from the
acoustic elements at the same time, so that we more or less
repeat to ourselves the words heard, thus supporting our
understanding with the help of kinaesthetic impressions'.[26]
The argument there is merely for an 'inner' join of word and
thing, the former being the *closure* of the latter (word-
concepts are closed, object-concepts are open, which is an
initial premonition of what will become the 'thing-presentation
= unconscious / word-presentation = conscious-preconscious'
emphasis of Freud's psychoanalytic work, which emphasis
itself is thus in turn a remnant, a left-over from the early
work on aphasia): word and thing are linked by the sound-
image alone and inner speech is the constant — or not, as in
aphasia — link of the two, the point of transmission of their
relation (the sound-image engages kinaesthetic impressions
that are the very history for the individual of object- and
word-concepts, of their production). With the discovery of
the unconscious and the elaboration of its theory (psychoanalysis), the knot of this link, this relation, tightens and is
displaced from a simple question of transmission; the history
of language, the terms of the development of thought and
consciousness and the process of the realization of the individual as human subject become coincidental, with the
unconscious — and inner speech with it inasmuch as such a
concept can stand in psychoanalysis — the fact and the
demonstration of that coincidence, of its effects. Evidently,
it is here, round the problem of this history, the interiorization of history as repetition, the balance from individual to
universal subject-form, that the Marxist critique of Freud
and psychoanalysis is made most strongly, and through a
consideration of language; as, for example, by Vološinov in
his 1927 essay *Freudianism*: 'Processes that are in fact
social are treated by Freud from the point of view of individual psychology . . . ', but, 'this "content of the psyche" is
ideological through and through; from the vaguest of thoughts
and the dimmest and most uncertain of desires all the way to
philosophical systems and complex political institutions, we

have one continuous series of ideological and, hence also, sociological phenomena.'[27]

The idea of language in Marx begins indeed from its stressed reality as social activity: language is 'practical consciousness', a term of the relation of men and women in social process, material production. At the same time, however (*therefore*), 'language is as old as consciousness',[28] which is exactly the problem developed by Freud, the area explored in his psychoanalytic experience and theory. For Marx, the three basic aspects of sociality — the satisfaction of needs, the satisfaction of further new needs and the reproduction of life — 'have existed simultaneously since the dawn of history and the first men, and still assert themselves in history today'.[29] For Freud, the unconscious is a kind of archaic present in language, the assertion of a history; thus the idea, briefly referred to earlier, of a material established during the historical development of speech and which has to be repeated in the case of the development of speech in each individual. What is strongly in evidence here, again, is the 'ontogeny recapitulates phylogeny' conception that is part of a historical thinking in the nineteenth century common to both Marx and Freud (one might remember in this respect the admiration shared by the two men for the work of Darwin). Moreover, just as Freud sees the origin and foundation of language in the sexual (itself an emphasis to be found in Darwin), so too Marx can regard the division of labour as 'originally nothing but the division of labour in the sexual act',[30] thereby joining the sexual, the social and language ('as old as consciousness', 'practical consciousness') in an original and actual concomitance. Simply, Freud offers to pose the question of language as a question of subjectivity and to grasp the sexual there, as sexuality (very different from 'the 'sexual act'), in that history of the construction of the individual, against the possible extrapolation from Marx of some notion of an instrumental clarity of consciousness to language for a given subject-agent (language merely a tool for communication that has no constitutive role in the production of consciousness and its terms), or, on the other side, against the reduction of language to ideology (language merely a superstructural category, merely the area of a false consciousness, and so equally without real constitutive force). Freud finds, that is, the productivity of language, its articulations, its divisions, its matter (recognizes what Marx intimates as the absence of ' "pure" consciousness', mind afflicted with 'the curse of being "burdened" with matter, which here makes its appearance in the form of agitated layers of air, sounds, in short of language'[31]), but does so with no idea of historical transformation (this is the final blockage of the ontogeny-phylogeny conception, moving from species universal to individual with nothing between but recapitulation, and where Marx, even as he retains something of that same thinking, separates from it in the working out of a new social-historical science, historical materialism): no idea of historical transformation save only for the individual in consciousness, the practice of the cure, the psychoanalytic situation — the room, the couch, the silence — set up to suspend, to bracket out, history, the social, to engage the sole history of the individual, the person, in every sense an *inner* speech.

It is that interiorization that Vološinov is concerned to challenge, insisting that processes treated by Freud from the point of view of individual psychology are fully social, that the content of the psyche is through and through ideological. Paradoxically perhaps at first sight, one of the strategies of Vološinov's argument against Freud is, in fact, an appeal to a reality of inner speech. What psychoanalysis describes as the unconscious is redefined as an aspect of the conscious, an 'unofficial' aspect that is in conflict with the 'official conscious'; the conscious is linguistic, that use of language which is inner speech ('Consciousness is in fact *that commentary* which every adult human being brings to bear on every instance of his behaviour'[32]); thus, as an aspect of the conscious, the unconscious (as Freud would call it) is linguistic and, since linguistic, a social and not an individual phenomenon. The argument, so to speak, has something right in its intention, wrong in its terms. Freud's account of the unconscious is itself, as has been said, not non-verbal in the way in which Vološinov suggests in order to expunge it in the interests of the linguistic and hence social, and the conflict between the 'official' and 'unofficial' aspects of the conscious is left without adequate explanation or content: Vološinov can see the area of the conflict as 'the sexual' but this is now outside of any theory of sexuality (hence, typically, one has no right at all to speak of infantile sexuality other than as meaning 'a set of strictly defined physiological manifestations'[33]) and tends towards a simple notion of social repression. The stress that 'the psyche in its entirety' is 'in every respect determined by socioeconomic factors'[34] remains unhelpful in its blanket generality and its imprecision with regard to what 'determined' might mean and to the mechanisms of the operation of such determination; the problem of the individual and subjectivity is not resolved by collapsing everything into the 'socioeconomic'. Certainly, the terms of the descriptions provided by psychoanalysis — 'the content and composition of the unconscious'[35] — need to be understood and questioned historically, considered in relation to 'historical time and class';[36] certainly, it is necessary to recognize that there is 'no fundamental dividing line between the content of the individual psyche and formulated ideology'[37]; but all this is not a reason (on the contrary) for erasing the specific domain of concern identified and approached by psychoanalysis, that of the construction of the individual, of the 'individual psyche', — or, to put it in a more Marxist perspective, of *the individual history of* historical construction.

Inner speech is still a valid point of exploration in this connection. Its theoretical development is, of course, not only in Vološinov. Initial psychological investigation is carried out in France in the late nineteenth century in the work of Egger (*La Parole intérieure*) and Ballet (*Le Langage intérieur*) and is bound up with the attempt to define the status of an inner speech as the carrier of thought, the point of the exchange of thought into its external expression.[38] It is indeed in Soviet psychology, however, that inner speech is decisively introduced and worked through, most notably with the researches of Vygotsky and Blonski (and in a context which includes in the 1920s an active presence of psychoanalysis: Pavlov himself had been favourably interested in psychoanalysis from as early as 1913; Luria — student, collaborator and friend of Vygotsky — was the secretary to psychoanalytic circles in Kazan and Moscow; and so on).

Vygotsky's treatment of inner speech is set out in *Thought and Language*, published posthumously in 1934. His concern is the relation of thought and language, and inner speech enters the argument in the terms of this concern as a kind of monitoring of thought, as 'the living process of the birth of thought in the word': 'Thought is not merely expressed in words; it comes into existence through them.'[39] As such, inner speech can be given a genetic description: in the beginning thought and language are independent activities, thought proceeding without language in very young children, as in animals (equally, the child's cooings and other vocalizations are speech without thought, mere acts to attract attention or whatever); around two years, pre-linguistic thought and pre-thought language meet and join to initiate a new kind of behaviour, verbal thought; at about seven years, after a period in which the child engages out loud in both social speech, for and with others, and egocentric speech, talking for itself in an activity of language that is in fact its use to direct and produce thought, the child learns to distinguish the functions of speech and internalizes the thought function of language, thus establishing inner speech. The latter can then be described as a 'a specific formation, with its own laws and complex relations to other forms of speech activity', Vygotsky indicating 'the extreme, elliptical economy of inner speech, changing the speech pattern almost beyond recognition'; 'a simplification of syntax, a minimum of syntactic breaking down, expression of thought in condensed form, a considerably smaller number of words' (inner speech is characterized by a basic predicativeness, the omission of the subject and the parts of the sentence related to it, and by a contextual sense of words, an intellectual and affective intensity beyond what Vygotsky calls their 'objective' meaning).[40]

Certain of the arguments of *Thought and Language* were criticized by Blonski in his *Memory and Thought* published in the following year. Blonski opposes the idea that thought and language have separate genetic roots and proposes instead the recognition of a common source, work: 'both speech and thought have developed from work; primitive speech was really action; primitive intellectual operations were actions'.[41] Equally, he challenges Vygotsky's hypothesis regarding the evolution of inner speech from the child's egocentric speech, placing as it does the origin of inner speech at a very late stage of development (six or seven years, well into school age) and thus leaving the child in a prior state of the absence of any such mechanism. For Blonski, inner and social speech are simultaneous, the former developing in relation to the latter as the initial activity of the repetition of speech heard, listening accompanied by an internal echoing to aid understanding (Blonski is here near to Freud's account of inner speech in *On Aphasia* mentioned earlier). This 'accompaniment' continues as the permanent reality of the process of thought for the individual, with the actual characterization of inner speech then coming back to a similarity with that given by Vygotsky: 'An extremely rapid and changeable flow of thoughts, making little sense for an outsider because of its jumps and incompleteness of reading and judgements, continually reverting to fragments of phrases or even to individual words which would surprise the listeners.'[42]

It will be clear that inner speech functions as a concept within a general context of the investigation of the nature of thinking, hence of the relation of thought and language. As such, it has a history which is longer than that of the psychological work outlined above, as long indeed as Western philosophy and with perfectly idealist emphases (Socrates in Plato's *Theaetetus* has a version of inner speech as 'the conversation which the soul holds with itself in considering anything'). Again, however, it has a real importance as a concept in connection with the problem of thought and language which is a fully, and necessary, materialist area of concern (the question jotted down by Lenin in the margin of Hegel's *Logic*: 'History of thought = history of language?'). What sense is to be given to — what are the operations and implications of — language as, in Marx's expression, 'the immediate reality' of thought? Vološinov, Vygotsky, Blonski engage, in different ways, that debate, the 'battle for consciousness' of the twenties and early thirties, the specification of the issue involved in moving 'from the social to the individual', grasping language and thought as 'subject to all the premises of historical materialism'.[43]

The debate is historically and theoretically important in cinema, is to be heard, for instance, in Eisenstein's 'all phases and all specifics of the thought process'. A more or less constant ambition for Eisenstein is the grounding of cinematic practice in the processes of psychological functioning and the establishment of the laws of the former from those of the latter. Inner speech is taken up in just these terms: 'the laws of the construction of inner speech turn out to be precisely those laws which lie at the foundation of the whole variety of laws governing the construction of the form and composition of art-works'.[44] The most important theoretical statement and assertion of inner speech is in a 1935 address, delivered to the All-Union Creative Conference of Workers in Soviet Cinematography, in which Eisenstein refers to work — probably by Luria — in the Moscow Neuro-Surgical Clinic and no doubt has Vygotsky's book very much in mind (Eisenstein appears to have been a member of a discussion group that included Luria and Vygotsky[45]). The tendency of his address, however, is towards a connection between inner speech and 'prelogical thinking' (thus quite distinct from Vygotsky's tying of inner speech to a development that makes of it a fully social relation of thought and language, a function of 'verbal thought'), referring this 'prelogical' idea to the anthropologist Lévy-Bruhl (whom Vygotsky indeed seeks to refute on one of the very points accepted by Eisenstein[46]). In 1932, Eisenstein could express himself in ways which suggest the 'thought and language' problematic of the contemporary inner speech discussion: 'How fascinating it is to listen to one's own train of thought, particularly in an excited state, in order to catch yourself, looking at and listening to your own mind. How you talk "to yourself", as distinct from "out of yourself". The syntax of inner speech as distinct from outer speech. The quivering inner words that correspond with the visual images.';[47] in 1935, it is apparent that his version of inner speech is independent of social language and involved in a fundamental 'psychic associationism': 'Since "inner speech" is prelogical and sensuous, [Eisenstein's earlier project] of stimulating abstract and ideological reasoning is abandoned; sensation and affect are now sufficient. . . . Now the spectator's reaction must be not thought but pathos, "ecstasy" . . . the very concept of montage is overhauled. Since the work of art must map the way we create felt concepts in life, montage's ability to render the dynamic flow of images makes it the sovereign formal principle.'[48] Eisenstein, moreover, sees himself quickly reproached with 'subjectivism', compared, even, to the hated Proust!

And yet . . . there are flashes in Eisenstein of something quite radically different, at least in potential implication. An interview in 1928 has the following exchange: ' "We have an incorrect attitude to the notion of symbol. It is wrong to assert that the symbol is now without life. The symbolizing force is a living one for it belongs to the essence of human reaction to sensation." / "Ah! so you're a Freudian!" / "No doubt. Cinema must take into account the consequences of the fact that every individual symbolizes unconsciously. It is not the achieved symbol that interests me but the symbol in process [*Symbol im werden*, literally "symbol in becoming"].'[49] Freudian? Certainly not on the whole (in the fascinating correspondence with Reich in 1934 Eisenstein sets out his objections to the importance accorded to the sexual in Freud) but constantly caught up none the less in the concerns of Freudian psychoanalysis (as stated previously, psychoanalysis is a presence in Soviet Russia in the twenties). The 'symbol in process' is one — excellent — definition of the unconscious recognized and described in Freud's work.

The symbol in process. The psychoanalysis of Freud and Lacan engages the unconscious as a kind of inner speech, where this latter is neither 'social' nor 'individual', still less the site of some universal symbolism (the 'achieved symbol'), but, exactly, linguistic in a new assumption of the — complex, heterogenous — reality of language as a site of history. For Freud, there is no escape from language, ontogenetically or phylogenetically: 'Thus, for Freud symbolism was always derivative of verbality. As the meanings of words change —

both in the ontogeny of the individual and the phylogeny of the species — so symbols accumulate in the unconscious of the individual and the race. Symbols are vestigial residues; here Freud [returns] to [the] promise of mastering archaic regression through the development of language. Symbols are the vestiges of a time when sexuality and language were themselves identified.'[50] There is no 'prelogical' in either of the senses given by Eisenstein (Lévy-Bruhl) or Vygotsky (the infant/animal 'biological', 'natural' forms): what one has, always, is another scene of shifts of meaning, slippages of identity, intensities of desire, a whole articulation (the unconscious structured in and as and like a language), a radical excentricity of any 'subject' (in that action of meanings, symbols in process). The thing-/word-presentation distinction does not plunge into some realm pre-language but into one where the identities assumed and derived in language (the *vision* of language) fail, the orders of the sign slide. 'Thing-presentations', the matter of the unconscious, are symbolic articulations, signifiers full of language in every sense, 'words' and 'things' intersecting (follow the analysis of any dream in *The Interpretation of Dreams*). Inner speech is then that history of language.

Simply, the point of all the difficulty, Freud and still less Lacan do not carry through to the end of that excentricity of the subject in language in that history, block that movement in what amounts to a fetishization of 'subject' and 'language' (what does psychoanalysis *believe* in today? subject and language). The real history with which psychoanalysis deals is still directly and immediately social, not 'before' or 'else-where' to social processes, ideological places. There is a material history of the construction of subjectivity and that history is also the social construction of the individual as subject, in a kind of necessary simultaneity, like the recto and verso of a piece of paper; between the psyche and the social, no 'fundamental dividing line' is to be drawn, not even with *lalangue* which can quickly become the separate realm of psychoanalysis, the term of its suspension of history.

It is very possible that in the long run the concept of inner

speech itself will be found to be caught up in theoretical and
ideological difficulties. Indeed, the inner/outer paradigm is at
once not without evident problems. 'Inner' easily tends towards a simply 'subjective' account of individual experience
in meaning and a consequent homogenization of the person
(inner speech becomes a kind of *property* of 'the subject',
'that interior recitation which constitutes our person'[51]),
in a way that is deeply conservative, indicating a realm of
separation — at best, as in Vygotsky, of unofficial resistance
— rather than a theory of action and transformation. Alter-
natively, by the very terms of the opposition set up, it
suggests the possibility of a theoretical reversal, inner into
outer, the 'through and through ideological' version which,
quite apart from the problems of defining the relations of
language and ideology and of the apparent extension of the
ideological as a general equivalence for the social, seems to
leave little place again for process and conflict — how to
explain difference, contradiction, tensions of 'inner' and
'outer', tensions *in subjectivity* — not just between an 'inner'
and an 'outer' sphere — that are crucial to any understanding
of the political importance of cinema, its potential, its
availability for use?

As far as the analysis of cinema and film is concerned, consideration of inner speech has so far been limited and, in fact,
disappointing. Its introduction here, again in the Soviet context, dates from a 1927 essay by the Formalist critic Boris
Eikhenbaum entitled 'Problems of Film Stylistics' in which
he emphasizes the inadequacy of the idea of film as a non-
verbal art: 'Cinema demands of the viewer a certain special
technique for divination, and this technique will of course
become more complex as the art of film-making develops.
Directors already make frequent use of symbols and metaphors, the meaning of which depends directly on current
verbal metaphors. Film viewing is accompanied by a continual
process of internal speech. We have already grown accustomed
to a whole series of typical patterns of film language; the
smallest innovation in this sphere strikes us no less forcibly

than the appearance of a new word in language. To treat film
as an absolutely non-verbal art is impossible. Those who
defend cinema from the imitation of literature often forget
that though the audible word is eliminated from film, the
thought, i.e. internal speech, is nevertheless present. The
study of the particularities of this film-speech is one of the
most important problems in cinematic theory.'[52] Subsequent
work has been largely occupied with Eikhenbaum's suggestion
of the dependence of visual on verbal metaphor, with demonstrating the use of image translations of linguistic tropes.[53]
Thus, for example, in *The Taking of Pelham 123*, the hope-
less and corrupt mayor of New York is sick in bed for most
of the time, quite unable to decide anything with regard to
the subway train that has been hijacked; at one point, we cut
to him just as he is having an injection in his buttocks and his
deputy walks in, 'Come on, Al, pull your pants up' — the
mayor, here as throughout the film, is *caught with his pants
down*. These 'literalisms' — the visual translation depends on
a literal fidelity to the linguistic metaphor — are the very
stuff of certain forms of film comedy, the films of the Marx
Brothers providing notable examples (in *At the Circus*,
the literalization of *the last straw that breaks the camel's
back*, done with a nice ironic twist through the agency of the
mute Harpo). Their analysis keeps inner speech close to a
simple recognition of stereotypes of thought, composition
and reading as the one to one conversion of fixed — achieved
— linguistic symbols.[54] Which is to say that we are still far
from an analysis engaging, on the basis of a concept of inner
speech, the process of the social and the individual through
language in the presence — the reception, reading, performance
— of a film. Paradoxically, moreover, the recourse to inner
speech so far has tended to privilege the visual, leaving sound
out of the picture (an appropriate enough metaphor); in the
discussions of and from literalisms, the terms are always only
the visual image and the linguistic expression. The paradox,
in fact, is the symptom of the weak version of inner speech
assumed: a version derived from Vološinov or Vygotsky or
Freud, and however different in each case, would have to
involve consideration of sound just as much as of image,
indeed would not be able to assume the film in terms of any

such given distinction as sound and image; the whole status of inner speech would change — no longer the point of a mechanical construction of a public unity of a film but the point of a complex investigation of the multiple existence of a film each time for a spectator at an intersection of constructions and intensities and slippages and times, of areas of activity and reality, contradictions, joins, displacements.

What is needed, still, and it is here that the status of inner speech could be thought through, the question of cinema and language taken up again today, is a theory of cinematic enunciation. Something of the framework of this, the model of films, might be laid out, initially at least, as follows.

A film is always finished, enounced; and finished, enounced, even in its enunciation which is given, fixed, repeated at every 'showing' or 'screening'. One has to think in this respect of the accomplished fact — the *fait accompli* — of film and the power of the image in that accomplishment (leading to those descriptions of film as characteristically an effacement of discourse; to the feeling of a loss of any historical sense, history constrained into the 'objective', into the form of a visibility and vision, where Marxism in its practice and its theory gives a history that is quite the reverse of 'visible'; and so on); the power which is there in the very regularity of the flow of images in time (smoothly, no resistance, a well-oiled defile for consciousness).

Yet, in that fixity, that givenness of the film, there is nevertheless, always, a present enunciation, the making of the film by the spectator ('making' here the join of the one and the other, the spectator making it as one makes a train, catching it, taken up in its movement, and as one makes, fashions something, articulating it, creating that movement): the whole enunciation in the seeing, listening to, following, reading, skipping, missing, interpreting, reinterpreting, remembering, forgetting, the film performance, from process to closure to process constantly, a veritable history of subjectivity in the symbolic divisions and unities and drifts, the symbol in becoming. Evidently, there is another enounced in this performance-enunciation of the film: all the meaning I am, that is me, all my identity, the history I have for-and-against the

film and in-and-across the very institution of the viewing of
the film, the institution of the regulation of the exchange,
the exchange at stake in the process of cinematic enunciation.
What we know predominantly are institutions of which the
force and the reason is *facilitation* of that exchange; the ease,
the flow, the assurance, the pacification of the passage across
from film to spectator, spectator to film in orders of identity,
hierarchies of meanings, simply in a stable timing, a 'bracketing
time'.[55] That verbal language is banished from the institution
of the enunciation — no speech as part of the performance
before or during or after the film (only the isolating, silencing
darkness) — is indicative, a part of the pacification; and thus,
in opposition, importantly reinstated in contemporary —
independent, avant-garde, political — attempts to produce
alternative institutions, different 'viewings', new 'hearings'.

All this is to come a long way from the first semiology and its
treatment of cinema and language, is to emphasize the need
now to understand the structured process of film in cinema,
to pose the terms for that understanding — in which language
remains a constant and crucial point of reflection, a junction-
problem for thinking cinema today.

Notes

Written 1979 and previously unpublished.

   1. Christian Metz, 'Le cinéma: langue ou langage?', in *Essais sur la
signification au cinéma* (Paris: Klincksieck, 1971) pp. 39—93; translation,
'The Cinema: Language or Language-System?', in *Film Language* (New
York and London: Oxford U.P., 1974) pp. 31—91. For an overall
account of Metz's initial semiological analysis, see my 'The Work of
Christian Metz', *Screen* vol. 14 no. 3 (Autumn 1973) pp. 5—28.
   2. The same kind of conclusion can be found in the — relatively few
— attempts to specify cinema in the terms of a Chomskian perspective
according to a competence/peformance model; cinema is a language

without competence: 'If, in cinema, there are no "bits of films" that can be excluded, it is because there are no audio-visual combinations that are unacceptable by virtue of some formal system.' Dominique Château, 'Texte et discours dans le film', in *Voir, entendre (Revue d'esthétique* 1976 no. 4) (Paris: Union Générale d'Éditions, 1976) p. 128. Certainly, the Chomskian model gives in one sense a more active version of language description ('creativity', 'transformation', the 'generative' production of sentences), but it remains based on an immobilization of language, precisely the inert of the formal system — 'grammaticality', the 'grammar'. Saussure's model is quite radically displaced at the same time that its ambition, the description of the linguistic system, is maintained; hence Chomsky's reference to Saussure's 'lucidity' and his stress that the competence/performance distinction 'is related to the *langue-parole* distinction of Saussure': Noam Chomsky, 'Current Issues in Linguistic Theory', in J. A. Fodor and J. J. Katz (ed), *The Structure of Language* (Englewood Cliffs, N.J.: Prentice-Hall, 1964) p. 52; *Aspects of the Theory of Syntax* (Cambridge, Mass.: M.I.T. Press, 1965) p. 4.

3. C. Metz, *Langage et cinéma* (Paris: Larousse, 1971) pp. 202, 111, 44, 51; translation, *Language and Cinema* (The Hague and Paris: Mouton, 1974) pp. 268, 149, 60, 69.

4. Françoise Collin, 'Polyglo(u)ssons', *Les Cahiers du GRIF* no. 12 (June 1976) p. 8.

5. Jean-Luc Godard, *Deux ou trois choses que je sais d'elle* (Paris: Seuil, 1971) p. 14.

6. Laura Mulvey and Peter Wollen, 'Interview', *Screen* vol. 15 no. 3 (Autumn 1974) p. 128 (the formulation quoted refers in context to the final section of Mulvey and Wollen's first film, *Penthesilea*, but is then, as it were, something of an imagination of the problematic of the subsequent *Riddles of the Sphinx*).

7. S. M. Eisenstein, *Film Form* (New York: Harcourt Brace & Co., 1949) p. 105.

8. Françoise Collin, art. cit. p. 3.

9. C. Metz, *Le Signifiant imaginaire* (Paris: Union Générale d'Éditions, 1977) p. 187.

10. Jacques Lacan, *Écrits* (Paris: Seuil, 1966) p. 799; translation, *Écrits: A Selection* (London: Tavistock, 1977) p. 298.

11. S. Freud, 'The Antithetical Meaning of Primal Words' (1910), *The Standard Edition of the Complete Psychological Works* vol. XI (London: Hogarth Press, 1957) pp. 155–61.

12. J. Lacan, 'L'Étourdit', *Scilicet* no. 4 (1973) p. 45.

13. J. Lacan, *Écrits*, p. 495; translation, p. 147.

14. S. Freud, 'Notes upon a Case of Obsessional Neurosis' (1909), *Standard Edition* vol. X (London: Hogarth Press, 1955) pp. 151–249; 'Psycho-Analytic Notes on an Autobiographical Account of a Case of Paranoia (Dementia Paranoides)' (1911), *Standard Edition* vol. XII (London: Hogarth Press, 1958) pp. 1–82, Cf. Freud's letter to Jung of 1 October 1910 ('I plan to introduce "basic language" as a serious

technical term . . . '), *The Freud/Jung Letters* (London: Hogarth Press and Routledge & Kegan Paul, 1977) p. 358.

15. J.-C. Milner, *L'Amour de la langue* (Paris: Seuil, 1978) pp. 22–3.

16. F. R. Leavis, *For Continuity* (Cambridge: Minority Press, 1933) p. 28.

17. Hanns Eisler, *Composing for the Films* (London: Dennis Dobson, 1947) p. 20.

18. H. Cixous, 'Entretien avec Françoise van Rossum-Guyon', *Revue des sciences humaines* no. 168 (1977) p. 488.

19. Irène Diamantis, 'Recherches sur la féminité', *Ornicar? Analytica* vol. 5 p. 32; Christiane Rabant, in 'Entrevue avec Moustapha Safouan', *Ornicar?* no. 9 (April 1977) p. 101.

20. J. Lacan, *Le Séminaire livre XI* (Paris: Seuil, 1973) pp. 96, 108, 182; translation, *The Four Fundamental Concepts of Psycho-Analysis* (London: Hogarth Press, 1977) pp. 104, 118, 200. Cf. present volume pp. 177–8.

21. Cf. S. Freud, *The Interpretation of Dreams* (1900), *Standard Edition* vol. V (London: Hogarth Press, 1953) pp. 418–25.

22. S. Freud, *On Aphasia* (1891) (London: Imago, 1953) p. 73.

23. S. Freud, *Moses and Monotheism* (1939), *Standard Edition* vol. XXIII (London: Hogarth Press, 1964) p. 99.

24. L. Wittgenstein, *Tractatus Logico-Philosophicus* (London: Routledge & Kegan Paul, 1961) p. 50 (4.1212).

25. Eisenstein, op. cit. p. 105.

26. S. Freud, *On Aphasia* pp. 91–2.

27. V. N. Vološinov, *Freudianism: A Marxist Critique* (New York: Academic Press, 1976) p. 24.

28. K. Marx and F. Engels, *The German Ideology* (London: Lawrence & Wishart, 1965) p. 42.

29. Ibid. p. 41.

30. Ibid. p. 43.

31. Ibid. p. 42.

32. Vološinov, op. cit. p. 85.

33. Ibid. p. 82.

34. Ibid. p. 86.

35. Ibid. p. 89.

36. Ibid.

37. Ibid. p. 87.

38. V. Egger, *La Parole intérieure* (Paris: Librairie Germer Baillière et Cie, 1881); G. Ballet, *Le Langage intérieur* (Paris: Librairie Germer Baillière et Cie, 1886).

39. L. S. Vygotsky, *Language and Thought* (Cambridge, Mass.: M.I.T. Press, 1977) p. 125.

40. Ibid. pp. 45, 145–6.

41. P. P. Blonski, *Memory and Thought* (1935), cit. A. N. Sokolov, *Inner Speech and Thought* (New York and London: Plenum Press, 1972) p. 48.

42. Blonski, ibid., op. cit. Sokolov, p. 49.

43. Vygotsky, op. cit. pp. 20, 51.

44. Eisenstein, op. cit. p. 130.

45. As reported by Annette Michelson from conversations in Moscow with V. V. Ivanov; cf. Harvey Denkin, 'Linguistic Models in Early Soviet Cinema', *Cinema Journal* vol. XVII no. 1 (Fall 1977) pp. 4, 13.

46. Vygotsky, op. cit. pp. 71–2 cf. Eisenstein, op. cit. pp. 135–6.

47. Eisenstein, op. cit. p. 105.

48. David Bordwell, 'Eisenstein's Epistemological Shift', *Screen* vol. 15 no. 4 (Winter 1974/5) p. 41.

49. Interview with Bruno Frei (1928), in S. M. Eisenstein, *Schriften* vol. 3 (Munich: Hanser, 1975) p. 260.

50. John Forrester, 'Language, Symbol and History in Freud's Psycho-Analysis' (Cambridge: unpublished paper, 1974) pp. 53–4. The present essay is indebted to Forrester's research at a number of points.

51. Roland Barthes, *L'Empire des signes* (Geneva: Skira, 1970) p. 99.

52. B. Eikhenbaum, 'Problems of Film Stylistics' (1927), *Screen* vol. 15 no. 3 (Autumn 1974) p. 14.

53. See notably Paul Willemen, 'Reflections on Eikhenbaum's Concept of Internal Speech in the Cinema', *Screen* vol. 15 no. 4 (Winter 1974/5) pp. 59–70.

54. Cf. Freud's initial considerations of symbolism in connection with conversion symptoms in hysteria, these being exactly the literalization of verbal expressions (a patient who takes something said to her as 'a slap in the face' expresses that feeling as a literal facial neuralgia); *Studies on Hysteria* (1895), *Standard Edition* vol. II (London: Hogarth Press, 1955) pp. 178–81.

55. 'The limitations of conventional narrative films: they cover a particular duration of time in which the protagonists transcend or are destroyed in the course of a single climax. Yes, it really is about bracketing time that I object to.' Yvonne Rainer, Letter, *Camera Obscura* no. 1 (1976) p. 96.

Chapter 10

The Cinematic Apparatus
Technology as Historical and Cultural Form

In the first moments of the history of cinema, it is the technology which provides the immediate interest: what is promoted and sold is the experience of the machine, the apparatus. The Grand Café programme is headed with the announcement of 'Le Cinématographe' and continues with its description: 'this apparatus, invented by MM. Auguste and Louis Lumière, permits the recording, by series of photographs, of all the movements which have succeeded one another over a given period of time in front of the camera and the subsequent reproduction of these movements by the projection of their images, life size, on a screen before an entire audience'; only after that description is there mention of the titles of the films to be shown, the *sujets actuels*, relegated to the bottom of the programme sheet.[1] This machine interest and its exploitation can be traced in a variety of effects and repercussions, from, say, Edison's lack of concern in the development of projecting apparatus (a business strategy based literally on selling the machine, projectors for audience viewing representing less of a market than kinetoscopes for parlour individual viewing) to the relatively long-lived assumption that the industry was effectively one of cinema rather than films, the latter being elements of the experience of the machine, a uniform product to be sold by the foot and the reel (an assumption which, paradoxically, unwittingly,

Edison had in fact seen beyond, fearing also that projection
with its large group diffusion would lead to audience satura-
tion and falling attendances for the interchangeable foot/reel
productions).

As though returning to something of those first moments,
theoretical work today has increasingly been directed towards
posing the terms of the 'cinema-machine', the 'basic apparatus', the 'institution' of cinema, where 'institution' is taken
more widely than the habitual notion of the cinema industry
to include the 'interior machine' of the psychology of the
spectator, 'the social regulation of spectatorial metapsychol-
ogy', the industry of the 'mental machinery' of cinema,
cinema as 'technique of the imaginary'. The last emphases are
derived from Christian Metz's essay 'Le signifiant imaginaire'[2]
which is decisively representative of this current turn of
theory. Metz's focus is the psychoanalytic constitution of
the cinematic apparatus, cinema as, exactly, 'imaginary
signifier': 'with that formula, my aim is to designate the still
poorly known set of paths by which the "exercise of cinema"
(the social practice of a certain specific signifier) takes its
roots in the large anthropological figures that the Freudian
discipline has so much helped to clarify: what relations does
the cinematic situation have with the mirror phase, with the
infinite movement of desire, with the position of voyeurism,
the primal scene, the twists and returns of disavowal, etc?';
'[the various studies undertaken in "Le signifiant imaginaire"]
were located at once on a site — in a "moment" rather — that
was not exactly that of the film, nor exactly that of the spectator, nor again that of the code (the list could be extended):
I placed myself as though up-stream to these distinctions, in
a sort of "common trunk" which covered all that at the same
time, which was nothing other than the cinema-machine
itself envisaged in its conditions of possibility.'[3]

The site or moment is a return to the machine, the apparatus: the facts of the Lumière programme are taken up,
examined, by Metz himself and by others — *camera, movement, projection, screen.* Or rather, the facts become new
facts, the terms are recast under the pressure of a theoretical
discourse that inserts new concerns, different conceptions for
an understanding of what the programme indicates as 'this

apparatus'. The shift is there, of course, in the use of the
term 'apparatus' itself: from the stress on the technological,
though in its account of the functioning of the machine to
furnish life-size reproduction of movement already beyond
anything of a 'purely technical' limit, to that on the meta-
psychological, though in its account of the specific struc-
turings and positions and relations inevitably engaged in
aspects of the technical mechanism of cinema.

The question can be posed, however, or can seem to be
posed, as to the status of the latter engagement. In the initial
— now 'classic' — elaborations of a semiology of cinema, the
situation of the technological was clear, even if potentially
problematic: 'the cinematic object is, in fact, immense and
heteroclite, sufficiently large for certain of its dimensions —
for example the economic and the technological — to exclude
themselves from the field of the semiological purpose'.[4] The
field of a semiology of cinema, its 'delimitable object', is the
analysis of cinematic language, where language is to be understood not as the technico-sensorial unity immediately grasp-
able in perceptual experience, the combination of matters of
expression, but as a particular combination of codes. Specificity is defined not via technology or technico-sensoriality
but in terms of codes, this particular combination; some of
the codes being themselves specific to cinema, a point at
which the technico-sensorial can reappear in the analysis
inasmuch as the specificity of the specific codes can be seen
to be connected with certain traits of a matter of expression
or the combination of matters of expression, derives from the
particular nature of the technico-sensorial unity. (Consider
here Metz's discussion of the specificity of cinema *vis-à-vis*
the audio-visual generally and television more especially[5].)

Apart from this reappearance, the technological emerges
only briefly, once the analysis of codes has been established
as the central concern of a semiology, in reference to 'technological codes': 'technological codes which are involved in the
very functioning of the cinematic apparatus (of the camera),
which are its programme (in the sense that one speaks of the
programming of a computer) and which constitute the very
principle of its construction, operation, adjustments. These
technological codes, although they have machines as their

"users", have been constructed by men (inventors, engineers, etc.); moreover, the structures which they impose on the information are again treated and mastered — but this time at the level of the decoding — by other humans, the cinema spectators who perceive the projected images and understand them. Among these codes, there is one which is so important it is even commonly considered to be the very principle of the cinema, its very definition: this is the complex system according to which the cinematic equipment (recording camera, film strip, projector) *"reproduces movement"* ... In this technical code (which is indeed the very code of the cinemato*graph*), the photogramme is the minimal unit, or at least one of the minimal units.'[6] The scope of the emergence, however, is limited. The discussion of technological codes effectively serves to further exclude the technological from the semiological purpose: it comes in the middle of a consideration of the common notion of the photogramme as the minimal unit of cinematic language which it helps to correct, the photogramme is a unit of a technological code, and to redirect, cinematic language is a combination of signifying systems or codes and analysis is thus not concerned with identification of 'the minimal unit of cinema'.

Located on a site or in a moment that is not that of the code, the subsequent attention to the cinematic apparatus, rather than to the cinematic language, might be taken as refinding the instance of technology, its insistence in a new form. In one sense, that attention does, as was said, come back to the first moments of cinema, to the basis of the apparatus itself; it stands up-stream to film, spectator, code, implicates large anthropological figures (the recourse to Plato's myth of the cave is indicative[7]), engages something of a primal scene of cinema (a history that is always there before the meaings of its films and as their ultimate return): in short, raises the psychoanalytic evidence of 'the apparatus'. Technology-apparatus-mental machinery: the question of technology, clearly, is no longer the old question, the whole notion of an 'instance' of 'technology' cannot be assumed, has to be interrogated critically from the concerns of the analytic description of cinema as technique of the imaginary, from the questions then posed as to the cinematic apparatus as historical and ideological form. Those questions today rest open, distant even, relatively unbroached by this current work in so far as its account of the apparatus has intimated problems of technology, history, ideology, and left them in its margins. What is probably Metz's own most direct statement in this area is thus, in fact, prior to the focus on the cinema-machine, at the close of a more classically semiological discussion of special effects and in the form of a straightforward adoption of position in a classic debate: 'In my view, *the technical* does not designate a kind of enclosed area sheltered from history. It is true that the technical, by the very fact that it works, proves the scientific (and not ideological) truth of the principles that are its foundation. But the *how* of its functioning (the ways in which the machine is regulated), which is distinct from its *why*, is nowise under the control of science and brings into play options which can only be of a socio-cultural order.'[8]

If it is conceded that there is no such thing as history in general, that history is a theoretical object distinct from what is declared 'historical' as a result of its occurrence in such and such a place at such and such a time, that facts are constituted as 'facts' from the point of their theoretical-discursive articulation,[9] those concessions are often in practice forgotten, the histories written in the same way, as of 'History', with questions of understanding collapsed into the mechanical assertion of chains of cause and effect, facts discovered and appealed to in the unconsidered ease of a blind circularity.

Historical considerations of technology are no exception to these practical failings; indeed, they are particularly encouraged in them by virtue of the status of technology as grounded in science and thus, given the powerful imaginary of the latter, in an evident reality of functioning progress (invention, modification, improvement, and so on), analysable in terms and with the factual guarantee of scientific development. Hence the force of the isolation of technology, its production in the histories as a self-generating instance, with the consequent assumption of either *technological determinism* ('research and development assumed as self-generating; the new technologies are invented as it were in an independent

sphere, and then create new societies or new human conditions . . . a self-acting force which creates new ways of life')
or *symptomatic technology* ('similarly assumes that research
and development are self-generating, but in a more marginal
way; what is discovered in the margin is then taken up and
used . . . a self-acting force which provides materials for new
ways of life'): 'Most histories of technology, like most
histories of scientific discovery, are written from these
assumptions. An appeal to "the facts", against this or that
interpretation, is made very difficult simply because the
histories are usually written, consciously or unconsciously,
to illustrate the assumptions. This is either explicit, with the
consequential interpretation attached, or more often implicit,
in that the history of technology or of scientific development
is offered as a history on its own.'[10] Corollary with such an
isolation is the simple acceptance of technical terminology,
of the terms proposed by the established technology itself,
as adequate analytic tools, their immediate and uncritical
translation into theoretical concepts, as though productive
in themselves of knowledge.[11]

The posing of the problem of determination is crucial to
the understanding given in the constructed history. Technological determinism substitutes for the social, the economic,
the ideological, proposes the random autonomy of invention
and development, coupled often with the vision of a fulfilment of an abstract human essence — and some of the wildest
versions of this latter are to be found in accounts of the
(then aptly named) 'media': 'through the art and technology
of expanded cinema we shall create heaven right here on
earth'.[12] Yet such a determinism cannot be merely, mechani-
cally, overturned, to leave technology as a wholly controlled
function of some other instance. The process of cinema, to
take the example of concern here, is that of a process through
which in particular economic situations a set of scattered
technical devices becomes an applied technology then a fully
social technology; and that social technology can, must, be
posed and studied in its effects of construction and meaning.
That formulation, however, is itself still problematic: the
process is that of a relation of the technical and the social
as cinema. The fantasy of the conventional histories with

their autonomous instance of technology and their endless problem of the 'invention' of cinema is exactly that cinema exists in the technological; cinema, however, is not a technological invention but a multiply determined development, a process; to say that 'film belongs in the first place to its inventors'[13] is not merely arguable on its own terms (Lumière and even Edison in this field, to take the two habitual 'founders of cinema', were exploiters and businessmen, developers rather than inventors) but limiting on, and ideologically so, a historical-materialist understanding. Cinema does not exist in the technological and then become this or that practice in the social; its history is a history of the technological and social together, a history in which the determinations are not simple but multiple, interacting, in which the ideological is there from the start — without this latter emphasis reducing the technological to the ideological or making it uniquely the term of an ideological determination. Approaches to this complexity are what is at stake finally in, say, the introduction of the notion of 'signifying practice' by Jean-Louis Comolli in his series of articles on 'Technique et idéologie' ('a materialist history of the cinema is impossible without the concept of *signifying practice*'[14]) or the implications of the description of the basic cinematic apparatus given by Jean-Louis Baudry ('the question can be posed as to whether the instruments — the technical base — produce specific ideological effects and whether these effects are themselves determined by the dominant ideology'[15]); approaches which raise questions of meaning and ideology and functioning, of sociality and subjectivity, immediately and thus which cannot espouse the realization-then-exploitation chronology that runs deep in thinking about the fully technological systems of communication, with its traces even in Brecht or Raymond Williams (the idea of radio or of radio and television as technologies developed 'without content'[16]).

Hence the necessity to engage not a history of the technology of cinema, but a history of the cinema-machine that can include its developments, adaptations, transformations, realignments, the practices it derives, holding together the instrumental and the symbolic, the technological and the ideological, the current ambiguity of the term *apparatus*.

Hence the necessity also to conceive that that history is a political understanding, to imagine that it can be grasped critically from aspects of contemporary avant-garde film practice, for example, or that it might be radically envisaged and recast by the questions posed by women to the machine in place.

Cinema, therefore. It is usually said that the creation of commercial cinema hinged on the conjunction of at least three areas of technical understanding and development: photography, persistence of vision, and projection; on their own terms, those areas can be given a long and uneven history of investigation and realization (which, of course, is still continuing, shifting; understanding of persistence of vision has been much transformed and the scientific status of the concept itself rendered increasingly dubious, and its contribution to the explanation of the illusion of movement in cinema greatly diminished). The introduction of the hold of the commercial in the conjunction of the technical areas is evidently crucial. Resting on an industrializable technological base, cinema, different to theatre, offers the possibility of an industry of spectacle. And spectacle is then evidently crucial with its introduction of the hold of meaning and vision and representation into, as a fact of, the industry itself. The series is not a chronology but a constant interlock: projection, for instance, which is at once 'early' (projecting devices were experimented in the mid-seventeenth century, Kircher's famous magic lantern) and 'late' (intensive work on projectors between 1893 and 1896, from the phantascope to the biograph), cannot but engage at one and the same time, and determingly, commerce and spectacle and the relation of the two (the possibility of a new theatre-novel-image industry, the possibility of a new theatre of the subject, representing, positioning, fixing: a veritable *speculation*).

The history of cinema can be written easily along the lines of the commercial or the technological or some simple combination of the two. Thus, for example, technological frameworks are seen as the major factors in the creation of cinema, with gelatine emulsions and continuous roll film as the decisive innovations which prompt technicians to depart from a

previous and limiting framework of operation, the public
success of the kinetoscope coming to give 'the final impetus
to the technological development of commercial cinematography'.[17] Thus again, for example, the subsequent development of cinema is seen in terms of the stages of its financial
control: competitive small business, conflicts between trusts
for overall control, control by banking finance.[18] The lines
can be shifted together – sound is the key to the establishment of the banks' control – and balanced out – 'although
technological innovation and the exclusive possession of
certain technological knowledge proved significant for the
pattern of development of the motion picture industry, innovations in marketing and corporate structure were at least
equally important in shaping the pattern'.[19] Invention and
business strategy become central focuses, with the former
varied in its sources and situations: many important inventions or realizations come from outside cinema (sound
systems, Technicolor), research switches from individuals or
groups close to the nineteenth-century mechanics of cinema
(interest in the science, the phenomena of vision, photography,
etc.) to highly financed research laboratories working in new
areas such as electronics to develop patents for the sponsoring
companies (firms such as Western Electric or General Electric
which set up the first industrial laboratory of this kind in the
USA[20]).

Histories along those lines leave another line which is, in
fact, that of the most common histories, histories of the
movies, written in terms of films rather than cinema, concerned with style, aesthetic innovation, 'the progress of film
as an art form'. Evidently, here and there, that line will be
involved in accommodations, propositions of the technological: 'Because film is a technological art, its production
confronts both mechanical and aesthetic problems.'[21] The
quotation shows the aesthetic line, its separation from the
technological, and the return of the latter as an additional
factor to be borne in mind, occasionally acknowledged. A
slightly different version can be seen in the following: 'As
the movie cannot exist apart from its apparatus, a satisfac-
tory definition of the medium's artistic nature depends on a
full recognition of its technological base.'[22] But what this

full recognition would mean (and whether, indeed, the problem is to be posed in this way at all), the relations and determinations, remains difficult, the effective history unwritten.

'It is technical advances which underlie stylistic innovations like hand-held techniques, depth of field photography, zooming, craning, and shooting by available light at night.'[23] The assertion has its obviousness – zooming requires the development of a single lens of variable focal length – and has the impasse of that obviousness, its impermeability to the further question then as to the determinations of the technical advances (as also to the criteria for the term 'advances' itself). Arriflex cameras were available in Hollywood in the late 1940s but there was no particular turn to hand-held sequences in response to the technical advance (nor in France at the same period in response to the Éclair Cameflex). With the emphasis given by such an assertion, technology becomes very much an autonomous instance, its explanations internal to itself in an ongoing movement of advance and modification consequent on advance: problems of loss of quality in post-synchronization mean that location scenes in the early thirties are shot with direct sound, microphones in use are omnidirectional and pick-up of background noise a difficulty, hence the introduction of slow-speed fine-grained Eastman background negative in 1933 which allows the possibility of good standard back projection again and thus the shift back to studio shooting for exterior scenes, and so on.

A different inflection within the same problematic is provided by the kind of work most clearly represented by the various writings of Barry Salt. Salt retains the technological base, which he describes in detail across the decades of cinema's history, but gives it an autonomy which limits its effects of determination: it is at once neither greatly determining – 'the constraints of film technology on film forms are far less than is currently supposed, though not negligible' – nor much determined – 'as for ideology, its connection with film technology is practically zero'.[24] The basic thesis is that of 'the dominance of aesthetic considerations over technical possibilities as far as the form of films is concerned';[25] technology, a pressure not a constraint, continually responds to the determination of aesthetic demands. Thus, for example, the trend towards longer shot lengths in the 1940s requires increased camera manœvrability and it is as a result of this requirement that the crab dolly is produced (Houston crab dolly 1946, Selznick crab dolly 1948). At the same time, technology is itself effective, as, for example, in the same area of shot length: various hindrances to assembling a film in the early thirties are relieved by developments such as the sound moviola and rubber numbering which allow shot length to decrease. Salt continues his discussion of this: 'Having reached this point about 1934—5, new technical developments began to have some effect on film photography, and at the end of the thirties a new trend towards longer takes was just starting to emerge independently of any technological pressures; a trend that was to flourish in the forties.'[26] The movement of the argument there is indicative: new technical developments have effects, a new stylistic trend begins: the determination is technical *or* aesthetic, the latter the general rule and the lacuna in this kind of history, a point beyond which there is no further explanation or the explanation only of a more or less crude psychology (the decisions of director-artists, what the audience demands, etc.).

Within the terms of this conception of 'the technological' and 'the aesthetic', finally, there will always be an endless series of adducible elements to carry the different inflections: demonstrating the aesthetic over the technological (Carl Mayer's notions of dramatic movement in his work with Murnau in 1923—4 leading to improvements in camera support technology), the technological over the aesthetic (the effect of CinemaScope on the film image — 'shallow focus, very wide angles, no definition'[27]), and including all the time moments of puzzle, of neither one nor the other, of inexplicable mystery (the lateness of the development of the optical printer).

In relation to the histories and arguments just described, there is a need to make certain immediate clarifications. Technology is generally taken as the systematic application of scientific or other organized knowledge to practical tasks; the knowledges and the devices they allow become the particular applied technology that is cinema. Within

cinema, techniques are the procedures involving elements
of the technology in specific ways, processes in the production and presentation of films. The terminology is wavering,
confusing, since not all of the techniques involved in the
production-presentation of films are dependent on technological processes for their operation; as an extreme example,
techniques of acting play a part in the production of many
films without necessarily being dependent on the technology
of cinema; a less extreme example might be said to be the
jump cut, a technique which does not depend on a technological process in the manner that, say, a zoom shot depends
on a certain type of lens.[28] The example of the jump cut,
however, is unconvincing — jump cuts are after all bound up
with the technology of cinema apart from which, unlike techniques of acting, they could have no possible realization —
and thereby at the same time indicative of the distinction to
be followed in discussion between cinema and film. What
Barry Salt is concerned with, for example, are film forms, the
various techniques — standard or individual — of films, with
cinema effectively left out of the account *because* it is a technology, the technology for the production of films which as such is
outside of any ideological determinations or effects and can
only be described technologically, in terms of its own history of
invention, advance, improvement, modification. Within cinema,
as it were, the question of the relation between technological determinants (the inventions, advances, improvements,
modifications) and techniques (the standard or individual
practices) in which technology is exploited is a question at
the level of films: the determination of the forms of films
by technical elements or/and the determination of the technical elements by the aesthetic requirements of film forms,
'technique' being the term that shifts between the one and
the other. Technology itself is then always found and finally
confirmed as an autonomous instance, with ideology involved
— should the argument envisage it — in the creation and
maintenance of the various techniques, even if (just because)
— again should the argument even pose the problem — technology is also acknowledged as bound up with the determinations of economic forces guiding its development in this or
that direction. Effectively, a kind of base/super-structure

model is deployed in which technology provides a base for techniques which are the point of the relations of ideology.

The question of films, of film forms, is important, and, moreover, as yet relatively unacknowledged in this context: what, for example, would be a textual analysis informed by reflection on technology/techniques (where the answer, of course, could not lie in the simple adoption in the analysis of technical terms, odd references to depth of field or whatever)? At the same time, however, a further question can be, has been posed (with consequences in return for the question of film forms): that of the applied technology cinema, the machine, of the apparatus, in fact, with reference to which large areas in themselves, and not merely a particular technique, become crucial focuses for discussion, camera, colour, sound, and so on; the question of the *limits* of cinema, historical and ideological, and the effects of the technology *there*: the apparatus as instruments, mechanisms, devices, *and* of the subject — as that history too.

Notes

Written for a conference on 'The Cinematic Apparatus', Center for Twentieth Century Studies, University of Wisconsin—Milwaukee, February 1978 published in Teresa de Lauretis and Stephen Heath (eds), *The Cinematic Apparatus* (London: Macmillan, 1980) pp. 1—13.

1. See the reproduction of an early Lumière programme in Georges Sadoul, *Histoire générale du cinéma* vol. I (Paris: Denoël, 1973) p. 290.
2. C. Metz, 'Le signifiant, imaginaire', *Communications no. 23* (1975) pp. 3—55 (quotations from p. 6); translation, 'The Imaginary Signifier', *Screen* vol. 16 no. 2 (Summer 1975) pp. 14—76 (p. 19).
3. C. Metz, introductory remarks to 'Métaphore/métonymie', *Le Signifiant imaginaire* (Paris: Union Générale d'Éditions, 1977) pp. 179—80.
4. C. Metz, *Langage et cinéma* (Paris: Larousse, 1971) p. 11; translation, *Language and Cinema* (The Hague and Paris: Mouton, 1974) p. 17.
5. Ibid. pp. 170—87; translation, pp. 225—48.
6. Ibid. p. 144 (cf. p. 177); translation, p. 191 (cf. p. 236).
7. Cf. Jean-Louis Baudry, 'Le dispositif', *Communications* no. 23

(1975) pp. 56—72; translation, 'The Apparatus', *Camera Obscura* no. 1 (1976) pp. 104—26.

8. C. Metz, *Essais sur la signification au cinéma* (Paris: Klincksieck, 1972) p. 192.

9. An emphasis equally valid in science, the science to which discussions of technology constantly refer as to an indisputable area of the observable, the factual, the real: 'observational reports, experimental results, "factual" statements, either *contain* theoretical assumptions or *assert* them by the manner in which they are used' Paul Feyerabend, *Against Method* (London: New Left Books, 1975) p. 31.

10. Raymond Williams, *Television: Technology and Cultural Form* (London: Fontana, 1974) pp. 13—14.

11. 'Any technical practice is defined by its objectives: such specified effects to be produced in such an object, in such a situation. The means depend on the objectives. Any technical practice utilizes amongst these means knowledges which intervene as procedures: either knowledges borrowed from outside, from existing sciences, or "knowledges" produced by the technical practice itself to accomplish its end. In every case, the relationship between technique and knowledge is an *external* relationship, without reflection, radically different from the reflected internal relationship existing between a science and its knowledges.' Louis Althusser, *Pour Marx* (Paris: Maspero, 1965) p. 172 n. 9; translation, *For Marx* (London: New Left Books, 1969) p. 171 n. 7.

12. Gene Youngblood, *Expanded Cinema* (New York: Dutton, 1970) p. 419.

13. V. F. Perkins, *Film as Film* (Harmondsworth: Penguin Books, 1972) p. 40.

14. Jean-Louis Comolli, 'Technique et idéologie' (II), *Cahiers du cinéma* no. 230 (July 1971) p. 57.

15. J.-L. Baudry, 'Cinéma: effets idéologiques produits par l'appareil de base', *Cinéthique* no. 7/8 (1970) p. 3; translation, 'Ideological Effects of the Basic Cinematographic Apparatus', *Film Quarterly* vol. XXVIII no. 2 (Winter 1974/5) p. 41.

16. B. Brecht, *Gesammelte Werke* vol. XVIII (Frankfurt am Main: Suhrkamp, 1967) p. 127 Williams, op. cit. p. 25. Cinema, of course, was not developed in the abstract; 'the reproduction of life itself' was not a subsequent discovery by Lumière; the description of what cinema would be, from the Lumière *'sujets actuels'* to animation, in Ducos du Hauron's ambitious 1864 patent for 'an apparatus designed to reproduce photographically a given scene with all the transformations to which it is subject over a given period of time' is not some freak — and neither is it the indication of cinema as an eternal dream of humankind: the technological and ideological move together as the very possibility of the development of the former as cinema; the pre-imaginary of cinema has its historical content from the problems of social definition and representation in the nineteenth century, the pressure for 'machines of the visible', and is itself a force in that development of cinema.

17. Reese V. Jenkins, *Images and Enterprise: Technology and the American Photographic Industry 1839–1925* (Baltimore: Johns Hopkins U.P., 1975) pp. 274–5.

18. H. Mercillon, *Cinéma et monopoles: le cinéma aux États-Unis* (Paris: A. Colin, 1953) p. 7.

19. Jenkins, op. cit. p. 298.

20. Cf. Douglas Gomery, 'Failure and Success: Vocafilm and RCA innovate Sound', *Film Reader* no. 2 (1977) p. 215.

21. John L. Fell, *Film: An Introduction* (New York: Praeger, 1975) p. 127.

22. Perkins, op. cit. p. 40.

23. Liz-Anne Bawden (ed.), *The Oxford Companion to Film* (London, New York, Toronto: Oxford U.P., 1976) p. 106 (article 'Camera').

24. Barry Salt, Letter, *Screen* vol. 17 no. 1 (Spring 1976) p. 123.

25. Salt, 'Film Style and Technology in the Forties', *Film Quarterly* vol. XXXI no. 1 (Fall 1977) p. 46.

26. Salt, 'Film Style and Technology in the Thirties', *Film Quarterly* vol. XXX no. 1 (Fall 1976) p. 32.

27. Lee Garmes A.S.C., interviewed in Charles Higham, *Hollywood Cameramen* (London: Thames & Hudson, 1970) p. 54.

28. Cf. Edward Branigan, 'Color and Cinema: Problems in the Writing of History', *Film Reader* no. 4 (1979) p. 19.

Chapter 11

Contexts

In the 1970s in France 'popular memory' became a key issue in cultural theory and practice. Michel Foucault, interviewed in *Cahiers du cinéma* stressed memory as 'an important factor of struggle' and, consequently, as cinematically productive, since defining a task for film-makers, an area of intervention.[1] The movement of popular memory has been blocked, and by a whole series of apparatuses, cinema included: 'People are shown not what they were, but what they must remember they were'; the point is to oppose that obliteration, the effects of those apparatuses, to return people their real memory, the terms of their struggle. 'Popular memory exists but has no means of formulation.' Thus the problem is one of a recovery and expression of history, with cinema seen as playing a potentially important part in its resolution, able to help towards that recovery and expression. Film practice will be archival, documentary in a literal sense of the word: the utilization and reinvigoration of a historical documentation; hence comments such as the following from *Cahiers* critics: 'to take up the question of the archive, it can be clearly seen how a film could be made which would utilize documents reflecting a repressed portion of popular memory in order to make it live again. The review *Le Peuple français*, for example, is a wealth of scripts.'[2] The focus of attention is to be what the historian Marc Ferro, the subject of another *Cahiers* interview under the rubric 'Cinéma et histoire', refers to as the 'obscure and everyday actors' of history, an interrogation of 'society itself';[3] and a film such as René Allio's *Moi, Pierre Rivière*, based on historical documentation published by Foucault, will have its importance and its theoretical success in this perspective — 'the everyday, the historical and the tragic' (the title of a note on the film printed in *Cahiers*).[4]

The reference to memory, in fact, must necessarily be complex. Rather as Freud describes hysterics as suffering mainly from reminiscences, Marx can be found in the famous opening section of *The Eighteenth Brumaire* castigating the dead weight of memory, the theatre of the past in which the Revolution of 1848 was performed: 'The social revolution of the nineteenth century cannot draw its poetry from the past, but only from the future. It cannot begin with itself before it has stripped off all superstition in regard to the past. Earlier revolutions required reminiscences of past world history so as to hide from themselves their own content. In order to achieve its own object, the revolution of the nineteenth century must let the dead bury the dead.'[5] Again, in the realm of artistic practice, the watchwords of a Brecht are not memory and recovery but, more urgently, crisis or destruction. Certainly there is room to distinguish between the official memory of the instituted history and the experience and struggles it covers over and represses; the point remains, however, that effective memory for struggle will not be a function of the past but of the present, will be a production. That that production must be the demonstration of something else — an opposition — can be agreed: the fact of 'mass communications' is a constant containment of meanings and positions and intelligibility (the variation of the same in cinema, the continually answering present of the television sound and image). 'Something else', nevertheless, is not simply 'outside', an immediate return to a past waiting to be found, a belief that sustains the intellectual nostalgia for the recovery of the 'unity' of a 'popular memory': 'a left ethnology proceeding through village chronicles and memoirs of the people, to transform a voyeuristic relation to the people into one of inheritance.'[6]

What needs particularly to be emphasized here is that history in cinema is nowhere other than in representation, the terms of representing proposed, precisely the historical present of any film; no film is not a document of itself and of its actual situation in respect of the cinematic institution and of the complex of social institutions of representation. Which is to say that the automatic conjunction of film and history-as-theme, as past to be shown today, the strategy for a cinema developed to recover 'popular memory', is an idealist abstraction, an ideal of film and an ideal of history. The present of a film is always historical, just as history is always present — a fact of representation not a fact of the past, an elaboration of the presence of the past, a construction in the present, for today, where the present is then equally always already historical, itself the process of that construction, a terrain of determinations and places, itself a political reality. Cinema is part of that present process, which is where *its* history, the history of cinema, is crucial to film. To make a film is always at once a problem of film and cinema, a problem of a — of this — signifying practice and its specificity (the latter including the terms of its articulation of the non-specific-to-cinema), its institution. When Foucault comments on the film *Moi, Pierre Rivière* that 'it was difficult and truly extraordinary to be able to reduce the whole cinematic apparatus, the whole filmic apparatus to such slenderness',[7] one has to reply that it is exactly in that supposed reduction that the apparatus is most thick, most ideologically consistent. The history of a film cannot be collapsed into the alibi of the document, the past as referent-guarantee (*Moi, Pierre Rivière* is full of 'cinema', not of 'the past'). Any relation of history in cinema risks simply reactionary effects if not passed through reflection on the current reality of such a practice, which reality includes the fact — the present history and institution — of cinema.

Representation: imaging, argumentation, deputation; the turn together — the bind of representing — of these different elements is important. The history of the individual as subject and as subject in and for a social formation is never finished. Its constant termination, the stable relation of subject in constructed meaning, a specific subject-construction, is the effect of representation, and an ideological effect: any social formation depends for its existence not only on the economic and political instances but also on a reasoning of the individual as subject, reproduced in images, identities of meaning, finding his or her delegation there. The term of this process is that of suturing: the join of the subject as unity of the recognition of sense, ground of intelligibility. Cinema is an institution of representing, a machine for the fabrication-maintenance of representation; it is as such that it is a crucial ideological investment, as such that it is developed and exploited, for a narration of the individual as subject in a narrative that is its mapping — again and again, the constant termination — within the limits of existing representations and their determining social relations. The category of this mapping is what can be called the 'novelistic': the location of the spectator subject of cinema in a unity which encompasses, from apparatus to final narrative image, the individual *as* individual view within given social orders of meaning that are returned as his or her place and action; with family relations taken as the arena of the social-individual construction-placing and of the necessary containment — possibility and limitation in one — of action; cinema as family machine (after and concurrent with the novel, prior to and concurrent with television, according to that pattern of taking-over in which one machine is replaced by another that includes it and thus allows it a certain displacement into margins of excess to be newly exploited and delimited, commercially and ideologically; as with cinema today, for example, turned to a violence and a pornography not available to television as the current central social machine), all tensions of change articulated within the dramas of the films produced and within the very functioning of the producing, the very institution of the representing.

What is now being realized, in fact, with regard to the history of the cinema, though its writing has not as yet shifted in consequence, is that that history is not to be understood via the concept of 'realism', ideas of 'progress towards realism', and so on, but first and foremost, in respect of terms of subjectivity, of the contract — of the contracting — of the individual as subject in representation, exactly the representing operation of cinema. Something of this can be fairly readily grasped, more-over, in the contradictions of property and expense to which the various technological innovations forming part of that history give rise. Family machine in its representing not in its ownership, cinema weights expense massively on the side of production, an area of capitalist (and/or national, state) invest-ment, with reception inexpensive, the price of the ticket, of one's 'place'. Innovations greatly reinforce this expense, hence this inaccessibility, of production (sound and colour are the ob-vious examples), creating indeed conditions of *national* inaccessibility, the collapse, weakening or sheer impossibility of even beginning to exist of many national film industries in the face of the monopoly capitalist expansion of Hollywood. At the same time, however, the wider implications of that expansion, expansion both in industries having interests that go beyond the sole market of cinema (the photographic industry, for example) and in the general ideological stake in representing for which cinema is only one factor among others, allow a crossing of cinema with technological developments — small gauges are a crucial instance — that recast it in different versions of the family machine, notably that of the home movie. What remains constant is the very fact of the produc-tion of the machines and the force of standardization achieved therein: standardization of the technological base, the actual machinery; standardization of the product, the film; stan-dardization of the subject, the relations-patterns of meaning assured. The relatively inexpensive product is as standardized — and above all in that 'variety' that is now sometimes acclaimed in it — as the expensive industrial one (not, of course, that the former is free of the hold of capitalist industry): the 'personal' is simply, as it were, restandardized, the super 8 home movie is a fully functioning *social* representing. The possibility, nevertheless, is that in the recasting, necessarily involving as it does new availabilities of property for family individuals, certain loosenings are there to be used, certain disappropriations-rerelations can be made — 16 mm, super 8 as terms for alternative groups, of a struggle exactly against the available 'cinema', the existing institution.

The film image completes on the individual subject as *its* spectator, point of a constant appropriation. How to resist an image, to refuse its belonging? 'It is with the images that captivate its eros of living individual that the subject comes to deal with its implication in the sequence of signifiers', writes Lacan,[8] almost as though describing cinema with its succession of images, the individual implicated there as subject, ceaselessly as the 'there' of the image. Cinema works to the utmost that regime of the privilege of the subject that has it that the image cannot but be *mine*, be *my* seeing, even when nevertheless it is seen — a seen — *for* me; which is the problem of belonging, the difficulty of contradicting 'my' image. The succession is then, of course, exploited to compound this closing — this closeness — of the image on the subject: matching of images as continuity, narrativization of that continuous matching as the steady assignment of a developing view, a stable memory, something for some one, some one for that something, these meanings, this vision. The desire for images is maintained and fulfilled in the very time of the succession, mapped by the realized film into the time of that desire, of the process of captivation: perpetual balancing of seeing-seen, identification with camera-identification with person or object, from shot to shot, and within the single shot itself via movement of human figures or camera creating new planes of fascination, a kind of extreme rendering of the scopic drive.[9] Which is the necessity in Godard or Straub—Huillet of the attempt to take away the subject of the image: images divided, crossed out, written over, multiplied in the single frame, returned to a television screen in Godard; images interrupted by black leader or, more interestingly, drawn out into an excessive time of vision and movement, something of a long chance of a real — the car sequences in *History Lessons*, the pans of *Fortini/Cani* — in Straub—Huillet.

The film image, then, cannot be accepted without questions as a simple point of departure for a political practice of cinema. Linked to a production of 'the visual', the illusion of a direct vision and the subject position-desire of that illusion, it must be posed as false. The visual in this sense does not exist: the image and its subject completion are produced in codes which include, amongst others, the codes of the specific machination — the operation — of the image in cinema, the codes of the constructed reality represented, and the codes of language itself (the whole problem, to go no further, of the nomination of visible objects, of their linguistic visibility). The image is never 'pure', never 'an image'; strictly speaking, indeed, the image is not an order of the visible but of the invisible, a speculation that adjoins real, symbolic, imaginary, the subject against difference, transformation, the history of the subject individual in process (symptom: the degree to which the coming of photograph and cinema has undermined the critical production of history, henceforth fixed as simply past, as spectacle). The problem cited by the Groupe Dziga Vertov in *Pravda* — 'sounds which are already right on images which are still false' — or *Vent d'est* — 'this is not a just image, just an image' — is always contemporary.

History is not to be recovered or expressed in cinema, is not a given; it is always to be gained in films, a political cinema to be developed in that struggle. On the assumption of this reality of history will depend the value for use of the particular films made. In the dominant institution of cinema, films are set as far as possible within the limits of a strictly regulated — economically and ideologically — context of exchange: the film is a mode of exchange of subjects, a universal representative (which universality is its representing operation). 'The relation between the film-text and the viewer is the prerequisite for political questions in the cinema.'[10] Alternative practices are alternative in so far as they transform the relations of representation *against* representing, against the universalizing conditions of exchange; representation held to use (a definition of Brechtian distanciation), that is, to division, disunity, disturbance of the (social) contract (of film).

Debate around films often stumbles over issues of effectivity, 'the real effect of a film', deadlocks on either 'the text itself', its meaning 'in it', or else the text as non-existent other than 'outside itself', in the particular responses it happens to engage from any individual or individual audience — the text 'closed' or 'open'. The reading (viewing, reception, understanding, reaction) of a film, however, must be seen as neither constrained absolutely nor free absolutely but historical, and that historicality includes the determinations of the institution cinema, the conditions of the production of meanings, of specific terms of address (of engagement of reading). The property of a film is not yours or mine, whether makers or spectators, nor its; it is in a conjuncture of questions of property across the three instances of preconstruction, passage and construction, through the many and different relations sustained by each and between them in the particular experience of the film. For a film practice, for a cinema, to begin to pose those questions of its property in a political definition of history and to pose history in a political definition of film and cinema is to begin to break exchange for use, universal for struggle, which after all — far from the unity of a popular memory — is the real and urgent task.

It is apparent now that the major error of the production of accounts of cinema and representation in conjunction with the appeal to the explanatory powers of psychoanalysis has been the location of a complete subject of cinema, via the description of the latter exclusively as single apparatus, instance, or whatever. Primary identification, voyeurism, and so on have entered the argument as static and absolute determinants, without history; in every case, there is primary identification, the all-perceiving subject, the phallic look. . . . The point is not to deny these descriptions (on the contrary, the present volume has been concerned in parts to develop some of them with regard to the institution of cinema) but to insist on their historical content (and thus on the historical content of the concept of 'subject' as a term in that account of the institution of cinema). We have to learn to understand and analyze the redistribution in specific conjunctures of the operation of cinema, the redeployment of limits — for example, the recasting of the instance of the all-perceiving subject (the spectator as primary identification, transcendental subject in the pure, all-powerful perception that cinema elicits in order to exist as signifier, the vision of its meaning[11]) *from the reality of a film practice in its material complexity, its possibility of contradictions.* Redeployment *and definition* of limits, since to grasp the former is to understand also that cinema is not a set of essences more or less actualized in its history (and in the usual descriptions generally more, given as always there), but a practice, a signifying practice, only in the historical and social relations and institution of which are such 'essences' *produced*, and cinema held to them, to a 'the subject'. It is in such a recognition that the questions of cinema envisaged here must be taken, followed through, posed for the work towards other cinemas, new films.

Notes

Previously unpublished but drawing, for a brief 'conclusion', on material to be found in parts of: 'Contexts', *Edinburgh 77 Magazine* (1977) pp. 37—43, and 'Questions of Property' (Martin Walsh Lecture), *Cinétracts* no. 4 (1978) pp. 2—11.

1. 'Entretien avec Michel Foucault', *Cahiers du cinéma* no. 251—2 (July—August 1974) pp. 5—15 (quotations in this paragraph from p. 7).
2. Pascal Bonitzer, in 'Entretien avec André Techiné', *Cahiers du cinéma* no. 262—3 (January 1976) p. 55.
3. 'Entretien avec Marc Ferro', *Nouvel Observateur* no. 652 (9—15 May 1977) p. 90.
4. J. Jourdheuil, 'Le quotidien, l'historique et le tragique', *Cahiers du cinéma* no. 271 (November 1976) pp. 46—7.
5. Karl Marx, *The Eighteenth Brumaire of Louis Bonaparte, Marx—Engels Selected Works* (London: Lawrence & Wishart, 1968) p. 99.
6. Jacques Rancière, 'Fleurs intempestives', *Cahiers du cinéma* no. 278 (July 1977) p. 18. The *Cahiers* critics themselves were later to take a distance from what was then seen as the 'Cinema and History fetish'; cf. J. Narboni, 'Là', *Cahiers du cinéma* no. 275 (April 1977) pp. 5—7; J.-L. Comolli, 'Le passé filmé', *Cahiers du cinéma* no. 277 (June 1977) pp. 10—11 n. 6.
7. 'Entretien avec Michel Foucault', *Cahiers du cinéma* no. 271 (November 1976) p. 53.
8. Jacques Lacan, *Écrits* (Paris: Seuil, 1966) p. 710.

9. Cf. Raymond Bellour, 'Énoncer', *L'Analyse du film* (Paris: Albatros, 1979) p. 273; translation, 'Hitchcock, the Enunciator', *Camera Obscura* no. 2 (1977) pp. 68—9 ('the two processes of identification which transfix the spectator: identification with the camera, identification with the object (the perpetual dialectic between being and having: identification and object-choice)').

10. Claire Johnston, 'Introduction', *Edinburgh '77 Magazine* (1977) p. 5.

11. The notion of the 'all-perceiving subject' constitutive of cinema was introduced by Christian Metz in 'Le signifiant imaginaire', *Communications* no. 23 (1975) pp. 32—5; translation, 'The Imaginary Signifier', *Screen* vol. 16 no. 2 (Summer 1975) pp. 48—52 ('I am myself the place where this really perceived imaginary accedes to the symbolic by its inauguration as the signifier of a certain type of institutionalised social activity called "the cinema". In other words, the spectator *identifies with himself*, with himself as a pure act of perception . . . as condition of possibility of the perceived and hence as a kind of transcendental subject, anterior to every *there is*.')

9. *Cf.* Raymond Bellour, 'Hermeneutics' of theory, in *Le Texte* *Musique*, 1973), pp. 27ff; and Louis T. Balthasar, ... the Enunciator ... to speak of ... 3 (1980) pp. 56-3 (the two processes of identifi-cation, which transfix the screen ... identify ahead with the cinema is in other respects the site where ... a particular dialectic between ... and lower identification and ...).

10. *Cf.* Roy Johnson, 'Introduction', *Einburg* 7', *Einburg* (1977) p. 2.

11. The notion of the subjective-viewing-subject constitutive of cinema was introduced by Christian Metz in the signifiant imaginaire, *Com-munications*, no. 23 (1974) pp. 3-55, transl. the 'The Imaginary Signifier', *Screen*, vol. 16 no. 2 (Summer 1976), pp. 14-76 (?) in myself ... is-place since the reality perceived imaginary as relate to the symbolic ... namely such as the quality of a certain type of institutional ... occur, actually called 'the cinema'. In other words, the spectator ... is identified with ?? with himself as a spectacle ... of perception ... as a condition or pre-filling of the perceived and hence of a kind of transcendental subject, anterior to every film.[^?])

Indexes

Films

Names

Terms and themes

This index is indicative rather than comprehensive inasmuch as many of the terms and themes listed (for example, 'narrative' or 'subject') are a constant preoccupation — *passim* — throughout the book. In such cases, only a few — major — references are given here.